Caribbean & African I

SOUTHWARK BLACK WORKERS GROUP
LIBRARY REFERENCE ONLY
352/354 CAMBERWELL NEW ROAD
SE5 0RW   Tel. 738 7105

MORGAN DALPHINIS

Caribbean & African Languages
Social History, Language, Literature and Education

Morgan Dalphinis

Karia Press

African and Caribbean Languages
Social History, Language,
Literature and Education.

First Published by **Karia Press** *in 1985.*

Copyright© Morgan Dalphinis, 1985.
(Except where indicated otherwise)

Photoset by Karia.
Book Design and layout by Buzz Johnson.
Cover concept and design by Buzz Johnson.
Printed by Whitstable Litho Ltd., Kent.

ISBN 0 946918 06 6 Pbk.
ISBN 0 946918 07 4 Hbk.

Karia Press
BCM Karia
London WC1N 3XX
United Kingdom

*To My Wife
Julie*

Contents

Papers and Poems used in the text	ix
Abbreviations	xi
Orthography	xii
Acknowledgements	xiii
Caribbean and African Languages: A General Introduction	1

PART I The Social History of Creole Languages

1	Introduction	21
2	Historical Background: the development of Patwa in St. Lucia	23
3	The Social History of Caribbean Languages: the St. Lucian Case	43
4	Creoles and Ideologies of Return	61
5	The Portuguese Creole of the Casamance, French and African Languages: Languages in competition in Southern Senegal	67

PART II Language

1	Introduction	83
2	Various Approaches to the Study of Creole Languages: the case for African influences	85
3	Lexical Expansion in Casamance Kriul, Gambian Krio and St. Lucian Patwa	97
4	A Syncronic Comparison of the Verbal Systems of St. Lucian Patwa and Guinean Crioulo	111
5	Island Carib Influences in St. Lucian Patwa	133

PART III Oral Literature

1	Introduction	157
2	Caribbean Creole Languages in Caribbean Literature	159
3	The African Presence in Caribbean Creole Oral Literature	165

4	The Writer and Audience: influence of the African Oral Tradition on Nigerian Literature (oral and written)	173

PART IV

1	Introduction	189
2	English as a Second Language [ESL] and the teaching of English to Pupils of Caribbean Origin in Britain	191
3	Oral Languages, Power and Education: a comparative survey of St. Lucian and English practices	199
4	Creoles in Voluntary Adult Education: the Caribbean Communication Project's experience	229
5	Recommendations for a Productive use of Creoles in Teaching	271
Bibliography		281

Notes: on papers, poems and reference work by the author which are used in the text.

'Various Approaches to the Study of Creole Languages with Particular Reference to the Influences of West African Languages upon those Creole Languages', paper presented to the *Africa Society*, King's College, University of London, 1976. Published in the Black Liberator, London, 1978 and CCP Occasional Paper No. 2, London, 1982.

'A Synchronic Comparison of the Verbal Systems of St. Lucian Patwa and Guinean Crioulo', paper presented to the *Comparative Seminar on African and Creole Languages*, School of Oriental and African Studies (S.O.A.S.), University of London, 1977(a).

'A General Introduction to Creole Languages', paper presented to the teachers at *Holloway Comprehensive School, London*, 1978.

'Lexical Expansion in Casamance Kriul, Gambian Krio and St. Lucian Patwa', paper presented to the Conference on *Theoretical Orientations in Creole Studies, St. Thomas, U.S. Virgin Islands*, 1979(a).

'Historical Background to the Development of Patwa in St. Lucia', paper presented to the *Comparative Seminar in Creole and African Languages*, S.O.A.S., University of London, 1977(b) and the *Conference on Creole Studies & Development*, Mahé, Seychelles, 1979(b).

'The African Presence in West Indian Creole Literature', paper presented at the *Centre for Urban Educational Studies*, London, 1979(c).

African Influences in Creoles Lexically based on Portuguese,

English and French, with special reference to Casamance, Kriul, Gambian Krio and St. Lucian Patwa, Ph.D., S.O.A.S., University of London, 1981.

'The Social History of Caribbean Languages — The St. Lucian Case', paper presented at the *Third International Conference on Creole Studies,* Vieux-Fort, St. Lucia, 1981.

'The Writer and his Audience — Influences of the African Oral Tradition on Nigerian Literature (Oral and Written)', paper presented at the *Modern Languages Association of Nigeria, Annual Conference,* University of Calabar, Nigeria, 1983(a).

'Portuguese Creole, French and African Languages — Languages in Competition in the South of Senegal', paper presented at the *Fourth International Conference on Creole Studies,* Louisiana, U.S.A., 1983(b).

'French Creole', Section one of the *Caribbean Communications Project Report,* produced as one aspect of the Preliminary Studies for the ILEA Afro-Caribbean Language and Literacy Project, on Further and Adult Education, © ILEA, 1984(a).

'Creoles and Ideologies of Return', paper presented to the *Conference of the Society for Caribbean Studies,* Heigh Leigh Conference Centre, Hertfordshire, May 1984(b).

'Oral Languages, Power and Education: A Comparative Survey of Saint Lucian and English Practices', paper presented to the *Conference on Languages Without a Written Tradition,* Thames Polytechnic, London, August/September 1984(c).

'Island Carib Influences in Saint Lucian Patwa', paper presented (in absentia) to the *Conference of the Society for Caribbean Linguistics,* University of the West Indies, Mona, Jamaica, September 1984(d).

'Recommendations for a Productive use of Creoles in Teaching, paper presented at the *Second International Conference on Intercultural Curriculum,* University of London Institute of Education, September 1984(e).

'French Creoles' in *Language and the Black Experience in Britain,* (forthcoming) edited by A. Wong and D. Sutcliffe, Blackwells, 1985.

'Gwo Piton, Piti Piton' in *Caribbean Quarterly,* University of the West Indies, 1985.

Abbreviations.

Complet.	– Completive aspect.
E.C.	– English Creole
ed.	– Editor.
Emph.	– Emphatic.
Eng.	– English.
e.g.	– For example.
F.C.	– French Creole
Focal.	– Focalizer.
fem.	– Feminine.
Fr.	– French.
Fut.(Im./N.Im.)	– Future tense/aspect (imminent/non-imminent.)
Hab.	– Habitual aspect.
J.C.	– Jamaican Creole.
Lit.	– Literary.
Loc.	– Locative.
mas.	– Masculine.
Mnka.	– Mandinka.
Neg.	– Negative.
Past.	– Past tense.
Perf.	– Perfective.
pl.	– Plural.
Port.	– Portuguese.
Prog.	– Progressive aspect.
Rel.	– Relative.
Rep.	– Repeat.
sing.	– Singular.
Specif.	– Specifier.
T/F.	– Twi/Fante.
U.	– Item(s) of unknown origin.
Wol.	– Wolof.
$\tilde{v}$	– Nasalised vowel.
<	– More than or derived from.
>	– Less than.
?	– Item(s) of unknown meaning and origin.
"... [ ] ..."	– Additions made by the writer to the original text.
"...."	– Literal translations, including grammatical analysis of (italicised) examples from Creole, African and other languages.
'....'	– Translation of non-English item(s).
*	– Ungrammatical item(s) in the language under discussion.

Orthography.

The St. Lucian Creole Alphabet (1981) has been used in the writing of all items in French Creole (Patwa).

The orthography of Cassidy and Le Page (1967) has been used in the writing of all items in English Creole.

The phonemic orthography of the International African Institute (I.A.I.) (i.e. the Practical Orthography of African Languages, I.A.I. 1930), with the following amendments, has been adopted for the phonemic transcription of African languages, throughout this book:

i) I.A.I. ŋ, ʃ, ʒ, ɔ and ɛ are represented by *ng*, *sh*, *zh*, *ò* and *è*, respectively, for ease of typographic representation.

The established orthographies of the language(s) concerned are otherwise used without alteration with the exception of the Hausa orthography in which ɓ, ɗ and ƙ are represented by *b'*, *d'* and *k'* respectively, also for ease of typographic representation.

The International Phonetic Alphabet (I.P.A.) has been adopted for all phonetic transcription.

Phonetic transcriptions are in square brackets and phonemic transcriptions are underlined.

Acknowledgements.

This book brings together various papers and poems written by me on the Social History, Language, Literature and Education in Caribbean and African languages between 1976 and 1984.

In this collection some changes to the original papers have been made in order to ensure accuracy and to improve their readability. The original content of the papers, however, remains the same.

The opinions expressed in this book are mine only and are based on fourteen years of thinking and research in Caribbean and African languages. In no way do they reflect the opinions of any of my past or present employers.

It would be impossible for me to attempt to thank all the individuals and institutions in Africa, Europe, America and the Caribbean whose help and encouragement have contributed to this book. I can only hope that lack of space is not equated with ungratefulness. This being understood, I would like to thank the *Folk Research Centre*, St. Lucia, the *Caribbean Communications Project,* the *I.L.E.A. Afro-Caribbean Language and Literacy Project* for permission to reproduce the papers originally published by them.

I would also like to thank Dr. David Dalby, Dr. D. Hudson, Dr. B. Cowen, Dr. P. Skehan, Mr. J. Norrish, Dr. J. Gundara and Dr. G. Brandt, all of the University of London; Mr. U. Reid (Linguistic Minorities Project), Mrs J. Little, Mr. J. Popeau, Mr. R. Payne and Ms. K Wiltshire, all of the West Indian Supplementary Service of the London Borough of Waltham Forest, Mrs O'Flynn of the English Language

Service, London Borough of Waltham Forest; Miss Y. Collymore, Mr. E. Whittingham, Miss P. Knight, Mr. G Brown and Miss S. Hamilton, all of the Caribbean Communications Project; the staff and pupils of Norlington Junior High School, London; Mr. G.S. Tseja, Vice-principal, Advanced Teacher's College, Ahmadu Bello University, Nigeria; Alhaji I. Abubakar, Commercial Manager, Jos Steel Rolling Mills, Nigeria; Mr. G. Kwanashie and Dr. D. Mohamed, both of Ahmadu Bello University, Nigeria.; Dr. U. Hassan, Bayero University, Nigeria , Miss L. Dalphinis, Mr. A.X. Cambridge, Mr. and Mrs Lawrence, Mr. Buzz Johnson, my friends and ancestors for advice and encouragement in the writing of various sections of this book.

To all the Creole speakers who consented to be interviewed: *grasia, tenki* and *mèsi* — 'thank you'.

My special thanks to the Dalphinis family in England, America and the Caribbean for their continued love and psychological backing. The mistakes are mine.

Morgan Dalphinis
London, March, 1985.

Caribbean and African Languages: a general introduction

When Fanon ascribed a basic importance to the phenomenon of language in his economic and psychological descriptions of French Creole speakers, in as early as 1952, many may have thought that he overstated his case. Today, thirty-two years later, his perspective is as true as it was thiry-two years ago. Indeed, it still remains true that to speak a language means more than to use a certain morphology and syntax, it means to support the whole weight of a culture and civilization (Fanon, F., 1970, p.13).

One could argue that this is the natural state of world events and that the language that we speak as our mother tongue is also the language of the civilization and culture that we wish to support.

In the case of the speakers of Caribbean Creoles, this is not the case because the language is itself, at least partly, a symbol of the historical conflict evident within Creole languages i.e. the conflict between the European enslaver and the African enslaved.

From the moment the first African was enslaved by Europeans in Africa, a new relationship was forced upon peoples of African descent everywhere. This social relationship has had long-term effects upon the high status of the languages of the enslaver and the related low status of the languages of the enslaved.

Africans speaking related languages of the Niger-Congo language family (in Western and Southern Africa) were taken to the Caribbean. Their mother tongues were suppressed through a system of dividing the speakers of the same languages, to make slave revolts more difficult, and a related system of punishments for using an African language including death, the whip, the chain-gang, etc. Despite this system, the Africans preserved the common grammatical core from their related African mother tongues and expressed these grammatical relationships, using the only vocabulary permissable within their respective slave societies, i.e. European language vocabulary.

Out of this gigantic human creative feat was born the Creole languages. Of the Caribbean Creoles, the great majority have their vocabulary base in either the French or English descendants of the Indo-European language family e.g. Jamaican Creole *dag*, cf. English 'dog', St. Lucian French Creole (Patwa) *Cheyen*, cf. French *le chien* — 'the dog' (See I & II below).

The grammatical structure of the Caribbean Creoles originate from the West African and Bantu language descendants of the Niger-Congo language family, eg. Wolof, Twi, Umbundu, Kikongo etc. (see III & IV below).

Due to immigration to Britain, a number of Caribbean Creole speakers are now resident in Britain, and the influences upon Creole languages in Britain from standard English, have increased in contrast to the influences of English as an international language upon Caribbean Creoles within the Caribbean (see V. below).

The similarities between the vocabulary of the Caribbean Creoles and the European languages from which much of their vocabulary is derived, are self-evident.

At the level of structure, however, the differences between Creoles and European languages mark the points of similarity between Creoles and African languages (see pp.8-11).

The similar use of adjectival verbs in Creole and African languages is, for example, also evident in Caribbean written literature as in the poem 'The Stone Sermon' (Brathwaite, E., 1969, pp.97-100):

>Sookey   Dead
>Noun +   Adjectival Verb
>
>cf. English: Sookey   is   dead
>   Noun + to be + Adjective

and in the short story 'A Reasonable Man' (Callender, T., 1975, p.90):

>Some times the dance-floor so crowded that every body butting
>   Adjectival   Adjectival
>into one another.   Verb   Verb
>cf. English: 'Sometimes the dance floor *is* so crowded that
>   to be + Adjective
>everybody *is* butting into one another ... (see also pt.III, ch.2).

In their uses of more aspect based pre-verbal markers e.g. Jamaican Creole *a* and St. Lucian Patwa *ka*, both used to indicate progressive action, Creole languages are similar to African languages also making use of more aspect based pre-verbal markers, rather than the more time-based tense markers of European languages, e.g. *will* as a marker of future tense in English.

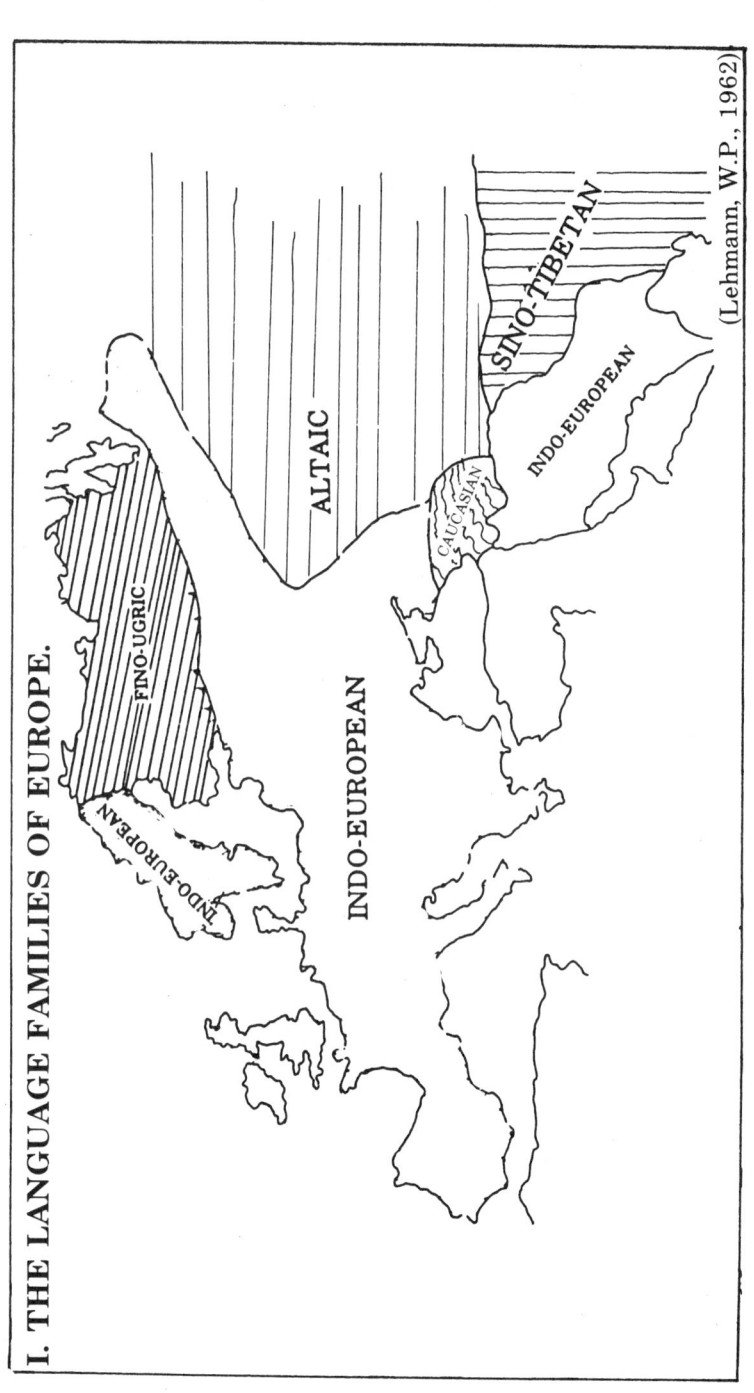
I. THE LANGUAGE FAMILIES OF EUROPE.
(Lehmann, W.P., 1962)

II. THE INDO-EUROPEAN LANGUAGE FAMILY.

```
                    INDO-EUROPEAN
                   /             \
                LATIN          GERMANIC
               / | | \          /    \
              /  |  |  \       /      \
        Italian Portuguese Spanish French  English  German
```

(Lehmann, W.P., 1962)

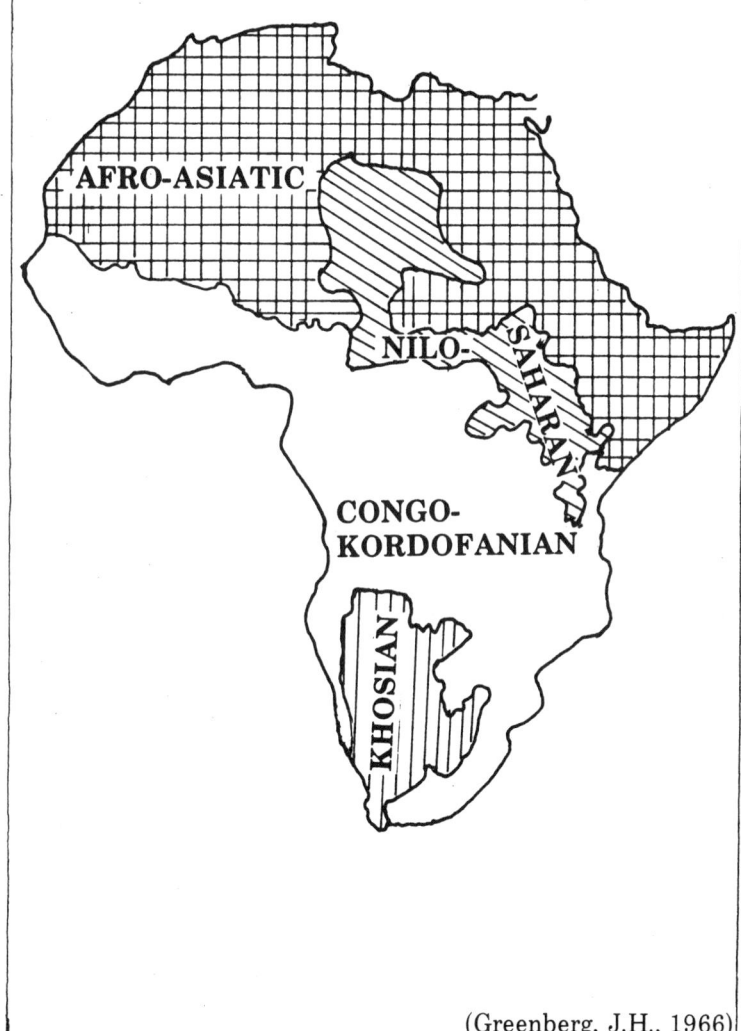

III. THE LANGUAGE FAMILIES OF AFRICA.

(Greenberg, J.H., 1966)

IV. THE NIGER-CONGO LANGUAGE FAMILY.

```
                        CONGO-KORDOFANIAN
                       /                 \
                  NIGER-CONGO         KORDOFANIAN
                 / |    |    \
                /  |    |     \
   WEST     MANDE VOLTAIC KWA  BENUE-    ADAMAWA-
   ATLANTIC                    CONGO     EASTERN
   |_____WEST AFRICAN_____|      |_BANTU_|
```

(Greenberg, J.H., 1966)

V. THE DEVELOPMENT OF CREOLE LANGUAGES

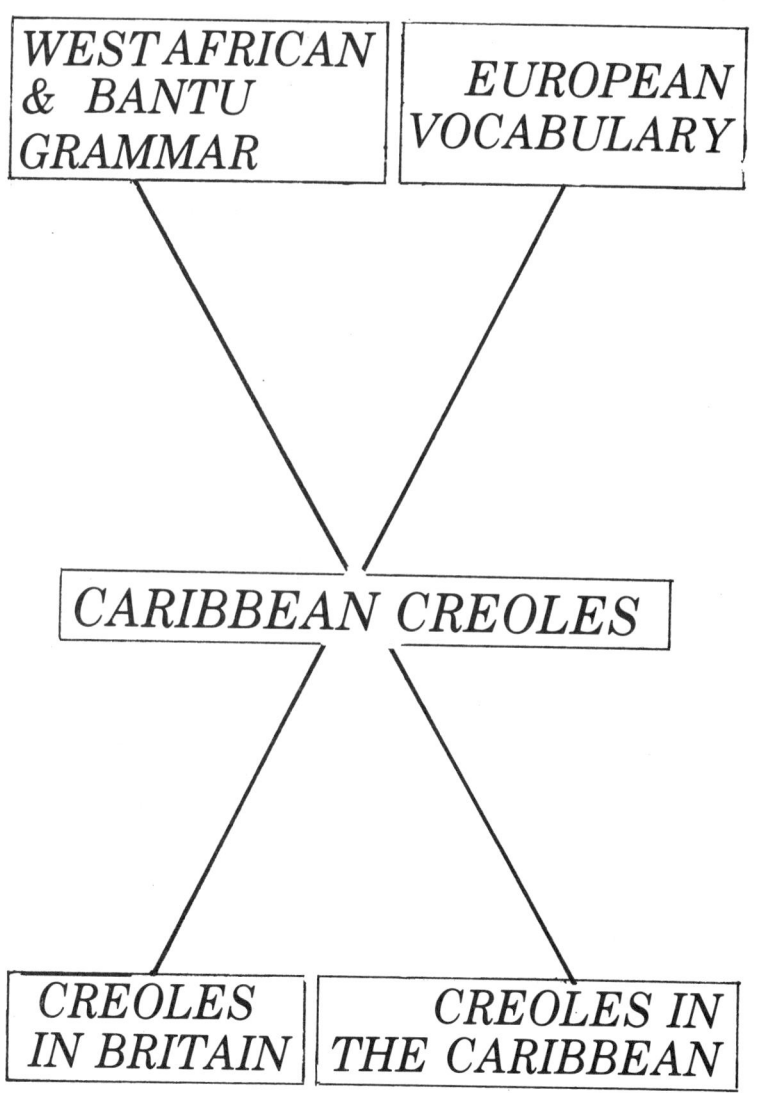

This use of a more aspect based perspective on events may explain other pan-Caribbean and pan-African views of time often referred to, ironically as 'African time' or 'West Indian time' or 'Black people's time' i.e. a view that events begin, or end, or are habitual, and, as a consequence, their description in clock terms is not as important as their progressive, habitual or other aspect. A friend who arrives, therefore, at 7.00p.m. for an appointment previously made for 2.00p.m., for example, may often claim that the appointment must be viewed in terms of 'African time' and not clock time.

This view of events is also shared with the American Indian e.g. the Hopi, whose verbal system and cultural perspectives are even more aspect based than that of Africans and Caribbeans (Whorf, B.L., 1956).

This use of a more aspect based verbal system in Creoles also affects Caribbean literature in which this Creole influence is also evident, in an absence of tense-marking on the verbs (see pt.II, ch.2, p.88).

The following eleven language features are also common to Creoles and African languages (in brackets below):

CARIBBEAN LANGUAGES   AFRICAN LANGUAGES

1. Stabiliser
sé   li   (F.C.)   garab   la   (Wolof)
"Stab.   him/her"   "tree   Stab."
— 'It is him/her'   — 'It is a tree'

2. PREDICATIVE ADJECTIVE
it   red   (E.C.)   è   bija   (Ewe)
"it   red"   "it   red"
— 'It is red'   — 'It is red'

3. EMPHATIC ELONGATION OF VOWEL
   i   kuwiii   (F.C.)   è   nyaaa   (Ewe)
"(s)he run"   "(s)he knows"
— 'He/She ran a lot'   — 'He/She is very intelligent'

4. EMPHATIC REPETITION
   i   ron,   i   ron   (E.C.)   munge   dawa   dawa   (Wolof)
"(s)he run,   run"   "(s)he   run   run"
— 'He/She ran and ran'   — 'He/She ran and ran'

5. GRAMMATICAL SAY/FOR

 i   di mwen kon ha   (F.C.)   fad'a   mini cewa (Hausa)
"(s)he tell me like this"   "tell   me   say"
  'He/She told me'   'told me'

6. PLURAL AFFIX

di man dem   (E.C.)   jòng   o   lu   ((Mandinka)
"the man pl."   "slave the pl."
 'the men'   'the slaves'

7. FRONT FOCALISATION

    li   sèl   vini   (F.C.)   Shi kad'ai ya   zo (Hausa)
"(s)he   Focal. come"   "he   Focal. he come"
 im wan nomo bin kam (E.C.)   — 'He alone came'
"(s)he one Focal. Past come"
 — 'He/She alone came'

8. TOPICALISATION

 liv la mwen ba ou   a, i wouj (F.C.)   Littafin da na ba
"book the I give you(sing.)it red"   "book the which I give
                                              ka, shi ja ne (Hausa)
                                              you(sing) it red be"
  buk we   a gi yu,   i   r d (E.C.)
"the book that I give you (Sing.) it red"
 — 'The book that I gave   — 'The book that I gave
    you is red'   you is red'

9. CATENATION

    i   pwan baton bat li (F.C.)   a   ye   buk o   ta
"(s)he take stick beat him/her"   "(s)he Perf. book the take
 i tek stik bit am (E.C.)   a   a ye   e busa
"(s)he take stick beat him/   "(s)he Perf. them beat"
her"
 — 'He/She took the stick and   — 'He/She took the book and
    beat him/her'   beat him/her'

10. SUFFIXATION OF THE DEFINITE ARTICLE AND PRONOUNS

liv la (F.C.)
"book the"
— 'the book'

liv mwen
"book me"
— 'my book'

jong ò (Mandinka)
"slave the"
— 'the slave'

nèg bi (Wolof)
"house the"

littafin na (Hausa)
"book my"
— 'my book'

11. NON DIFFERENTIATION OF THE 3RD. SING.

i —'(s)he/it' (E.C. & F.C.)

o (Kikongo)
è (Ewe)
i (Twi/Fante)
— '(s)he/it'

Of these features, repetition at the sentence level (above) is also related to repetition at the word level in both Creoles and African languages.

Cf. kuyon kuyon (F.C.)   with dòfdòf (Wolof)
    "stupid stupid"   "stupid stupid"
    — 'very stupid'   — 'very stupid'

This use of repetition for emphasis may well be related to repetition as part of the 'act of creation' in African and Creole literature (see pt.III, ch.4)

The vocabulary of Creoles, despite their European origin in form are often continuities of African language meanings (see pt.III, ch.2).

The Creoles have traditionally been the means of providing a platform for the discussion of local events, for example, in the following St. Lucian song in which the relationship between a man (Siril) and a woman (Sentonya) are discussed:

Sa Ki Soté Pak Milé-a

Sa   ki soté   pak   milé a
"Those who jump fence mule the

Those who Jumped the Mule's Fence

'Those who jumped the mule's fence,

Sète	*Sentonya*	*épi*	*Siril,*		It was Sentonya and Siril,
It was	Sentonya	and	Siril		
an	*bèl*	*tifi*	*kon*	*Sentonya*	A beautiful girl like Sentonya,
a	beautiful	girl	like	Sentonya	
I	*ka*	*soté*	*pak*	*milé a,*	She jumped the mule's fence,
(s)he	Prog.	jump	fence	mule the	
I	*ka*	*manjè*	*lachè*	*Siril,*	She ate Siril's flesh,
(s)he	Prog.	eat	flesh	Siril	
I	*ka*	*kouyé*	*Siril*	*M.C.,**	She called him a pig,
(s)he	Prog.	call	Siril	M.C.*	
Yo	*pòtè*	*plent*	*kont*	*li,*	They took her to court,
they	bring	case	against	him/her	
Sètè	*a*	*nom*	*ki*	*té témwen,*	It was a man who was the witness,
it was	a	man	who	Past witness	
Kont	*yo*	*wivé*	*duvan*	*bawo,*	When they came before the judge,
when	they	arrive	in front	judge	
Yo	*mandé*	*li*	*ki*	*lèta 'y,*	They asked her what her trade was,
they	ask	him/her	what	trade him/her	
I	*di*	*lèta*	*'y*	*sè péyé,*	She said that her trade was to pay,
(s)he	say	trade	him/her	be pay	
Sè	*bay*	*gouté*	*ki*	*ka pasé,*	It was to give (sexual) tastes,
be	give	taste	which	Prog. pass	
Bay gouté,					Give tastes (repeat four times),
(repeat four times)					
Bay	*gouté*	*ki*	*ka*	*pasé,*	Give tastes which pass away,
give	taste	which	Prog.	pass	
Bay	*gouté,*				Give tastes (repeat four times),
give	taste				
Bay	*gouté*	*ki*	*ka*	*pasé,*	Give tastes which pass away,
give	taste	which	Prog.	pass	
Bay	*gouté.*				Give tastes (repeat twice).'
give	taste				
(repeat twice)					

* Short for *mal kochon* — 'male pig'

(The St. Lucian Creole alphabet, 1981, is the orthography used for transcribing the song and all other items in Patwa (French Creole) throughout this book. See Orthography and Abbreviations.)

In more recent times, newspapers with only Creole articles have developed mainly in the French Creole speaking islands e.g. the newspaper *Gwif an Tè* — 'Fingernails in the Earth' in Martinique and *Balata* — 'A Hardwood Tree' in St. Lucia.

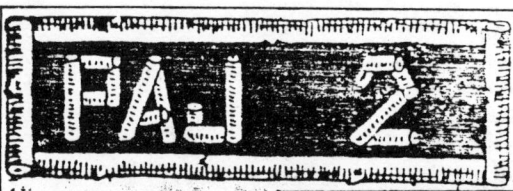

An Sent-Lisi, i ni anchay bon mizisyen ki ka jwé mizik twadisyonal pou anchay tan ek yo pwotjiwé tout kalité mizik pou tout bontan ki ni an vilaj yo épi lòt tikòt. Mé i ka fè nou byen lapenn lè nou ka we yo pa ka wisouvwè kalité lonnè-la yo vo la. Ek sa sé davwè yo pòkò fè yon rèkòd, enben jwé asou radyo, enben alé Lanméwik enben Langlitè; épi davwè yo pa ka genyen lavi yo asou mizik tousèl; èk davwè yo sé jan isi èk nou konnèt yo tèlman byen. Nou ka pwen yo pou sa yo yé san wè adan sé mizisyen-sala sé mapipi

Leonard Jones ni swasant an. Ek kon tout lòt mizisyen ki ka jwé mizik twadisyonal, i pa ka bat tanbou tousel. I ka alé lanmè, i ka fè ti jaden'y, èk lè i ni tan, i ka fè nas pou fè an ti lavi. Mé lè pyès sé bagay-sala pa maché, sé asou tanbou i la fè an ti liv sik.

Leonard lévé adan an fanmi dansé èk chanté. Ek i koumansé jwé tanbou a douz an. Kon pwès tout mizisyen Sent-Lisi, Leonard pa wisouvwè pyès lison an mizik. Manyè i apwann, sé pa kouté épi

koutoumba, èk sé di kalité bélè- la kon anlè, bélè, èk bélè i èk i vini an mapipi Lè i té ni vent an, i té an bat tanbou-la èk moun té konnèt li an péyi-la. Anfen, Leonard ka bay pwès tout bontan an plas-la. Kon Leo di, i ka jwé an débò swayé ki ni anchay (débòt) èk an mawon sé an ti plézi, la mou bwè èk dansé asou tanbou). I ka jwé bay tout kon chayé kann, kannot sòti gwar mennen bò lanmè. Ek

In the following extract from *Balata*, a traditional St. Lucian musician, Leonard Jones, discusses his life (see above). The section of the extract in the rectangle can be translated as follows:

> 'Leonard Jonesis sixty years old. And like all other musicians who play traditional music, he does other things than only beating the drum. He goes to sea, he does a little gardening, and when he has time, he does a little fishing to eke out a living. But when none of these activities work, it's by drumming alone that he can make a little money.'

Caribbean written literature, however, continues to be the source for a Creole use of English, particularly where direct speech is being used by the author. In using the latter, the author (like D.H. Lawrence in his use of Yorkshire varieties of English) has no choice but to use the Creole and Creolized forms of everyday Caribbean language and life. However, where the author is describing events without a use of characters in dialogue i.e. in reported speech, Standard English is used, as in the following extract (Callender, T., 1975, pp.78-79):

REPORTED SPEECH

He took a deep long breath and plunged under the water again. Scraping his knees every now and then, he slowly worked his way towards the cluster, averaging his progress by the number of strokes he made. He surfaced again, and a beam of light skimmed over the spot where he had just come up. It was now moving away from him. He dived again. And now he reached one of the rocks that formed the cluster. He reached out and grabbed a sharp jutting portion of it. The insweeping waves threw him against it and bruised his body, bloodied his gripping hands, but he did not lose his hold. He remained there whilst fingers of light patterned their search upon the sea and the sky and the rocks, and he shivered from fright and fear that, after all, he might not be able to escape them.

Three thousand dollars, he thought. That was a lot of money. That was the price they'd set on his capture. A lot of people will be looking for me in the hope of getting that, he thought. Three thousand dollars!

He stiffened and looked up. Above the noise of the waves on the rock, he could distinguish men's voices. And now he could hear the scrabbling noise of someone clambering up on the rock. He drew in his breath and pressed his back against the jagged side of the rock, waiting, his eyes staring upward. The rock rose behind and above him as he gazed from its base upward to the top edge silhouetted against the dark blue of the sky. He saw a pair of heavy boots, black and sharp against the sky, descending. He held his breath more deeply and his fingers clawed upon the rock behind. There was a splash. The policeman had dropped upon the rock platform below, and staggered as he landed, the light of the torch dancing crazily around at the impact. And then . . . the torch dropped from his hand into the welter of the waves. The policeman was close to him, so close that he could touch

DIRECT SPEECH

him, but the torch was gone, and the policeman couldn't see in the overhanging darkness of the rock.

The policeman swore under his breath, then shouted "Hi!"

"Hinds?" someone replied.

"Yeah. I loss my light, man."

"You ain't see nothing?"

"Hell, I don't know where he could have gone. I thought I was in front of him. You think he gone back in the opposite direction?"

"He was running this way, man."

"So the smart thing to do is to head the other way as soon as he get in the water . . . ."

"You might be right. Hell, why I ain't think of that before?"

"Hold on. I coming up to you. This place dangerous, man. A man could slip off one o' these rocks and drown easy, easy."

"Well, come up and lewwe go. We going have to wait till morning. We can't do nothing more now."

The policeman scrambled up. The voices receded. The sea pounded on the rock as before.

The man waited for a few moments. Then he walked gingerly along the treacherous platform and slipped into the water. In the distance he could see faintly the retreating figures of the policemen. Under cover of the rocks, he headed for the shore. He swam warily, for the sharp teeth of the reef were not easy to avoid.

At last he reached the shore. The barking of the dogs had receded into the distance, and he ran along now, all caution gone.

— o — o — o — o — o —

As seen above, the underlined items in the extract are indicative of Creole influences.

ITEM IN EXTRACT	CREOLE INFLUENCE
Man	Man as a form of address
ain't nothing	use of double negatives typical of both Caribbean and Black American speech
think, get	the Creole verb, like the verb quoted in the text is unmarked for tense
going have	catenation of verbs in a series is also typical of Creole languages (see above).

Despite their rich cultural heritage Creoles have been devalued of prestige, in the same way that their speakers have been, for at least five hundred years.

The efforts of Creole speakers in bridging the communication gap between themselves and Europeans for centuries, has, for example, never been valued. Creole speakers have often mastered European languages, in addition to their Creole languages, in an effort to decrease the communication gap. Europeans, by contrast, have contributed next to nothing in this communication effort and only very few Europeans speak any Creole, let alone any African language. The burden of communication has been the Black man's burden (Dalby, D., 1970).

This devaluation of Creole languages and their speakers continues to the present day when Creoles are still viewed by some as the inferior dialects of European languages, but not as languages of an independent origin, or, in some cases, not even as languages in their own right.

In the present day context of continued cultural aggression against all things Black and African, these views can be contextualized. The main idea is to deny all credit to all positive elements of African civilization in that these are incompatible with views on world-wide White supremacy. The negroid features of some ancient Egyptian statues have been effaced due to similar urges. In modern times television programmes have been made which 'prove' that jazz was a White American creation. A Caribbean hair style is not to be called a 'Corn Row' but by the name of a White actress 'Bo Derick' and the reggae song 'Red Red Wine' could only become famous on an international (White?) level when it was sung by a mainly White reggae group — UB40, and not when sung by its original Black performers. Who knows, soon television programmes will soon be made to 'prove' that reggae was originally a White British creation?

These negative views continue in the British Educational System within which there is little teaching of Caribbean literature, irrespective of the high number of pupils of Caribbean descent within that educational system.

In the Caribbean context, the self-hatred of Africans was

engendered in a racial/class system within which mainly pink and brown-coloured people were, traditionally, allowed to hold political and economic power. In this socio-racial context *sang mêlé* (mixed bloods) like Josephine could become the wife of Napoleon Bonaparte. The majority of dark-brown and Black inhabitants of the Caribbean could only hope for subservient roles at the bottom of the social pile.

Creole languages in the Caribbean have, therefore, traditionally been devalued by their own speakers who may point to these languages and at times their own African features and say that these are the cumulative reasons for their poverty and underdevelopment. They mistakenly equate cause with effect.

In more recent times some positive views on African, Caribbean and Black American culture have changed some of these older views to a limited extent. Research and folk societies in the Caribbean, e.g. The Society for Caribbean Linguistics and Folk Caribbean e.g. The Society for Caribbean Linguistics and the Folk Research Centre, St. Lucia, have done much to raise the valuation of Creole languages in Caribbean minds. Members of these societies have, for example, produced dictionaries of Creole languages as well as guidelines for educational systems catering for Creole speakers.

The post-'independent' period and the ideology of 'independence' for many Caribbean territories has also had some positive effects in the valuation of Creole languages, in that Caribbean politicians, formerly with both their culture and pockets tied to Europe and America, suddenly had to attract the support of Creole speakers at the ballot box. The standard and international English which would have made any colonial Caribbean governor famous was now a liability, as the voters now spoke Patwa, Bajan, Creolese, Creole and West Indian Talk. The Caribbean politicians therefore changed their language, at least in the oral mode.

The cost of educational materials for 'independent' Caribbean territories also had another effect useful to Creole languages. If politicians supported, at least with their lips, the idea of Caribbean culture, then educational materials should, in 'independent' Caribbean territories, reflect this culture. Caribbean writers would feature in this process and would, therefore, use Creole in their works (see above). The Caribbean attempt to deny itself culturally and linguistically therefore failed.

In Britain and the Caribbean we are, therefore, all faced with the question: seeing that after five hundred years of slavery we have failed to exterminate Creole language, what do we do about them now?

In both Britain and the Caribbean the answers have been the

same: assimilate them and/or compromise them, but do not allow them any independent footing. For example, the teaching of, or about Creole languages is not mentioned in teacher-training in Britain, except as an anecdote to Sociolinguistics or as an example of the need for a policy of Multi-cultural Education in Britain. In St. Lucia, on the other hand, there has been some government support for the development of the St. Lucian Creole alphabet. However, there have been, to date, no moves to introduce the alphabet into the St. Lucian Educational System.

Five hundred years after the conquest and we have learned nothing except how to better serve our conquerors. We fear ourselves:

Sèpan	di	sé	pa	sa	ki	ka	chwé
"Snake	say	be	not	that	which	*Prog.*	kill
mwen	hayi	men	sa	ki	di	mi	li!
I	hate	but	that	which	say	look	him!"

— 'The snake says that it is not the one who kills that I hate but the one who shouts there (s)he (i.e. the snake) is!'. For example, eight years ago, the study of Caribbean languages was thought of as a strange preoccupation summed up best by the reaction of a member of a Caribbean government who, on seeing two of my papers on Creoles, said to me, "You mean there is that much to say about Patwa?" The reactions of some Europeans were also both incredulous and hostile in that they seemed to feel challenged by the very idea that Caribbeans have any cultural heritage worth serious consideration.

Today, eight years later, there is some small improvement in attitudes. Caribbeans now want to know more and more about themselves and many Europeans also want to become experts on Caribbeans. The system, however, which is designed to oppress Caribbean peoples, has not changed, firstly because many Caribbeans, sadly, do not want to take the hard and lonely path towards independence: economic, cultural or otherwise. Either the chorus is 'It's the white man's fault' or 'White people are the best and we should not rock the boat'.

Secondly, many Europeans do not like the idea of real equality with Caribbeans, whether in language or otherwise. Either the chorus is 'Blacks are inferior anyway' or 'Let us pretend that we are offering equality by giving a few token jobs to a few safe blacks, but let's not rock the boat with changes that affect the economic or the political'.

It is only within this context of the struggle for the improvement of the material conditions of Africans and their descendants inside and outside Africa (a) by their own efforts and (b) by a wish for equality with Africans by those who at present profit from their oppression, that any meaningful improvement in the role of both Caribbean and African languages can be expanded. Out languages are the symbols of our struggles, our defeats and our victories.

If we are to return proudly, on the other side of the grave, to face the spirits of the ancestors like men and women, we must, on this side of the grave, justify their previous struggles and sacrifices on our behalf by reconstructing the political and economic context within which our culture can have its respected place.

There can be no defence of African and Caribbean culture except through a continuation of our struggle.

Let us eat the kola nut of truth so that present bitterness may one day become refreshment.

Indeed, some of the deepest 'truths' for me are still, even after learning five other languages, only expressible in my mother tongue ie. Patwa, as in the following poems by myself:

Gwo Piton Piti Piton Large Piton Small Piton

Tjèk fwa adan lavi	Sometimes in life
Lavi ka ba nou wòch,	Life gives us stones,
Lavi ka ba nou fè.	Life gives us iron.
Tjèk fwa adan nan vi,	Sometimes in a life,
Woch ka pété douvan jyé'w,	Stones burst before your eyes,
Fè nan difé cho lavi ka kwazé'w,	Iron in the hot fire of life crushes you.
Men chonjé:	But remember:
Sé woch asou wòch	It is stone upon stone
Ka fè gwo piton, piti piton,	Which makes the large *piton* the small *piton*,
Difé asou difé ka fè gwo piton sòti piti piton.	Fire upon fire which makes the large *piton* emerge from the small *piton*.
Mòn lavi ki nou ka monté,	Mountains of life that we climb,
Ban nou fè nan tjè,	Give us iron in the heart,
Wòch lavi nou ka pléwé,	Stones of life that we cry of,
Ban nou difé nan tjè.	Give us fire in the heart.
Gwo piton piti piton,	Large *piton* small *piton*,
Antwé nan tjè-nou.	Enter our hearts.
Kité nou défan sa Kawayib	Let us defend what Caribs
Défan ban-nou.	Defended for us.
Wòch lavi, difé lavi.	Stones of life, fires of life,
Gwo Piton, Piton nou la! Nou la!	*Gwo Piton, Piti Piton* we are here! We are here!
Gwo Piton, Piton nou la! Nou la!	*Gwo Piton, Piti Piton* we are here! We are here!
Gwo Piton, Piti Piton . . .	*Gwo Piton, Piti Piton* . . .
Gwo Piton, Piti Piton . . .	*Gwo Piton, Piti Piton* . . .

(in the south-west of St. Lucia (The Caribbean) there are two volcanic hills which rise almost vertically from the sea. The larger hill is called *Gwo Piton* and the smaller hill, *Piti Piton*. The descendants of the St. Lucian carib are to found in the areas near *Gwo Piton* and *Piti Piton*.)

Inspiwasyon

The heavens ache,
All the songs that might have been,
Lightening blue,
With thunder's cry,
Blue to touch,
Blue plunder of the earth.

But they were not sung,
The blue did not touch.
Heart-ache of colonial slavery
Voices held in prison,
Prisoners holding in an ache.

The cry is all around.
And you cannot escape
To blue clouds,
To calm seas,
To deep philosophy
Here where philosophy is action.

Mwen té pé palé
Men yo tjwé vwa mwen.
Mwen té vlé volé
Men yo koupé zèl mwen.
Lang mwen ka bat sèlman
Kon koutim, kon tjè mwen.

Ki tan ki tan vwa-a
Kai viwé.
Jibyé blé èspwa,
Cyèl blé lapé,
San tonnè, san zéklè,
Men épi zyé klè.

Déviwé an jou ti bèl péyi,
Bèl péyi èspwa,
Déviwé an jou bèl vwa,
Déchenen mwen,
Libéwé tèt mwen.

Kité mwen sav ankò
Difé katjil,
Kité mwen sav ankò
Katjil èk aksyon,
Ansam, ansam,
Blé tonnè,
Blé plézi
Inspiwasyon.

I could have spoken
But they killed my voice.
I wanted to fly
But they cut my wings.
My tongue only beats
Like a habit, like my heart.

When oh when will the voice
return.
The blue bird of hope,
The blue sky of peace,
Without thunder, without lightening,
But with clarity.

Return again one day the beautiful country,
Beautiful country of hope,
Return again beautiful voice,
Unchain me,
Liberate my head.

Let me know again
The fire of thought,
Let me know again
Thought with action,
Together, together,
Blue thunder,
Blue pleasure
Inspiration.

Part I.
The Social History of Creole Languages.

1. Introduction.

The Social History of Creole Languages

Creole languages, perhaps more than any other language type, are closely tied to the societies in which they were created and are at present used. This may be due to the fact that from their very origins they were created as a result of social pressures i.e. the social pressure for communication between ethnic groups who did not understand each other and so developed a pidgin (the first stage towards the formation of a Creole) for inter-ethnic communication.

In the case of the Caribbean Creoles the social pressures for communication were mainly between African and European ethnic groups.

The social context for the Caribbean Creoles was the Atlantic Slave Trade, involving the enslavement of Africans by Europeans for economic profit.

As well as being a social context for exploitation, however, the Caribbean Creole social context is one of African resistance, readaption and perpetuation of African culture in the teeth of an attempt to enforce European culture upon captured Africans.

Out of this social carthesis of African cultural continuity in the New World, was born the Caribbean Creole languages as an embodiment of the history and social structure of its speakers.

'Historical Background: the development of Patwa in St. Lucia' situates the development of Creole in St. Lucia within such a socio-historical context between 1639 and 1948, with a particular emphasis upon the contribution of nineteenth century St. Lucia maroons to the development of St. Lucian Patwa.

'The Social History of Caribbean Languages: the St. Lucian case', while accepting the historical background of St. Lucia as having a predominating effect upon the St. Lucian Creole language (Patwa), analyses the modern relationships between language and society in St. Lucia, many of which have attributable historical causes.

'Creoles and Ideologies of Return' examines further the different political ideologies which have resulted from the different social histories of three Creole societies, in Casamance (Senegal), Gambia and St. Lucia. The use of each Creole language as a social symbol is also outlined.

This analysis is taken further in 'Portuguese Creole in Casamance, French and African Languages : languages in competition in southern Senegal'. In this chapter, social conflicts inherent in the creation of this Portuguese Creole are also evident in the present-day development of this Creole.

The large extent of overlap between social conflict, language change and creativity in Creole languages suggests a model of language competence and cognition in Creoles in which social conflict, involving languages in competition, are themselves central to language and cognitive competence of Creole speakers.

2. Historical Background: the development of Patwa in St. Lucia.

The earliest available reports[1] on the history of Saint Lucia index the island's history as one of turbulence and a frequent change of rulers. The English settlers brought to St. Lucia in 1639 were promptly chased off by the native Caribs; the Caribs in their turn were practically wiped out[2] by the French invading from Martinique, under the leadership of Governor Duparquet in 1640. Between 1640 and 1650, St. Lucia was firstly owned by the "Compagnie des Isles d'Amérique" (Company of American Islands) and then by a Monsieur Dizel du Parquet who bought the island, as well as a few other islands from the "Compagnie" which was now bankrupt:

> Le 12 mai 1648... la Compagnie... accablée de dettes... décide de liquider son association en vendant son avoir: les Ilês. Dizel du Parquet acquiert le 22 Septembre 1650 Martinique, Sainte Lucie, la Grenade et les Grenadines pour 41500 livres.[3] (The 12th May 1648. .. the Company... overwhelmed by debts... decides to liquidate its association by selling its assets: the Islands. Dizel du Parquet acquired Martinique, St. Lucia, Grenada and the Grenadines on the 22 September 1650 for 41500 pounds).

From 1650, the ownership of the island was contested by the British and French alone by means of treaties and, more often by wars; in 1664, Lord Willoughby sent 1000 Barbadians to St. Lucia who overpowered the French settlers, but, two years later, were overpowered themselves by diseases and "native wars".[4] In 1667, the French retook the island and in 1674 reannexed it to the French crown as a dependency of Martinique and, though French ownership was contested by the British in the years that followed, a peaceful arrangement was reached whereby the island was to be used for restricted purposes only.

This arrangement was shattered in 1739 by the deployment of

French troops on the island of the Marquis de Caylus; in 1748, peace was again arranged between the British and the French at the treaty of Aix-la-Chapelle, where St. Lucia was declared neutral. This neutrality was broken by the Seven Years War which followed, during which St. Lucia surrendered to the British admiral Rodney; at the end of this was St. Lucia was given back to France.

However, like Helen of Troy, St. Lucia was destined to be the scene of further conflict between her eager suitors; in 1762, the British "occupent sans coup férir la Grenade, Saint Vincent et Sainte Lucie"[5] (occupied Grenada, Saint Vincent and Saint Lucia without a shot being fired) with a force led by Douglas and Rodney . In 1778, presumably after another period of French control, Rodney again retook the island, but, in 1783, it was restored to France at the Treaty of Versailles. The see-saw struggle continued, and in 1794, during the French Revolution, the British admiral Jervis took the island for Britain; it was subsequently recaptured by the Republican Victor Hughes for France at the Peace of Amiens. Eleven years later, in about 1813, St. Lucia was ceded to Britain. The following are the conquests, either by war or by treaty: Caribs: one conquest; French: seven conquests; British: eight conquests.

From Rinchon[6] we ascertain that the slave population of St. Lucia in 1780 was approximately 20,000, and from Frossard[7] that the slave population in 1787 was 16,689, but by 1833, according to Rinchon,[8] the slave population was only 13,348; this figure agrees with Curtin's 10,000 "and rising" graph indicating the number of slaves imported into St. Lucia between 1776 and 1834.[9]

From the reports of the Protectors of Slaves between July 1826 and December 1829,[10] we get the figure of 14,300 slaves for the 1826 population of S. Lucia, as well as interesting details about the past slave-society of St. Lucia. The overall impression of these records is the high requency of the 'crime' of running away; for example, between the 1st June and the 31st December of 1826, "Absconding, running away"[11] was the 'crime' committed most by the most slaves, i.e. by 120 male slaves and 20 female slaves, while 5 slaves were punished for "harbouring runaways" during the same period. Running away was also the 'crime' committed by the most slaves between the 1st January and the 30th June of 1827, i.e. by 131 male and 26 female slaves;[12] as it was also for the period between the 30th June and 31st December 1827, during which 97 male and 13 female slaves absconded and ran away; as well as for the period between the 1st January and the 30th June in which 83 male and 13 female slaves ran away.

Given the many forested areas in St. Lucia, the mountainous terrain in some areas which has only been opened up by road communication in fairly recent times;[13] running away was quite a feasible strategy, and, given the already existing bands of "Maroon" or runaway slaves in these forests, a more pleasurable existence than slavery. It is from this experience that we get the word *mawon* — 'runaway', and the phrase *nèg mawon* — 'runaway slave', in St. Lucian Patwa. Unfortunately, in recent times these terms have the abusive meaning of 'ignorant, fool, silly', in all of which are also partly coreferential with 'black' and 'African' in St. Lucian society.

Running away or Marronage was obviously not without its pains[14] as it was often undertaken for a period of a few months only in many cases, for example, the slave "Pierre who ran away for 5 months" and the slave Angelique who ran "away for more than a month in the woods"; both alluded to in the Half Yearly Returns from 30th June 1827 to the 1st January 1828 inclusive, of the records of the Protectors of Slaves.

The names of some of the slaves in these records, as well as indicating the probable mockery of the masters, for example "Petit Pascal" (Little Pascal), "Janvier Jaloux" (Jealous January)[15] are also possible indices of the areas in West Africa from which they were taken; for example the names St. Rose Mustapha and Louisa Galba (compare Hausa Garba) indicate an Islamic West African origin; the names Nanny,[16] Cuffy and Ado, on the other hand, indicate the possible presence of Akan slaves from the Gold Coast, while the names Lucie Ibo[17] and Charles Congo[18] speak for themselves. The names Mandingo[19] and Pierre Senegal[20] on the other hand, indicate a Senegambian origin.

The records of the minutes of the St. Lucian Privy Council from 1826 to 1832 and the records of the Minutes of the Executive Council from its formation in March 1832 to February 1834 are not very indicative of such possible origins of the St. Lucian slaves, but are extremely good indices of the tremendous effect of Maroon *mawon* culture amongst the St. Lucian slaves; we are told that there "were a good many Maroon Slaves in the island" and that the British rulers in about 1826 were wondering:

> whether it would not have a good effect if it were to serve his Proclamation offering a free pardon to all who should return to their owners within a certain period, after which a General Detachment would be ordered out for their apprehension.[21]

This General Detachment was to some extent successful; for example:

> the Maroon Negro Henry killed by a detachment regularly authorised to go in pursuit of Maroon Slaves.[22]

The importance placed upon their effectiveness is evident. The authorities found it:

proper to establish at Castries and Soufrière in addition to the present Police a Brigadier and 3 Archers at each of these towns with a salary of £3000 livres each per Annum and £2000 livres to each of the said archers in addition to the usual fees granted by Law for the capture of Runaway Slaves.[23]

Given that the "Allowance" of a high official such as the Protector of Slaves was £7,000 livres,[24] it is an indication of the importance placed upon the threat of the *nèg mawon* to St. Lucian plantation society that, as seen below:

3 archers	@ £2,000 per year for Soufrière =	£6,000
3 archers	@ £2,000 per year for Castries =	£6,000
1 Brigd.	@ £3,000 per year for Soufrière =	£3,000
1 Brgd.	@ £3,000 per year for Castries =	£3,000
	Total:	£18,000

£18,000 should be spent purely upon counteracting the Maroon threat.

The threat of the Maroons is further indicated by the fact that "fees granted by law for the capture of Runaway Slaves" were made in addition to the salary of these Regular Detachments which must have been in existence in parts of the island other than Castries and Soufriere. Note that these Regular Detachments for Castries and Soufriere:

> should be exempt from the performance of all Militia duties.[25]

Given the strength of Maroon culture in St. Lucia, it is likely that the development of Patwa owed as much, if not more, to the slaves than to the masters. As a common language of the St. Lucian slaves it must have been an extremely important means of communication for the runaways and for the perpetuation of runaway culture. Bands of slaves living in the forests away from plantation society are likely to have contributed other dimensions to the development of Patwa than those of plantation society where the culture of the masters was paramount, both in the minds of the plantation slaves and those of their masters.

Further, given that running away, as suggested earlier, was carried out for short periods by many slaves, it is likely that even the slaves who spent most of their lives on the plantations would have had some acquaintance with the Maroon culture of the perpetual runaways.

Given that British political domination in St. Lucia had lasted since 1813, it is likely that in 1827 some of their linguistic dominance and, as a consequence, some of their political dominance was avoided by the Maroon slaves speaking Patwa.

A French connection of the St. Lucian Maroons as a dimension of their perpetuation of an Afro-Caribbean alternative to plantation society culture and language is based upon fact as well as conjecture; for example, the famous case of the "Negro named Cyrile[26] who had escaped from Martinique" in 1828 and even had the audacity to perform actions causing him to be:

> accused of having been concerned in poisoning some Slaves at Martinique and had also been in the habit of Selling Drugs without Licence since his arrival.[26]

in St. Lucia, having disembarked upon the coast in a canoe; apart from indicating the easy communication available between St. Lucia and neighbouring Martinique (24 miles), it is only an individual example of the Martinico-St. Lucian Maroon route. This route is ironically alluded to in Patwa: *pas pa tè* — 'pass by land', an ironic name for Martiniquan immigrants in St. Lucia[27] which preserves the comment that the first Maroon immigrants in St. Lucia *té pasé pa glo* — 'had come by water'.

As well as Curtin's[28] short note that St. Lucia was looked upon as the haven of many Runaway Slaves, the Privy and Executive Council records are specific; for example, in 1830 the:

> Honourable members called his Excellency's attention to the frequent arrivals in this Island of runaway slaves from Martinique and their numbers being started to have increased to an alarming extent, and fearing that some evil consequences may arise there from, that they may materially affect the morality of the Slaves in this Island... to his Majesties government that the colony may be relieved of them,[29]

while even as late as 1832, the Privy and Executive Council still indicate the problem of the tradition of Martinico-St. Lucian Marronage in St. Lucia:

> The Council proceeds to the further consideration of the proclamation for repressing and discouraging the ingress of Fugitive Slaves from Foreign Settlements.
> The evidence of Refugees who have arrived from Martinique previous to the passing of the act proposed.[30]
> The Council proceeded to the further consideration of a proclamation for the refusing and discouraging of fugitive slaves from foreign settlements.[31]

Whatever the illusions of the Martinique slave about greater freedoms available in St. Lucian plantation society, the difficulty of inter-communication within St. Lucia in the recent past[32] was a feature which made Marronage in St. Lucia as feasible as Jamaican Marronage in the Blue Mountains; as the records for 26th May 1832 indicate:

> the frequency of the Crime of Running Away amongst the slaves of

this Island and the Physical Circumstances of the Country rendering it difficult, if not impossible to arrest fugitive slaves, it is necessary.. to repress this practice.

This Martinico-St. Lucian link, though possibly justifying the statement of a French colleague at the Études Créoles (Creole Studies) Conference of 1976 at Nice ("La perpétuation de la Créolophonie est une perpétuation de la Francophonie"—the perpetuation of French Creoles is a perpetuation of French language and culture), indicates also the presence of common factors among the slaves, from the linguistic to the genetic, other than the French language. Slaves from both Martinique and St. Lucia, both living in the St. Lucian forests as Maroons, would have to develop a culture substantially different from Martiniquan and St. Lucian plantation societies in order to guarantee their mutual survival. These common factors would of necessity be of an Afro-Caribbean dimension.

The Relexification thesis which points to the common syntactic structure[33] between the Kriul of Senegambia and the Caribbean Creole languages, and which holds that the French Caribbean Creoles and Creoles in which the Kriul syntactic structure has been preserved, but the Portuguese-derived lexical items have been replaced by French-derived lexical items, would find good grounds for justification in this historical context. What is more common to both St. Lucian and Martiniquan slaves, apart from a common African origin in Senegambia where the Afro-Portuguese middlemen[34] did much of their slave trading in the Kriul language? The meeting of Martiniquan and St. Lucian *nèg mawon* in the relative isolation from St. Lucian and Martiniquan plantation culture, provided by the St. Lucian landscape, was only a possible opportunity for high relexification of Kriul structure by French-derived lexical items common to both Martiniquan and St. Lucian slaves.

This common origin, culture and language is of pertinent relevance to the St. Lucian historical situation where in the earliest years in which St. Lucian Patwa was first being developed, namely between 1640 and 1813, the changes of ownership between British and French slave-masters were frequent. For this frequency of change between British and French domination not to have affected the basic structure of St. Lucian Patwa, and to have left its structure nearly equivalent to the Martinique Creole language (developed mainly under French domination) necessitates a preservation of linguistic structure other than English or French in the linguistic competence of St. Lucian and Martinique slaves. An African sub-stratum[35] theory, and a straight Relexification hypothesis can both be easily accommodated by such historical evidence

This Martinico-St. Lucian slave route is also alluded to by living

Martiniquans whose slave-master ancestors had sent a slave to St. Lucian by boat in order to save this slave from severe punishments in Martinique.[36]

This route was not one-way only, and whatever illusions the Martiniquan slaves held of St. Lucia as a haven, the St. Lucian slaves only duplicated them in their zealous attempts to run away to Martinique; for example, such an attempt, although unsuccessful, is referred to in the Privy and Executive Council records for the 6th of October 1832.

> Eight of the slaves of his Estate, the Roseau, were missing last night, and are supposed to have embarked in a canoe for Martinique.[37]

They were apprehended by seamen authorised to do so, as indicated by the testimony of one of these seamen:

> About five this morning I came up with the Boat, detached to Seaward, which had met with a Canoe off the Margot des Roseaux with Thirteen Slaves on Board — twelve belonging to the Perle Estate and one to the Bois d'Orange Estate.[37]

The possible mutual influences between the St. Lucian and Martiniquan Creole languages can however only be further attested by an analysis of the past records for Martinique in which I should expect some reference to St. Lucian *nèg mawon* in Martinique and Martiniquan *nèg mawon* successfully escaping to St. Lucia. The link of French culture between these slaves is, however, not an argument to be ignored; as early as 1639 when French troops invaded St. Lucia from Martinique, the first Martinico-St. Lucian links were forged; this was followed by the 1674 reannexation of St. Lucia to the French Crown as a dependency of Martinique and culminated with a period of French cultural ascendency between 1651 and 1793 where, with a gap in 1667, for the English governor Faulk's last year of office,[38] 36 French governors ruled St. Lucia. The governor most responsible for the French cultural and material development of St. Lucia in this period was the governor Laborie.[38]

The cultural supremacy of France within St. Lucia as well as being alluded to in 1814, when St. Lucia could be described as French in "language, manners and feeling",[39] is also well attested; the French place names of the island, for example, Vieux-Fort, Dauphin and Gros Islet, and, even under British domination, French titles such as ' "Procureur du Roi"[40]   as well as French names for English currency were used by the British administrators themselves: "the sum of   £200 *livres*"[41] (my emphasis).

Political co-operation between French-ruled Martinique and British-ruled St. Lucia in 1827 was so cordial that at least one case of repatriation was amicably dealt with:

> a slave now at Martinique ... and it is satisfactorily proved that the Slave name Pauline is a Creole of St. Lucia and all her relations are still here and as on a preceeding occasion his Majesty's Government were pleased to recommend that another slave in similar circumstances should be allowed to return to the island and be registered as a slave of this Colony ... in the meantime that the Slave be allowed to return to the island.,[42]

In fact, so cordial was this relationship that a potential conflict between a French schooner and a British vessel in St. Lucian waters was avoided:

> the very handsome conduct of Capt. Jacob, Commander of the Sloop Jeremie, in declining to receive any remuneration for the injury done to this vessel by the act of Captain Irailland, of the French Schooner Argus in consequence of the large family of Captain Irailland.[43]

In fact, even an account of this encounter was also given:

> to the governor of Martinique and a very satisfactory explanation ... had been made both to the British flag ...

Despite this extreme cordiality between the French rulers of Martinique and the rulers of British-dominated St. Lucia, the extreme cultural dominance of France in St. Lucia and the resultant cultural rejection of British values is not one to be underestimated, even up to this present day, after many years of British political domination.

According to the records even by 1827,[44] fourteen years after the advent of British rule, both the Laws of France and of England were important in the legislature of this now British territory:

> the age of Majority should be reduced to 21 years as was at present to the rule both in England and France.[45]

Even concerning the length of time within which contracts might be annulled, French custom is alluded to in detail:

> ... the term settled by many of the ancient customs of France exclusive of the customs of Paris.[45]

By 1832 the question of French cultural dominance is undisputed even by the British rulers, who argue that the office of Judge of the Police court in St. Lucia necessitates knowledge of French law; for example, the complaint of a leading St. Lucian citizen in 1832 is one of descrimination being practised against him because of his alleged lack of knowledge about French law, "... justified his opinion of my unfitness for the Office of Judge of the Police Court first, because he conceives me ignorant of the French Law".[46] Indeed in the institution of the law, nowhere else are the Francophone rites of justice copied in more detail than in the

British-ruled St. Lucia of 1832; the title of the Chief Justice is that of the Chief Justice in France — the *Sénéchal* ("performed by the Senechal or President of the Court"),[47] and even his jurisdiction, the *Sénéchausée* was mimicked in St. Lucia: "the Court of the Sénéchaussée".[48]

Given this extreme influence of French institutions and culture in the St. Lucian past, the defensive attitude of the past British rulers towards French culture in St. Lucia is not surprising. This, by the way, follows from the fact that even under British rule many of the masters of the plantations and the members of the élite were French. For example, the "Honourable Gaillard Delablanque"[49] and "Mr. Le Chantre the Deputy Grelfier of the Court".[50]

This dominance of French culture is one that was possibly shared by the St. Lucian slaves as well as the St. Lucian slave-masters. Given the Latin/French ideology of assimilation as compared to the Germanic ideology of racial separation of the British, it is not surprising that the slaves should have had greater access to French rather than British culture. St. Lucian situated French culture, therefore, has possibly always had an influence upon the St. Lucian slave-masters in any wish to identify themselves as autonomous and separate from the Metropolis, whether English or French.[51]

As far as the slaves were concerned this possible greater access to French culture was firstly no doubt easier for slaves originating from a Kriul-speaking Senegambia as the Latin culture and language of the Portuguese mulattoes was closer to French than it was to English. Note for example the greater similarity between Patwa *bon* and Kriul *boniitu* as compared to English [gud] (all meaning 'good').

This access to French culture has resulted in a mainly Afro-French culture in St. Lucia. For example, when a Césaire speaks of "a bowl full of oils, a candle-end with a dancing flame",[52] are we brought to an African present and past of non-Christian icon- and ancestor-worship or to the Catholic past and present of the French, or to a new culture in which both are reflected?

The St. Lucian *fèt lawòz* (feast of the rose) itself is indicative of the Afro-French cultural syncretism; whatever the French origins of this fête (feast), the sudden rhythmic dancing in a room around tables on which jars full of roses were placed, to the chanting of *wòz, lawòz, wòz, lawóz* (rose, rose, rose, rose), shows a definite African element in the mode of performance despite its European content.[53]

Given this cultural and linguistic access of the St. Lucian slaves to Afro-French culture, it only follows that Patwa was the language of revolt, African perpetuation and of African religions in St. Lucia, the words *voudou* (Voodoo), *tjenbwa* or *kenbwa* (sorcery), for example, were and are identified with Patwa rather than English in St. Lucia. Breen's description of a group of about twelve slaves about to be hanged for the 'crime' of revolting against slavery is also exemplary in that he describes one such slave about to be hanged, who sheds "a single tear" which for Breen[54] indicated a sudden realization by the slave that *kenbwa* would not save him.

Breen's other description of a slave who, because he believed the herbalist who told him that he would be invulnerable to harm, willingly allowed himself to be condemned to certain punishment, is another aspect of the African experience which only has lexical indices in Patwa.

An analysis of past language policies in St. Lucia also indicates the cultural ascendancy of France in the island and the resultant linguistic syncretism between French and African languages in the development of Patwa; the first comment evident on language policy in the records is in 1832 when St. Lucia was under British rule:

> On the Governor's enquiring what proportion do the Slave proprietors or managers of this Island understand the French language only, bear to those understanding English, they were calculated at about two thirds.[55]

This carte blanche for the ascendency of the French language in a British-ruled territory is reflected by the practice of translating laws from English into French for the purpose of what is possibly the majority of the population — French-speakers:

> ... It had hitherto been the usage of the Royal Court to have all Laws translated into French previously to their being registered in the Royal Court, *and in no former instance had any Law been registered in the English Language* (my emphasis)

In such a multi-lingual society, the frequent use of interpreters was a logical consequence:

> Mr. Taggart the Sworn Interpreter being sent for, admitted that he received the Law of 2nd November 1831 as also that of 20th June 1831 for translating into French... Mr Taggart replied that having other translations to make, he did not think that he could individually translate those orders in Council *in less than three or four weeks* (my emphasis)[56]

The arguments between interpreters and their employees as well as being a testimony to human quarrelsomeness also indicate that the standard of French spoken in St. Lucia was of a high if not meticulous standard; for example, we note a case where, pertaining to "the Registry of this Translation", it was suggested "that the registration should only be provisional in consequence of the numerous errors contained therein".[57]

Even if this wish for linguistic perfection is explained as the necessary care devoted to the translation of all official documents, one has to admire the wish to preserve the French language in a British territory where all such documents would be read by French-speaking slave-masters, whose memories of France should have begun to fade.

Language-use, as well as being effective (for example: the "using in the public court house language calculated to excite the slaves of the Island to Rebellion" by the "protector of slaves"[58]) was, for this period, unquestionably a French-benefiting affair. For example:

> ... the Order in Council of the 2nd November 1831, be promulgated in the French language, which they are of the opinion will supersede the necessity of publishing further on that head ...[59]
> [the] Sitting of 26th May 1832 ... bearing the date 2nd November 1831, was directed to be published in English and French for the information of the community.[60]

The implied value attached to bilinguals, e.g.:

> I have the occassional assistance of a young Gentleman versant in both languages,[61]

and what seems to be cutting criticism within this context:

> Mr Grant knew nothing either of the laws of France, *or its language*[62] (my emphasis),

also point to the importance of French in St. Lucia of 1832.

Whatever its influences, whether French, West African or Portuguese, it is evident that, as well as the neighbouring island of Martinique, other islands were influenced by the Afro-French culture and language of the St. Lucian slaves, as well as influencing the St. Lucian slaves by means of this same language and culture. For example, Trinidad French Creole, which is now a dying language, was probably influenced by the past ingress of "refugees" from St. Lucia:

> The Procureur General began to make an observation that the removal to Trinidad could not be viewed by the Refugees at present in this island as any punishment, because a great many of these persons have quitted St. Lucia and returned to that Colony, where they had established themselves.[63]

As with the case of Martinique, the influences were mutual; St. Lucia was the catch-point of runaway slaves from as far afield as Trinidad:

> The Honourables Peter Smith, Peter Mater and Gaillard Delabenque strongly objected to the Refugee Slaves being punished for that offence, being sent to Trinidad, as they conceive it will *tend in no way to deter them from visiting this colony*, but they approve of their being sent to Sierra Leone at the Expense of Government[64] (my emphasis).

The development of St. Lucian Patwa could only have benefited from the ingress of Trinidadian slaves some of whom also spoke a French Creole.

This reference to St. Lucia as a haven for runaway slaves is an interesting myth. Like all myths it must have had substance as well as popular currency amongst slaves from neighbouring islands. It is obviously nothing to do with the leniency of French as opposed to English slave-masters, as slaves from French-ruled Martinique and British-ruled St. Lucia both wanted to flee to the island opposite (St. Lucia for Martiniquan slaves and Martinique for St. Lucian slaves).

Perhaps an explanation would be the classic psychology of "the grass is greener on the other side" and the necessary illusion for all slaves throughout history, from Spartacus's band or the Israelites to the more recent African slaves, that somewhere in this world or the next is a 'promised land' which just has to be better than the one the slave finds himself in. After all no future land either in time of space could be any worse.[65]

Psychology apart, the terrain of St. Lucia, which even in present times is difficult, high mountains and deep forested valleys in most areas, with the exception of areas near the coast where the deltaic alluvial deposits of rivers have created areas of flat land. This was probably definitely a defendable or inhabitable haven for the slaves who managed to run away into these valleys within St. Lucia, and, on the theory that nothing succeeds like success, it is not surprising that slaves from other islands, among them Martinique and Trinidad, would take a chance for survival's sake and go to where at least the fable of an alternative to slavery was said to originate — St Lucia.

Given the prominence of St. Lucia as a runaway catchment area, the Maroon *mawon* influences upon St. Lucian Patwa by groups of slaves living in the forest is not to be underestimated; possibly the present-day predominance of Patwa in rural areas, (*hòtè*), as opposed to its slow death in the urban area of Castries, has been influenced by this situation as well as by the natural wish to master international languages, English being the most accessible, by any urban, as opposed to rural, population. Another possible outcome of this past situation is the genetic classification *nèg jiné* (Guinea African)[66] 'blue'-black negroes who are often mainly of rural origin; e.g. from the rural area of Desrisseaux (*dèwiso)* in St. Lucia.

This reference to the possible exportation of St. Lucian slaves to Sierra Leone, if it was acted upon ("approve of their being sent to Sierra Leone at the Expense of the Government"[67]) may possibly explain the origin of some of the French-derived lexical items in Sierra Leonean Krio as well as reasserting part of the geographical dimension in which African-derived Creole languages had their most prominent influences.

Apart from this suggested punishment of being sent back to Africa, other punishments were devised to restrain the culture of Marronage in St. Lucia itself such as "a rigid penal enactment to repress this practice"[68] entailing a system of corporal punishment for the first and second offence and "Chain Gang for life on the third offence for both men and women slaves".[69] The severity of these punishments in fact only index the audacious traditional tenacity of the African in surviving under any circumstances; despite these threats they continued to search for freedom by running away from slavery.

The Journals of the Legislative Council from 1835-1839 bear out the previously described historical background to Patwa. For example, the 1835 "Ordinance respecting refugee slaves from Foreign Colonies which was read ... repressing and punishing the illegal intrusion of fugitive alien Slaves into the Colony of Saint Lucia".[70] They also allude to the tradition of Marronage in St. Lucia as well as testifying to the Martiniquan connection in St. Lucian culture:

> The Procureur General laid on the Table a Draft Ordinance respecting Martinique refugees.[71]

and to the maintenance of French culture in a British-ruled St. Lucia; for example, the maintenance of the Catholic Church, introduced into St. Lucia by the French rulers, seems to be of importance even under British rule as seen from the same records.[72]

These records also indicate the high probability that many of the rulers of St. Lucia after 1813 were French not only in "culture and manners" but in blood also. This is also testified by the possibly French influences on the use of English by the Clerk making the various records, for example, the "Procureur General"[73] (compare the English "procurer").

These journals, however, indicate other interesting dimensions of the history of language in St. Lucia. For example, the entrenched nature of Marronage in St. Lucian culture seems to have had a great influence upon even subsequent plantation society itself as even "Aprenticed Labourers" began to follow this African slave innovation.

> An Ordinance preventing and punishing persons harbouring and employing *runaway* Apprenticed Labourers[74] (my emphasis).

The first reference to Anglo-French conflict in St. Lucia on the basis of differences in culture is referred to in 1835: ". . . the impossibility of administering the existing French Laws" by a court designed for British laws; ". . .by a court constituted totally different from that to which the execution of these laws was originally confided".[75]

From about 1835 St. Lucian society becomes transformed away from a classic slave-orientated and slave-concerned society[76] towards a proletariatizing society concerned with the laws of supply and demand for labour and with the question of whether economic profit can still be derived by the importation of labour as well as the need of investors to ascertain the price of labour:

> The Sugar Planter in this Colony has no prospect in view of improving his condition by bringing into the colony free labourers[77]. . . . an apprentice is . . . rated at twenty one pounds sterling each.[78]

This possible economic non-viability of the importation of free labour has no doubt been responsible for the present lack of any large population of Indians or Chinese in St. Lucia at present; the numbers of those imported were not large enough for them to form ethnic minorities capable of having a distinctly separate identity in St. Lucia. The island's descendants are predominantly of African, European (mainly French), Indian, Amerindian and Chinese genetic stock, in that order of importance; race relations have consequently usually been good as these minorities have never constituted a threat to the status of the generally African-descended population and economic power is in the hands of Mulattoes, 'Blue'-blacks, Whites, Indians, Syrians and Chinese alike. This is not to say that the society is at present, or has been in the past, free from racially defined conflicts; it is merely that given the frequent inter-marriages across these ethnic boundaries, no individual or group can be free of blood-ties with other ethnic groups.

The Mulatto/'Blue'-black traditional jealousy and enmity, although still evident, is dying a slow death, firstly because given inter-marriage mulattoes cannot remain pale for long — they soon become brown. It is often the disease of mental inferiority-complexes disguised by superiority-complexes and evident in statements such as: "My grandfather was white and white people are much better than black people"[79] which present the past and present areas of potential conflict in St. Lucian society for *all* ethnic groups.

Although this seems extra-linguistic, it is of paramount importance in the consideration of African-influenced Patwa in St. Lucia which has traditionally been looked at as the language of the 'inferior' blue-blacks,[80] the 'savages', the dreaded link with the

African exported *nèg jiné*, and was officially discouraged, for example "the Mico teacher who used to go in the street by night flogging any boy heard speaking Patwa", and the Barbadian educationalist who referring to Patwa said: ". . . After all Patwa is not a language".[81]

However, given what we all know about the past structure of 'Caribbean societies: whites at the top ruling the blacks at the bottom, with the miscegenated mulattoes as the 'middle' class, it is not surprising that this past and present attitude to Patwa is the logical consequence. However, it is easy for an educationalist to see the uselessness and psychological drag consciously and unconsciously placed upon the minds of the future leaders of St. Lucian society — the present-day children, by negative and hostile attitudes to Patwa.

This attitude towards Patwa is, logically, extended to the voudou and *kenbwa* practices in the island; these vestiges of African religions are looked on with fear and again characterized by all that is 'evil' and 'blue-black' in St. Lucia; for example, the St. Lucian priest who took it as his God-given duty to warn an islander about his grandfather, because his grandfather was a local herbalist.[82]

However, this overtly hostile attitude to these religions, many of whose rites are conducted in Patwa, is often only traditional African lip-service, as even some of the educated elite, though Western-educated, also find that some of their needs can only be satisfied by the herbalist.

Further, as Alleyne[83] points out, this hostility to Patwa can be given the indices of class, in which case the elite often speak Patwa as a second language while the mass speak in Patwa most of the time. This has the result that the mass, when not needing to pacify their inferiority-complexes by saying that *voudou* and Patwa are bad, in the presence of a social superior, are themselves practitioners of *voudou* and Patwa; all the petty scandals of the colonized destroying themselves instead of the originators of their colonization only find fulfilment in paying the herbalist to send a spell on their 'enemy' or to get rid of a spell sent upon them by their 'enemy' and are all avidly conducted in Patwa.

Patwa-orientated *voudou* and the associated practices of faith-healing are not always in terms of doing harm; for example, the majority of herbal medicines in St. Lucia, their mixture and their uses are often locked in the secrecy-orientated brains of St. Lucian herbalists, while faith-healing by prayer and rubbing with soft-candle are also successful practices without evil consequences.[84]

Alleyne, in giving his class-indices to the use of Patwa, however, suggests that because of traditional dislike of Patwa preached by the elite, Patwa will die out. I agree with him that Patwa could die out, but not for this reason. As long as the society is as rigidly stratified as it is, with upward mobility being extremely exceptional, then this traditional alienation of Patwa by the elites as the language of the poor only serves to perpetuate Patwa among the poor, who will have no alternative language or culture as long as class structure is as rigid and upward mobility as unlikely as Alleyne suggests. The social rejection of one group by another often only serves in making that group look within itself for the things that it desires. In linguistic terms as long as English-taught education is reserved for the elites only, the mass will have no part to play in it, and will consequently only use the language in they conduct most of their social intercourse — Patwa.

Sadly, the alienation of some of the elites from Patwa culture only marks their alienation from their own history, characterized as it was by all the exuberance of African and Latin culture as indicated for example in the traditional dress of St. Lucian women:

> ... you have the head-dress set-off by the brilliant colours of the Madras henkerchief, erected into a pyramid or cone ... the embroidered bodice ... the striped jupe ... a profusion of bracelets and bouquets of foulards and favours.[85]

The whole tragedy of anyone alienated from their past is that they may not be able to propose solutions to problems of the present; there is no doubt in any linguist's mind that some of the past and present difficulties of St. Lucian children in the acquisition of the English language are derived from negative attitudes by the educational system to their mother-tongue — Patwa.

The Administration Reports of 1895-1904 make it clear that this past hostile attitude towards Patwa was firstly part of past language policy: "Patwa is to be used as little as possible"[86] in primary schools, which, although recognizing the necessity to have recourse to Patwa for: "... better understanding of an item", "... where the explanation of a word or sentence cannot be conveyed in English it is certainly allowable to explain it in Patois", was still unfortunately based upon limited information; for example, the linguistic phenomena of simplification[87] which characterize both the historical derivation and the morphology of many Creole languages seem to be totally lost upon the administrator who possibly despairingly writes of the linguistic behaviour of St. Lucian children in primary school: "... the omission of initial and final letters is still too common".

A linguistic analysis would indicate that a population who, from their very origins as slaves in Senegambia possibly learnt Crioulo — a modified Portuguese, then in St. Lucia learnt Patwa — a modified French, would possibly find it normal to modify English by dropping the inflections which would play no part in the non-inflected African or Creole languages they were used to. The ironic fact is that even if Patwa does die as a result of this past language policy, it is extremely likely that aCreolized English having Patwa structure will result. The tragedy of the Caribbean linguistic Othellos, both past and present, is that they love the languages of their past slave-masters "too well".

However, as to the results of the linguistic aspect of educating the St. Lucian child in English, the Administration Reports indicate a detailed knowledge on the part of the administrators; although the children: "know their books by heart... it was possible to take away the book, and he or she would continue to the end of the lesson without missing a word". Yet "when particular words were pointed to here and there, they could not tell what they were". Given that English was a foreign language to these children, it is only logical, for me at any rate, that though they were as adept in oral retention as were the present older generation of St. Lucian Catholics in fervently reciting the Latin Mass, they had as little background in this foreign language as did the older generation of Latin.

However, as long as social structure in the Caribbean is based upon the false premise that Whites are superior to Blacks: "In the third vital statistics for the West Indies . . . the proportion of Blacks was higher than the census figures reveal"... "this is due to preference for the designation 'Coloured' to the designation 'Black' ",[88] then hostile and ignorant attitudes are the logical consequence, after all, where such a psychology is prevalent, who would be so illogical as to admit to being a *nèg jiné*, an ancestor of *nèg mawon*, practitioner of *voudou* and a speaker of Patwa. This inferiority complex of the man is indexed by the labelling of his language as inferior.

To believe that one has been made in the image of the devil with 'bad' hair with a 'dark' complexion is to believe also that one speaks a 'bad' language. Our ancestors, African, French, Indian, Carib and Arawak deserve a better future:
nou ni pou vini pli konfòtab an lapo nou èk an lang màman nou épi lang papa nou — Patwa (we have to become more comfortable in our own skins and in the language of our mothers and fathers — Patwa).

Notes

1. Ridgeway, A., 1945.
2. According to Ridgeway, they were totally wiped out, but even as a child in St. Lucia, I was under the impression that they were to be found in the area around Canaries, and were skilled at making implements in clay such as pots. Being myself part-Carib, I am slightly doubtful that they were "wiped out"; and further, Kuczynski, in his Demographic Survey of the British Empire, gives census figures for St. Lucia in 1946 where he alludes to 13% Carib population.
3. Martin, G., 1948, p.14.
4. Ridgeway, A., 1945. Presumably this is a reference either to the Caribs who were supposedly "wiped out", or to factional wars among the Barbadian invaders.
5. Martin, G., 1948, p.133.
6. Rinchon, D., 1929, p.96.
7. Frossard, 1789, Volume 1, p.346.
8. Rinchon, D., 1929, p.103.
9. Curtin, P.D., 1969, pp.65-66.
10. The Public Records Office, London, henceforth P.R.O.
11. Reports of the Protectors of Slaves from July 1826 to December 1829, pp.58-59.
12. Ibid., p.61.
13. See Alleyne, M.C., 'Language and Society in St. Lucia', 1961, pp.1-2.
14. See the experience of Montejo in 'Autobiography of a runaway slave'. See bibliography.
15. Reports of the Protectors of Slaves, 1826-1829, p.21.
16. Ibid., pp.31-32, 40, 47.
17. Ibid., p.4.
18. Ibid., p.35.
19. Ibid., p.8.
20. Ibid., p.47.
21. Records of the Privy and Executive Councils (P.R.O.), 1826-1834, pp.24-25, 30, 38.
22. Ibid., p.46.
23. Ibid., pp.46-47.
24. Ibid., p.25.
25. Ibid., pp.46-47.
26. Records of the Privy and Executive Councils, 1826-1834, p.7.
27. See Breen's 'History of St. Lucia'. See bibliography.
28. Curtin, P.D., 1969, pp.65-66.
29. Records of the Privy and Executive Councils, 1826-1834, p.52.
30. Ibid., p.9.
31. Ibid., p.11.
32. See Alleyne, M.C., 'Language and Society in Saint Lucia', 1961, pp.1-2.
33. Dalphinis, M., 1977(a), 'A Synchronic Comparison of the Verbal System of Saint Lucia Patwa and Guinea Crioulo', seminar paper, School of Oriental and African Studies, Univ. of London.
34. Rodney, W., 'A History of the Upper Guinea Coast'. See bibliography.
35. Comhaire-Sylvain, S., 1936.
36. Personal communication.
37. Records of the Privy and Executive Councils, 1826-1834, pp.58-60.
38. Ridgeway, A., 1945.
39. Alleyne, M.C., 1961, p.2.
40. Records of the Privy Council, 1826-1834, p.43.
41. Ibid., p.46.
42. Ibid., p.24.

43. Records of the Privy Council, 1826-1834, pp.36-37.
44. Ibid., and the Records of the Minutes of the Executive Council from its formation in March 1832 to February 1834.
45. Records of the Privy and Executive Councils for 1827, p.14.
46. Records of the Privy and Executive Councils for 1832, p.27.
47. Ibid., p.97.
48. Ibid. p.89.
49. Ibid. p.11.
50. Ibid. p.53.
51. See Alleyne, M.C., 1961, p.3.
52. Césaire, A., 1969, p.47. This 'Catholic' practice is part of both Martiniquan and St. Lucian culture. See also the 'Petit Larousse' dictionary: "veine".
53. Apart from the tables, there was nothing else in the room; the doors were kept wide open, and anyone wanting to celebrate could enter, dance, chant and leave whenever he/she felt like it. See also Breen's reference to *lawoz*.
54. See Breen's 'History of Saint Lucia' and Alleyne's article of 1961.
55. Records of the New Legislative Council for 1832, p.57.
56. Records of the New Legislative Council for 1832, pp.53-56.
57. Ibid. Note, however, that the 'errors' may have been simple mistranslations in the text.
58. Ibid. p.60.
59. Ibid., p.64.
60. Ibid. p.68.
61. Ibid. p.80.
62. Ibid. p.42.
63. Ibid., pp.11-12.
64. Ibid., p.11.
65. Another advantage in running away to another island would be that no one on the 'new island' would be able to identify the immigrant slave. If the slave had committed any 'crimes' on his/her home island then going to a new island would have been a very sensible strategy.
66. This word indexes the wide area of West Africa called the Guinea (*Jiné*) Coast during the Atlantic Slave Trade, that is unless the word is taken to mean Djenna, where there was a slave port.
67. Records of the New Legislative Council, 1832, p.11.
68. Records of the New Legislative Council's sitting of May 1832, p.75.
69. Records of the Legislative Council, 1835-1839, p.5.
70. Ibid., p.49.
71. Ibid., p.39 and p.42.
72. Ibid., p.23.
73. Ibid., p.39.
74. Ibid., p.47.
75. Ibid., p.46.
76. See Dr. Eric Williams' 'Capitalism and Slavery' for an excellent economic analysis of the transformation from a slave-based economy towards a more proletariat-orientated economy in the Caribbean.
77. Journals of the Legislative Council, 1835-1839, p.90.
78. Ibid., p.88.
79. Conversation in St. Lucia, 1972.
80. Dalphinis, M., 'Various approaches to the study of creole languages, with particular reference to the influences of West African languages upon these creole languages'; paper given to the *Africa Society*, King's College, Univ. of London, 1976.
81. Alleyne, M.C., 1961.
82. Personal communication.
83. Alleyne, M.C., 1961.

84. Personal communication.
85. See Breen's 'History of Saint Lucia'. See bibliography.
86. Administration Reports, 1895-1904, p.20.
87. I am using 'simplified' in a purely linguistically defined and non-pejorative manner.
88. Kuczynski, R.R., 1948, gives the following census figures for 1946: "70,113 persons;... 343 were White,... 58.07% Black,... 37.63% mixed; 2,651 (2,635 East Indian) or 3.79% Asiatic; 13% Carib". This figure of 13% Carib testifies to my disagreement as to their total extinction in St. Lucia, and, if in recent times they have 'disappeared', they are still, like all the other ethnic groups in St. Lucia "Natives of [our] Person".

3. The Social History of Caribbean Languages: the St.Lucian case.

This chapter gives special attention to the Africa/Caribbean social and historical dimensions which characterised the development of proto-Patwa pidgin in St. Lucia and the sociolinguistic framework developed for analysing synchronic Patwa and its social context.

Historical Overview

The main ethnolinguistic groups involved in the social development of St. Lucia were Island Carib, Africans, Indians and Europeans. Of particular importance, in the formation of proto-Patwa grammatical structure[1] were the Island Carib and Africans.

Island Carib
The earliest known inhabitants of St. Lucia, the Arawak, were colonised by the more war-like Carib invaders from the American mainland who killed off the Arawak men and took over their women. This resulted in a social/language division which was to also characterise later African/European social contacts in St. Lucian.

The Arawak women continued to speak Arawak amongst themselves, and the men, Carib. Their offspring, the Island Carib, spoke a language of Arawakan structure with Carib vocabulary. With the genetic mixture resulting between African maroons and Island Carib in St. Lucia, a few African language items were loaned into Black Carib and a number of Island Carib items into Patwa.[2]

Africans
The main initial source (1600-1700) of Africans in St. Lucia was from Senegambia. Supportive evidence includes:

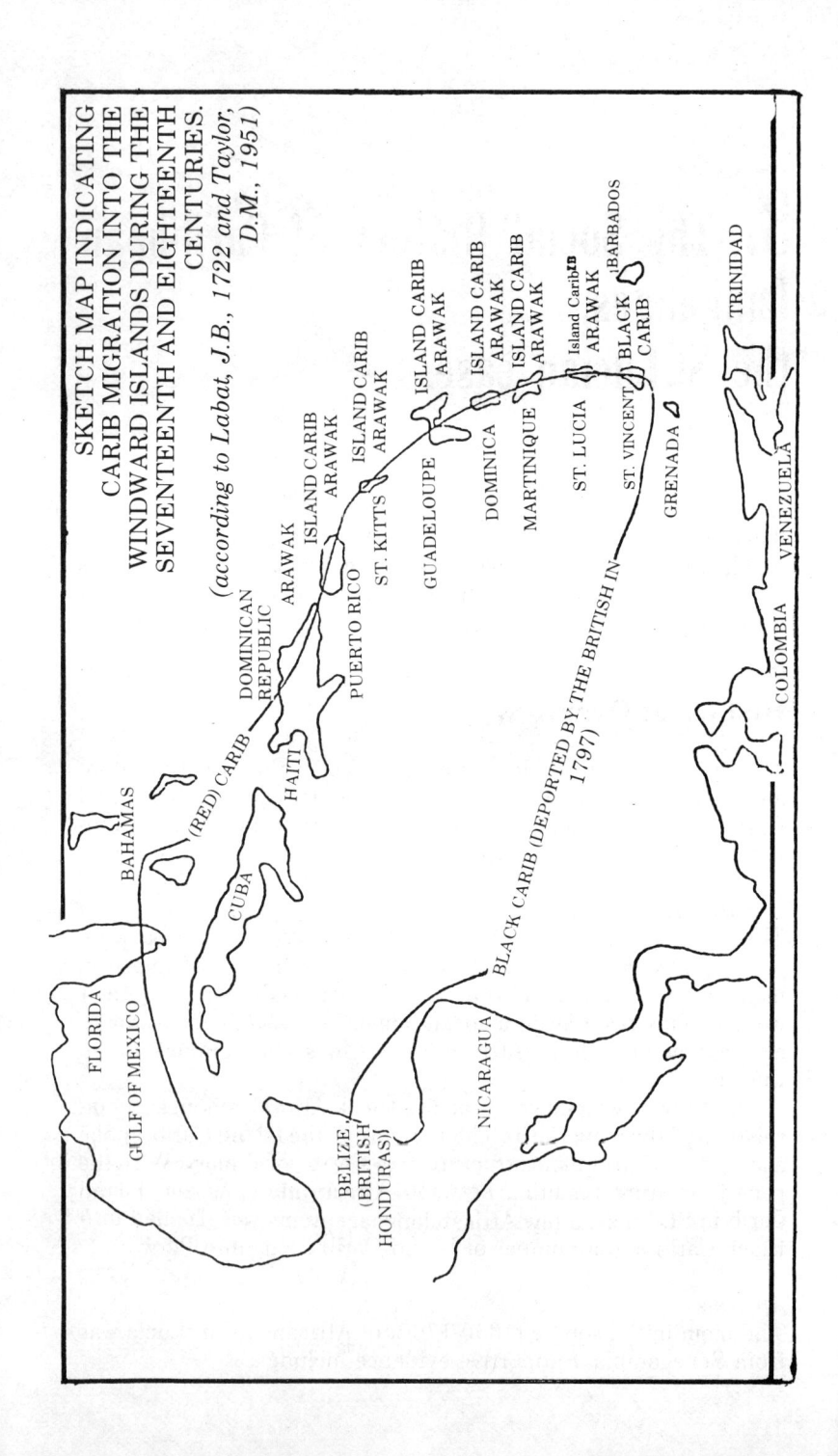

SKETCH MAP INDICATING CARIB MIGRATION INTO THE WINDWARD ISLANDS DURING THE SEVENTEENTH AND EIGHTEENTH CENTURIES.

(according to Labat, J.B., 1722 and Taylor, D.M., 1951)

(a) The Compagnie des Indes d'Amerique which had transformed its Senegambian assets into La Compagnie du Sénégal, had, as well as being responsible for the exportation of Senegambians to the French Caribbean, also nominated the governors of St. Lucia until 1674. It is unlikely that both responsibilities were not closely related.
(b) A list of slaves described as possibly the oldest of the French Atlantic Slave Trade[3] underlines such Senegambian origins.[4]
(c) Lists of Senegambian slaves from ships in Senegambian waters indicate Guadeloupe, Martinique[5] and St. Lucia as destinations as late as 1819.
(d) Slaves from Martinique who had taken part in the French Revolution were shipped to Senegal for imprisonment in 1824. This suggests a traditional Afro-French shipping lane.
(e) A number of Patwa grammatical items reflect Mandinka/Wolof[6] influences.[7]

These Senegambians featured mainly as house slaves while, during the same period, Ewe/Fon slaves were imported into St. Lucia, via Martinique, for use as field slaves.[8]

The main subsequent sources (1700-1800) include Zaire (Congo) and Angola. Supportive evidence was found both in Patwa oral literature[9] and in lists of St. Lucian plantation slaves in 1815, where older slaves are from Senegambia and younger slaves are from Kongo/Angola.[10]

The *Nèg Jiné* (Guinea Africans) referred to in Patwa oral literature are likely to have been of Ewe/Fon origin and the *Nèg Kongo* of Congo/Angolan origin.[11]

With the acquisition of St. Lucia by the English in 1834, other slaves of Akan and Eastern Nigerian origin featured more prominently in St. Lucia.

Free Coloureds
The results of Euro-African genetic mixture, the St. Lucian Free Coloureds were in higher number in and around the urban centres of Castries and Soufrière.

Although they became an important economic force in the island in 1823, they were forced to petition the 'English' legislature of St. Lucia in 1824 in order to end racial discrimination practised against them on the basis of earlier French/St. Lucian laws. Due to the ameliorations gained by the Free Coloureds from an 'English' legislature, and the Anglophone origins of some of their leaders, the Free Coloureds remained pro-English and anti-French (/Patwa/ African).

Barbadians
Again mainly centred in the urban Castries area, these, the

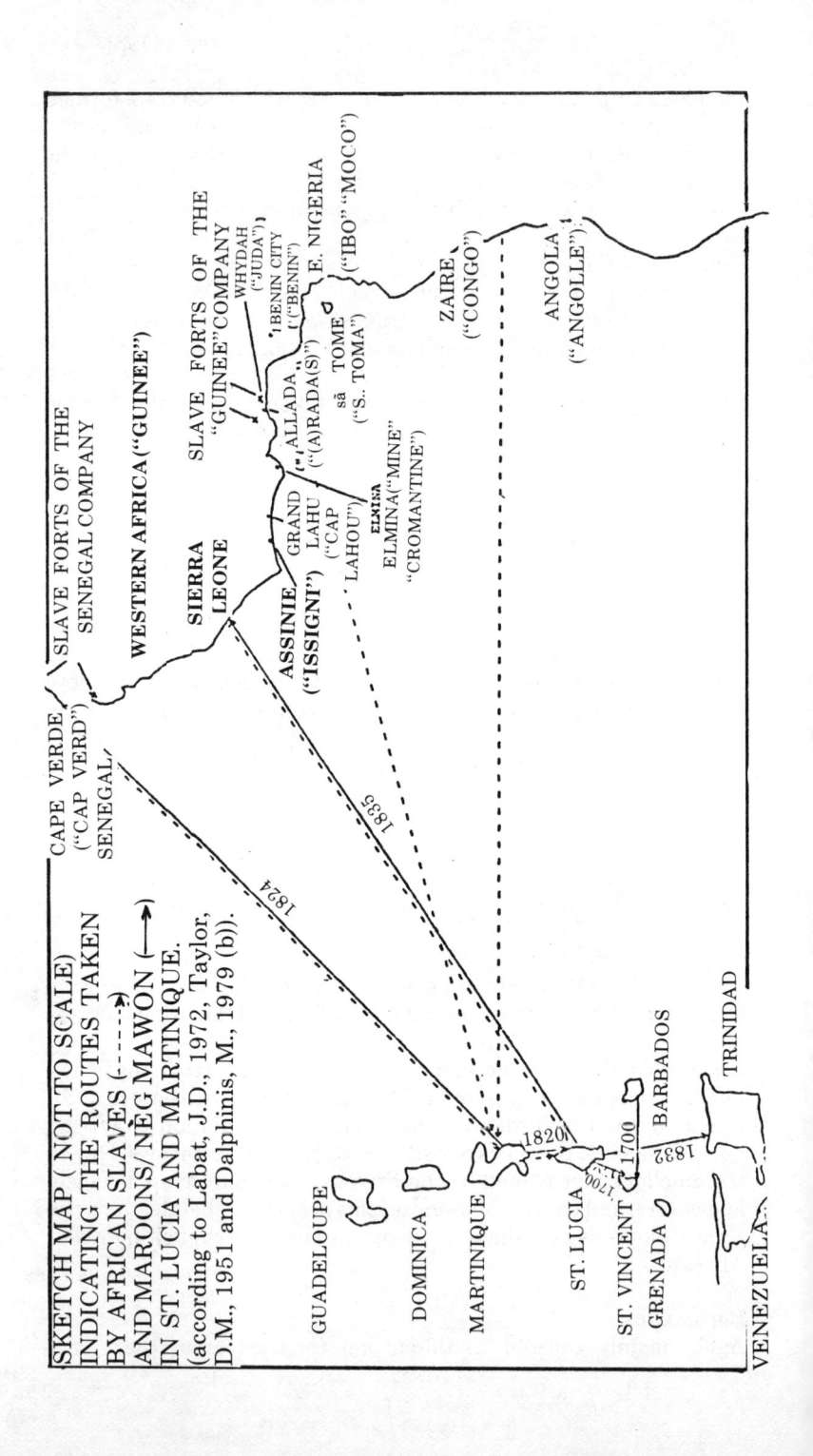

SKETCH MAP (NOT TO SCALE) INDICATING THE ROUTES TAKEN BY AFRICAN SLAVES (------) AND MAROONS/NÈG MAWON (———>) IN ST. LUCIA AND MARTINIQUE. (according to Labat, J.D., 1972, Taylor, D.M., 1951 and Dalphinis, M., 1979 (b)).

CAPE VERDE ("CAP VERD")
SENEGAL
SLAVE FORTS OF THE SENEGAL COMPANY
WESTERN AFRICA ("GUINEE")
SIERRA LEONE
SLAVE FORTS OF THE "GUINEE" COMPANY
ASSINIE ("ISSIGNI")
GRAND LAHU ("CAP LAHOU")
ELMINA ("MINE") "CROMANTINE"
ALLADA "(A)RADA(S)"
WHYDAH ("JUDA")
BENIN CITY ("BENIN")
sā TOME ("S. TOMA")
E. NIGERIA ("IBO" "MOCO")
ZAIRE ("CONGO")
ANGOLA ("ANGOLLE")

GUADELOUPE
DOMINICA
MARTINIQUE
ST. LUCIA
ST. VINCENT
GRENADA
BARBADOS
TRINIDAD
VENEZUELA

1820
1700
1700
1832
1824
1835

historically latest immigrants (1901-1905), featured as dockworkers, teachers and criminals. Their traditional attitudes were pro-English and anti-Patwa.

Sociolinguistic Overview

Methodology
In order to analyse whether any correlations existed between the selected social categories used to describe St. Lucian society[12] for example, male versus female, rural versus urban, and their related synchronic Patwa varieties, Patwa speakers were asked to translate English sentences into Patwa in a 'formal' interview situation and to recount Patwa oral items in an 'informal' situation.[13]

The use made of a set of selected African/creole grammatical features, for example, front-focalisation, was contrasted with the social categories selected in both speech styles.

The results of these contrasts were interpreted in terms of the following important definitions:
Creolization: the use of any of the African/Creole grammatical features is taken as a positive measure of 'creolization' in the speech of all speakers.
Decreolization: a non-use of one or more of these features in favour of grammatical structures reflecting non-creole languages (i.e. European and/or African)[14] is taken as a negative measure of 'decreolization', likewise in the speech of each speaker.

In formal speech a selected number of these structures were analysed for each of the selected African/creole features. When a feature was used a positive score was given and *vice versa*.

In informal speech a similar procedure was adopted with the exception that the use (resulting in a positive score only) of the selected features was counted positively throughout the oral literature responses of the speakers.[15]

In the results for both speech styles a mid-point between the highest and lowest scores[16] (by any speaker) was used to measure the percentage (%) of speakers in each social category whose use/non-use of the selected grammatical features was below this mid-point in the case of each selected feature.

Sociolinguistic differences of 19% and under were defined as insignificant for the purposes of this study. The significant results of such were represented in table form.[17]

Sociolinguistic Analysis

The results for formal speech,[18] particularly in relation to the urban/rural social categories were the most apparent sociolinguistic differences, i.e. when urban/rural residence was contrasted with the African/creole features of *Front-Focalisation* (*sèl*) and *Plural Affix* (*sé*).[19]

Front-Focalisation in Terms of Residence
Rural speakers displayed a greater degree of hypercorrection,[20] resulting in a lower use of this creole feature. 14/17 (i.e. 82%) rural speakers scored below -3 (representing half of the negative score) while 17/30 (i.e. 57%) urban speakers scored below -3.

It is likely that urban speakers, being more familiar with the bilingual use of Patwa and English in the urban situation, were more used to the 'formal' situation which characterised the use of the linguistic section of the questionnaire used.[21] Consequently, the formal Patwa of urban speakers, not being as marked by hypercorrection towards English as that of rural speakers, was characterised by a higher use of this Patwa/Creole feature.[22]

The rural milieu is the primary domain of Patwa. For example, of the 14 monolingual Patwa speakers interviewed in informal speech only one (P9) was urban in residence while only one of the ten second-language Patwa speakers (P52) was of rural residence.[23]

The use of English, the language of external prestige in St. Lucia, is connected with the urban setting. The use of Patwa by rural speakers in a situation where English is simultaneously used[24] is marked by a lack of familiarity with this context and the wish to use as 'correct' a Patwa as possible, i.e. a Patwa with a reduction of its non-English grammatical features. Such a 'correction' of Patwa results in the suppression of Patwa/Creole features. These general tendencies were also reflected in an analysis of the total negative (decreolized) score for both front-focalisation and plural affix in terms of residence: 10/16 (i.e. 63%) rural speakers scored below -10 (representing half of the total negative score) while 13/30 (i.e. 43%) urban scored below -10.

Plural Affix in Terms of Residence
Of all the selected social categories, only residence resulted in any significant sociolinguistic correlation[25] with the use of plural affix. 7/28 (i.e. 25%) of urban speakers scored below -7[26] (indicating half of the negative score), but 8/17 (i.e. 47%) of rural speakers scored below -7.[27] This would suggest the high sensitivity of urban/rural social differences in St. Lucia given similar meaningful interaction with front-focalisation.[28]

Conclusions

The general lack of variation in the selected grammatical features suggests that Patwa is not in a process of major decreolization. It is instead undergoing a process of relexification in which the lexicon of a second European language (English) is replacing French lexicon in the Patwa structural mould, for example:

Patwa:	gasòn	a	ka	manjé	piman
	"boy	the	Hab.	eat	pepper"

— 'The boy eats pepper'

Relexified	bòi	la	ka	manjé	piman
Patwa:	"boy	the	Hab.	eat	pepper"
	bòi	la	ka	it	pèpa
	"boy	the	Hab.	eat	pepper"
	bòi	la	dòz	it	pèpa
	"boy	the	Hab.	eat	pepper"
	di	bòi	iting		pèpa
	the	boy	eat Hab.		pepper

all also meaning 'The boy eats pepper'.

Although such relexification was not subjected to a formal sociolinguistic analysis, as were the selected grammatical features, some general sociolinguistic tendencies were nevertheless evident in the data for both formal and informal speech:
(i) younger speakers, e.g. P17 and P18 (<21) relexified more than older speakers, e.g. P6 and P8 (42>).
(ii) urban speakers, e.g. P12 and P19 relexified more than rural speakers, e.g. P47 and P25.
(iii) speakers of 'middle' (and 'high') prestige, e.g. P13 and P45 (speakers of 'middle prestige') relexified less than 'low' prestige speakers, e.g. P3 and P5.

Rural/urban differences often had a greater influence upon relexification than did differences in social prestige, e.g. P45, a rural speaker of middle prestige, relexified less than P13, also of middle prestige, but of urban residence.

This relexified Patwa is different from, though convergent with, Barbadian/English Creole; cf. the following Barbadian/English Creole sentence with the relexified Patwa variants above:
di boi iting   pèpa
the boy eat Hab. pepper
'The boy eats pepper'

Some writers have referred to both as being the same.[29] Midgett

by contrast writes about the:
> formation and increasing usage of a colloquial style of English, having certain grammatical correlations with Patois which is in many cases its functional equivalent.[30]

Midgett nevertheless denies the presence of English Creole in St. Lucia.[31] Le Page, however, does differentiate between a St. Lucian (English) Creole of Barbadian origin and a Patwa-influenced English within a process he describes as 're-creolization' in the direction of English in St. Lucia.[32] Patwa and relexified Patwa alone are given special attention here.

The results of the contrast between the varying grammatical features and the selected social categories indicate the importance of the rural/urban differences in the use of Patwa.[33] These rural/urban differences are themselves partly the result of a history within which Castries, the urban centre and political capital, also became, during the nineteenth century, the traditional centre of English as spoken by a small English élite and a larger 'middle' social group of Free Coloureds (*Gens de Couleur*), i.e. mulattos and freed African slaves who owed many of their social advantages to Britain.[34] The leaders of the Free Coloureds were themselves immigrants from neighbouring islands including English/English Creole-speaking Antigua.[35] The English Creole of some of these Free Coloureds was expanded by later Barbadian immigrants during the twentieth century.[36]

This has led to the following approximate order of distribution in the oral use of Patwa, relexified Patwa and English on a scale of the domains below:

Language	Domain
English	Formal education, international communication, government and commerce, urban.
Relexified Patwa	Urban (Rural)
Patwa	Rural (Urban)

As suggested above and elsewhere, this rural/urban linguistic division is both historically and genetically important and can be summarised thus:
Patwa/English
rural (*hòtè*)/urban (*vil*)[37]
'African maroon (*nèg mawon*)/mulatto or 'European' *(milat* or *bétjé).*

Both Carrington and Midgett[38] indicate the alternating use made of Patwa and English by Patwa bilinguals as markers of familiarity/non-familiarity and/or solidarity/non-solidarity between the speakers. This alternating use of Patwa and English as well as relexified Patwa can also be analysed[39] in terms of their respective internal and external prestige[40] when used by speakers of different social groups amongst themselves:

Internal Prestige	External Prestige
(Informal speech)	(Formal speech)
High Prestige Speakers — Patwa	English
Mid-Prestige Speakers — Patwa/Relexified Patwa	English
Low Prestige Speakers — Patwa	Relexified Patwa

As suggested above, the domains of Patwa and English are exclusive (i.e. in informal and formal speech respectively), but relexified Patwa can have prestige in both domains of speech, depending on the speaker's social prestige. Relexified Patwa in fact occupies a 'middle' social status in that it is viewed by speakers of 'low' social prestige as a 'better' Patwa and is used by them in formal situations. By contrast, it was only used in informal situations by 'middle' status speakers, who were aware that it was not a 'better' Patwa, but who used it in informal speech in contrast with the English they used in formal speech.

This formal/informal division in attitudes reflects dual trends in St. Lucian culture. Leiberman,[41] for example, using the methodguise technique,[42] indicated that while Patwa speakers would rate Patwa as inferior to English in answer to a direct question as to their relative status, they would rate someone speaking Patwa in more positive terms, for example, of trustworthiness, friendship, etc., than when the same person spoke English.

This duality of attitudes is partly the result of dual historical influences. Similar to Ziguinchor Kriul-speakers,[43] St. Lucian Patwa-speakers are now in contact with a language and culture which did not have a formative role in the development of their own Creole. Their dual language attitudes reflect both the increased influences of English as an international language reinforced by the regional influences of a mainly Creole English-speaking CARICOM,[44] in contrast with a wish to cling to familiar St. Lucian traditional values, of which Patwa is a symbol.

Such an analysis of the various domains of Patwa, relexified Patwa and English, and their respective physical, genetic and social distribution, would suggest a closer correlation between ethnic origins and language, especially in the light of other research:

> St. Lucia has roughly four colour distinctions for classifying people: white (European and/or creole), red, brown and black. The prestige

associated with these terms ranks from high to low respectively... There are relatively few European whites, creole whites, or red skins in Soufrière, although they are found in higher proportion in Castries.[45]

As previously indicated, however, ethnic differences were not found to be important in the use/non-use of the selected grammatical features by the Patwa speakers recorded.[46]

Where the Patwa-speakers interviewed by the researcher were of Barbadian descent, and did not fully identify with St. Lucian values, a limited and/or passive competence in Patwa was evident, for example, in the case of P26. Where speakers were of African/St. Lucian descent but wanted to assimilate as closely as possible with European culture, the use of Patwa was suppressed despite some level of competence in the latter by the speaker.[47] Most Patwa speakers, who are now bilingual in English,[48] share this attitude to varying degrees dependent upon their self-identification with various aspects of European culture. Urban and 'middle' prestige speakers more familiar with European culture used Patwa with greater confidence in formal speech than did rural and 'low' prestige speakers.[49] The reverse is true in informal speech where Patwa monolinguals, rural and 'low' prestige speakers made more confident and competent use of Patwa oral literature than did urban Patwa speakers.[50]

Some attempts are, however, being made to encourage a positive attitude to the use of Patwa by Radio St. Lucia, which now broadcasts the news and a number of agricultural and cultural programmes in Patwa.[51] The Folk Research Centre (St. Lucia), directed by Fr. Patrick Anthony, has been foremost in popularising Patwa as a vehicle of folk-culture in St. Lucia through a series of radio programmes and its publication *Research Notes*. The Folk Research Centre is also attempting, through its field-workers, to teach Patwa monolinguals to write in both Patwa and English.

This new wave of enthusiasm towards the use of Patwa over the radio is, however, resulting in the use of a specialised Patwa in many of the broadcasts. This is as a result of the use of French items taken from French dictionaries by broadcasters from Castries[52] whose knowledge of Patwa lexicon was at times relatively limited,[53] and the need to make use of specialised vocabulary to describe items and events formerly outside the traditional domain of Patwa, for example, world nuclear disarmament.[54]

Appendix

Table 1. List describing Slaves brought from Cape Verde to Le Havre (24 September 1677)[55]

No.	Noms	Noms Retablis*	Age	Taille		
1	Sambaré		23 ans	5 pieds	3 pouces	
2	Gamby		19	5	3	
3	Manhuel		22 "	5 "	5 "	
4	Sansiques		20 "	5 "	5 "	
5	Colas		24 "	5 "	7 "	
6	Samba Guiaye	Samba Gaye	22 "	5 "	5 "	
7	Mallyguiaye	Malik Gaye	26	5 "	4 "	
8	Diamba Guiama	Demba Thiam	25 "	5 "	6 "	
9	Comtisilla	Conté Sylla	24 "	5 "	6 "	
10	Lanoir Secq	Anouar Secq	23 "	5 "	6 "	
11	Dianbaguaingue	Demba Gning	25 "	5 "	6 "	

*Names mainly reconstructed by Mr. Mokhar Diop.

Table 2. Origins of the St. Lucian Plantation Slaves, 1815*

Ethnic Group/ Region of Origin		Slaves by Age <21	22>	42>	60>	Age Unknown
Senegambia:						
Cape Verde (River)		4	4	1		
Senegal			1	1	5	1
Mandinka		7	39	64	46	
Bambara			1	2	3	
Jenna			1			
Susu ('soso(s)')**				9	2	
Pulaar ('Voula', 'Poulard(e)', 'Fuller', 'Boular')		2	15	6	3	
	Sub-total	13	61	83	59	1
Angola:						
Angola		1	7	3	1	
Mayumba ('Mayombr')			2			
Congo		51	186	79	20	1
Mondongue			1		1	
	Sub-total	52	196	82	22	1
Dahomey:						
Arada ('Rada', 'Aiada')			12	8	4	
Ado			2	3		
	Sub-total	0	14	11	4	

* According to the *Registry of Plantation Slaves* for St. Lucia in 1815 (P.R.O. document no. T71, piece no. 379) and counted by the researcher.

** Modern names (mainly from Curtin, P.D., 1967) are given for the various ethnolinguistic groups and regions. Where the name(s) in the actual document are different they are put in quotation marks and bracketed (as above). The sub-headings Senegambia:, Angola: etc. are my own.

Note that this is an extract from the longer list in Dalphinis, M. 1981, pp405-408.

Table 3. Patwa Speakers and their Social Categories

Speaker number*	Sex	Age group	Prestige	Rural (R) Urban (U)
P1	F	<21	Low	U
P2	M	42>	Low	U
P3	M	22>	Low	U
P4	F	42>	Low	U
P5	M	22>	Low	U
P6	M	42>	Low	U
P7	F	22>	Low	U
P8	M	42>	Mid.	U
P(9)	F	42>	Low	U
P10	F	42>	Low	U
P11	F	42>	Low	U
P12	M	22>	Low	U
P13	F	<21	Mid.	U
P14	M	22>	Low	U
P15	M	22>	High	U
P16	M	<21	Mid.	U
P17	F	<21	Low	U
P18	M	<21	Low	U
P19	M	22>	Mid.	U
P20	F	<21	Low	U
P21	M	22>	Mid	U
P22	F	42>	Low	U
P23	F	22>	Low	U
P24	F	42>	Low	U
P25	M	22>	Low	U
P26	F	22>	Mid.	U
P27	M	42>	Low	M
P28	F	42>	Low	R
P29	F	42>	Low	U
P30	M	42>	Low	U
P(31)	M	42>	Low	R
P(32)	F	42>	Low	R
P(33)	M	22>	Low	R
P34	F	22>	Low	R
P35	M	42>	Low	R
P(36)	F	42>	Low	R
P37	F	22>	Low	R
P38	F	42>	Low	R
P39	M	42>	Low	R
P(40)	F	42>	Low	R
P41	M	22>	Low	R
P(42)	F	42>	Low	R

Speaker number	Sex	Age group	Prestige	Rural (R) Urban (U)
P(43)	M	22>	Low	R
P(44)	M	42>	Low	R
P45	F	<21	Mid.	R
P(46)	M	42>	Mid.	R
P47	M	<21	Mid.	R
P48	M	42>	Low	U
P49	F	42>	Low	U
P50	F	42>	Low	R
P51	F	42>	Low	R
P52	M	22>	Low	R
P53	M	42>	Low	R
P54	M	<21	Low	U
P55	F	22>	Low	U
P(56)	F	42>	Low	R
P(57)	F	42>	Low	R
P58	F	42>	Low	R
P(59)	F	42>	Low	R
P60	M	22>	Low	R
P61	M	42>	Low	R

*First Language Patwa speakers are in bold type; Patwa monolinguals are also bracketed.

Table 4. Front-Focalisation (Feature 3) in Formal Speech

Negative Score	Speaker Number by Residence	
	Rural	Urban
0		
-1		
-2		54, **2, 5, 6, 8, 11,** 17
-3	**34,** 52, **39**	26, **3,** 15, **16, 19,** 23
-4	**53, 61, 27, 35, 44, 28, 38, 45, 50, 51, 37**	30, 29, **49,** 55, **10,** 13, 20, 22, 25, 7, 12, 14, 18, 21, **1**
-5	**47, 58**	4, 24
-6	**60**	
	82% at below -3	57% at below -3

Table 5. Plural Affix (Feature 8) in Formal Speech

Negative Score	Speaker Numbers by Residence	
	Rural	Urban
0		
-1		26
-2		
-3		
-4		
-5	**41**	54, **6, 11,** 24
-6	**61, 34, 38, 53,**	23, **18, 12,** 7, **30,** 15, **8, 16,** 55
-7	52, **27, 37, 47**	**49,** **25,** 29, **21,** 3, **10, 14, 22**
-8	**51, 58, 39,** 45	**13,** 5, **20**
-9	**60, 28, 35**	**19, 1, 2, 4**
-10	**50**	
	47% below -7	25% below -7

Notes

1. Dalphinis, M. 1981 (PhD Thesis) is used as the major reference work for this paper.
2. See map below.
3. Delafosse, M. and Debien, G., 1965, p.319. See table 1 of the appendix.
4. See above.
5. As St. Lucia was peopled by settlers and slaves from Martinique, the origins of their populations are likely to have been convergent.
6. Two major Senegambian languages.
7. Dalphinis, M., 1979(a).
8. See map above and Dalphinis, M., 1981, pp.384-385.
9. Dalphinis, M., 1981, pp.512-514, for a list of Umbundu (an Angolan language) items in the oral literature of St. Lucian Patwa speakers.
10. See table 2 of the appendix for an extract from a summary of these lists.
11. Dalphinis, M., 1977 & 1981, p.384 & p.386.
12. See table 3 of the appendix for a table of the social categories of the Patwa speakers interviewed.
13. See linguistic vocabulary in the appendix to this chapter.
14. In reference to the African creoles: Casamance Kriul amd Gambian Krio.
15. The sociolinguistic differences in informal speech were not large. The results for informal speech were, therefore, not given a major focus in this study.
16. As the potential scores for each selected feature varied, so too did the mid-point.
17. See tables 4 and 5 of the appendix. Note that in these tables each speaker is symbolised by a number.
18. The sociolinguistic contrasts for informal speech were less apparent.
19. Described in detail in Dalphinis, M., 1981, pp.9-41.
20. See pt.II, ch.3, pp.97 & 99.
21. See above.
22. See table 4 of the appendix.
23. See table 5 of the appendix.
24. As in response to the linguistic section of the questionnaire.
25. I.e. resulting in differences of 20% and more between the resultant socio-linguistic groups.
26. As only one score occurred between -1 and -4, -7 was taken as the mid-point representing half of the total negative score.
27. See table 5 of the appendix.
28. Described above.
29. Carrington, L.D., 1969, Leiberman, D., 1974.
30. Midgett, D., 1970, p.166.
31. Ibid., p.165.
32. Le Page, R.B., 1977.
33. See the sociolinguistic analysis above.
34. See the Historical Overview above.
35. Gaspar, B., 1979, p.12.
36. Cf. Le Page, R.B., 1977, p.115, who also suggests that this Creole was Barbadian-influenced.
37. Dalphinis, M., 1977, p.16. The rural dimension is given a political analysis by Romalis, R., 1975, p.228.
38. Carrington, L.D. and Midgett, D., 1970.
39. These conclusions are based on observations of Patwa/English speakers during fieldwork in St. Lucia in 1979 and on analysis of my own communicative competence as a mother tongue Patwa speaker.
40. See the appendix for a definition of prestige, external prestige and internal prestige.

41. Leiberman, D., 1974.
42. Lambert, W.E., 1967 in Pride, J.B. and Holmes, J., 1972, pp.336-349.
43. Dalphinis, M., 1979(a).
44. I.e. Caribbean Community of which St. Lucia is a member.
45. Leiberman, D., 1974, pp.34-35.
46. Dalphinis, M., 1981, p.454. This past direct correlation between decreolisation and 'de-negrification' was however definitely an important one in past St. Lucian society, in which the use of French and then later English by the Free Coloureds, would probably have been preferred to Patwa as a means of obtaining the upward social mobility they hoped to gain, by becoming assimilated into French and then British culture in St. Lucia.
47. Such speakers refused to be interviewed in Patwa and said that they did not speak Patwa.
48. In contrast to previous years when most St. Lucians were monolingual Patwa speakers. See Carrington, L.D., 1967, p.17.
49. See Sociolinguistic analysis above.
50. Idem.
51. E.g. the weekly radio programme *Viva Sènt lici* — 'Voice of St. Lucia', on which the researcher gave a talk on Patwa in Patwa in April 1979.
52. The radio station is in the Castries area where most of the broadcasters live.
53. Given the greater use of English and relexified Patwa in the urban centre.
54. The impact of Patwa/English bilingualism upon problems of literacy in St. Lucia have been documented by Dalphinis, L.B., 1981.
55. Delafosse, M. and Debien, G., 1965, p.319.

4. Creoles and Ideologies of Return

The following Creole societies are briefly analysed from the perspective of Afro-Caribbean links and ideologies of return: i) Casamance Portuguese Creoles (Senegal), ii) Gambian English Creoles, and iii) St. Lucian French Creoles.

Casamance Portuguese Creoles

Afro-Caribbean Links
This group was marked by the absence of any overtly African or Caribbean self-associations.

Like other parts of the Afro-Portuguese network dispersed in relatively small groups throughout Senegambia, as well as in other parts of Africa such as the Congo, Angola and Mozambique, the Afro-Portuguese of Ziquinchor and Casamance claimed their European ancestry despite the fact that, genetically, they were more African than European.[1]

Their main links with the Caribbean was that of procurers of slaves for the Atlantic Slave Trade. The slaves procured were mainly from the victims of inter-African conflicts, for example, the Bainuk victims of Balanta genocide, and Dyola and Manding colonialism.[2]

Ideologies of Return
The Afro-Portuguese Creoles had no ideologies of return, neither to Europe nor the Caribbean. Having inherited the past profits and continued profitability of the Atlantic Slave Trade from their Portuguese grandfathers and their mainly Mandinka grandmothers, they were a ruling group/'tribe' in Casamance and thus could not think of changing their social position beneficially, by 'returning' elsewhere.

Indeed, they continued to see themselves as 'Portuguese' representatives of Portugal who would fight for the rights of Portugal against other intruders. For example, Honorio Pereira Barreto, the Afro-Portuguese army commander in Portuguese Guinea (now Guinea Bissau) between 1839-1859 saw himself as the Portuguese defender of Guinea against French military incursion despite lack of military support from Portugal:

> ... il était inutile d'écrire au gouvernement portugais sur les insultes que nous recevions en Casamance... mille fois j'ai été découragé dans cette lutte de ma petite personne contre les autorités français de Gorée et du Sénégal, soutenues par leur gouvernement.[3]

> (... 'it was useless to write to the Portuguese about the insults we received in Casamance... I had been discouraged a thousand times in this struggle of my little person against the French authorities of Gorée and Senegal, supported by their government'.)

Gambian English Creoles

Afro-Caribbean Links
The English Creoles or Liberated Africans of the Gambia are themselves part of the product of Afro-Caribbean links.

They were slaves from slave ships stopped by the British anti-slavery blockade of West Africa who were resettled in the Gambia.

They identified with the British rulers of the Gambia, partly due to political necessity as none of the indigenous Senegambian groups would accept such 'Sons of Slaves' as their equals:

> ... the section, which makes all children born to a slave free will be a great assistance in stamping out slavery altogether. The natives laugh at this section. 'A child born from a slave must be a slave, and (*sic*) cannot be anything else, is to them a sound natural law which cannot be set aside by any law of man...[4]

Many of these Gambian English Creoles were descendants of West Indians, disbanded from the West India Regiment, who settled in the Gambia, for example, the Coles, Williams, Spoldings, Bidwells, Stapleton and Benjamin families of Banjul, The Gambia.

Perhaps, partly due to these genetic links with the Caribbean, some of the Gambian Creoles actively participated in Garveyism and the Universal Negro Improvement Association.

In fact, in order to curtail such activities, the British administration in the Gambia (1922-1942) withheld the passports of one Trinidadian and one Barbadian involved in forming branches of the organisation in the Gambia and Senegal.[5]

The fear of at least one such West Indian, who preached the message of rebellion from the pulpit, also had its echoes in the Gambia:

African Orthodox Church, whose head is Bishop George Alexander McGuire, D.D. A native of the Island (sic) of Antigua B.W. Indes... he made his listeners believe that Almighty God, Jesus Christ, and the Virgin Mary was (sic) as black as the ace of spades...
I hereby declare that this African Orthodox Church... is seditious against the Government of Great Britain... [6]

Ideologies of Return
Like the Portuguese Creoles of Casamance, the English Creoles of the Gambia had few economic motivations in wanting to 'return' anywhere. Although they had begun their history at the lowest rung in Senegambian society, they rapidly inherited the place of the British, and became the Western educated and 'English' speaking modern elite of the Gambia.[7]

St. Lucia French Creoles (Patwa Speakers)

Afro-Caribbean Links
As suggested in the map (pt.I, ch.3, p.46), rebellion and Maroons in St. Lucia (Patwa/French Creole *nèg mawon*) has kept the link with Africa alive.

The French Creoles of St. Lucia and Martinique ran to the hilly interiors of their islands as part of their resistance to slavery. Upon this tradition of maroonage, the ideas of the French Revolution — *Liberté, Egalité, Fraternité*, caused the overthrow of the planter class, the erecting of the guillotine, a 'reign of terror' and six years of a revolutionary St. Lucia (1789-1795).

The metropolitan 'empires' of Britain and France struck back in St. Lucia and Martinique respectively. In the case of Martinique the revolutionaries and maroons were re-exported to Senegal.

At the end of slavery these African links were continued in the St. Lucian case by the importation of indentured labour from Sierra Leone.

The most profound link with Africa, however, remains in the French Creole language of St. Lucia which is of an African grammatical structure, in its African religious practices, for example *kèlè* (cf. Mandinka *kèlè* 'war')[8] and in its Afro-French culture.[9]

Ideologies of Return
Like all ex-slaves torn from Africa, not by their own choice, the romantic element of how life might have been in Africa remains in the St. Lucian psyche.

The degradation suffered, and still suffered by Africans in the New World and in Europe, increases the desire to return to an Africa where the same type of degradation, it is hoped, is not suffered.

The low economic status of Africans and their descendants in contrast to most Indo-Europeans and their descendants in countries visited by the French Creoles also increases the idea that economic equality or even economic superiority for the African and his descendants only exists in Africa.

However, by far the most profound effect is that Africans do not cease to be African or at least African influenced once they have gone to another environment. The kèlè ceremony in St. Lucia in which a ram is sacrificed and its blood used in incantations to the African ancestors, is as African as similar practices of ancestor remembrance and/or worship in Africa. Similarly the attitude to death amongst the St. Lucian Creoles is that of a joyful return to the ancestors in Africa/Guinea.[10]

Language as Social Symbol and Ideology

Language in all three Creole societies, although all being clearly the results of the fusion of an African grammatical structure with different European language vocabularies, index differences in social/political ideologies.

The Portuguese Creoles saw themselves as Portuguese and thought of their language as Portuguese; the Gambian Creoles saw themselves as ex-slave representatives of Britain and thought of their language as a variety of English. In the case of both Casamance in Senegal and Banjul in Gambia, to speak Creole was to be a member of the ruling social group.

In St. Lucia, to speak Patwa (French Creole) was to identify oneself with the 'lower' elements of the society despite the fact that 99% of the population speak Patwa. Conversely, however, to speak Patwa is to continue to be influenced by the African customs in St. Lucia and to continue African resistance and rebellion in the face of a world-wide 'whitewash'.

Notes

1. Jajolet de La Courbe, M., 1686, in Cultru, P. (publisher), 1913, p.192 and Moore, F., 1738, p.71.
2. Fernandes, V., 1506-1510; D'Almada, A.A., 1594; Monod, Th. Da Mota, A.T.; Mauny, R., 1951, pp.71-75 and Dalphinis, M., 1981, pt.I, ch.1.
3. Barreto, H.P., 1839-1859, document no.51, in Walter, J., 1947, p.168 and translated by Roche, C., 1976, p.71.
4. National Archives, Banjul, reference no.2, piece no.50.
5. Activities of Universal Negro Improvement Association, National Archives, Banjul, Secret File, no.727.
6. Colonial Secretary's Office, Confidential Minute Paper, National Archives, Banjul, reference no.3/59; file no.727, dated 21st. June, 1922.
7. Dalphinis, M., 1981, pt.2, ch.1.
8. Ibid., pt.III.
9. Idem.
10. Idem.

5. The Portuguese Creole of the Casamance, French and African Languages: languages in competition in southern Senegal.

Introduction

The Portuguese Creole of the Casamance (*Kriul*), spoken in southern Senegal, indicates from its origins up to the present day the global struggle between 'majority' and 'minority' and languages. In the case of Creole languages generally, it is a struggle against the metropolitan languages within which the original Creole lexical sources are based.

In the case of Kriul, like that of Patwa[1] (the French Creole of Saint Lucia), it's a struggle against a 'majority' language with which the Creole has no common lexical base. In the case of Kriul the struggle is against French, while, for St. Lucian Patwa, it is against English.

Weinreich has examined the question of languages in contact.[2] Descriptive linguists suggest that this kind of contact only exists in the minds of linguists. The generative linguists, on the other hand, see the question of linguistic contacts as an aspect of a theory of performance.[3] This is why we suggest here that contact, as well as competition between languages, are the essential elements in the origin and perpetuation of Creole languages; and that this competition is an aspect of the competence of the Creole speaker. We will examine this hypothesis, using Kriul as an example.

Ethnic Groups

Between 1506 and 1510, Valentim Fernandes indicated at least three main ethnic groups in the Casamance: Mandinka, Dyola and Balanta.[4] During the nineteenth century, four important ethnic groups were described: Mandinka, Dyola, Balanta and Bainuk. The

Dyola sub-groups (amongst others Fulup, Bandial, Hulon, Bayot and Karon) were also described on the northern and southern banks of the river Casamance.[5]

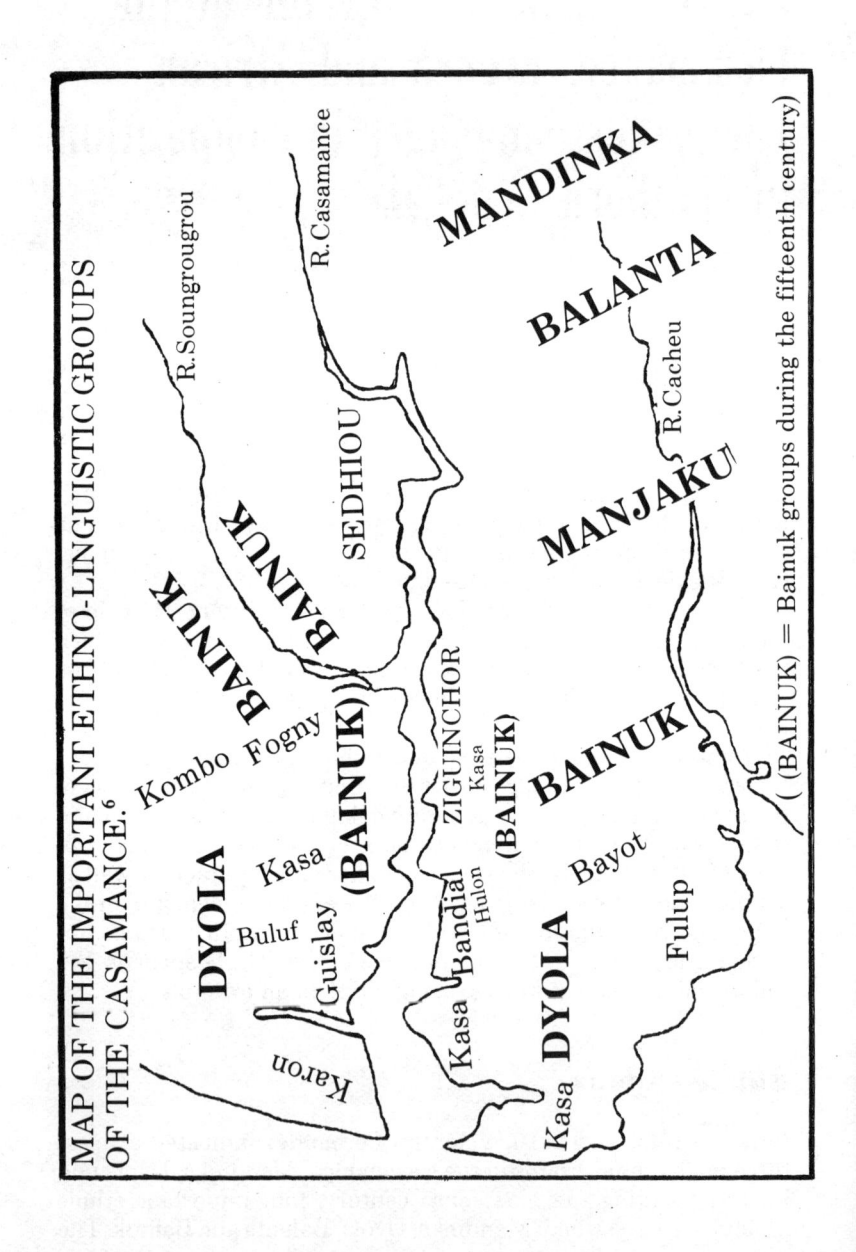

MAP OF THE IMPORTANT ETHNO-LINGUISTIC GROUPS OF THE CASAMANCE.[6]

((BAINUK) = Bainuk groups during the fifteenth century)

Bainuk

This group was dispersed on the north bank of the river Cacheu, and on both banks of the Casamance and Soungrougrou rivers. The Bainuk of the south bank of the Casamance were depopulated by Balanta and Dyola attacks during the fifteenth century:

> Balantas qui leur [Bainuk] font une geurre acharnée, et les Feloups (Dyola) qui cherchent à s'entendre vers leur fertile et pittoresque pays . . .[7]
> ('Balanta who made fierce war against the Bainuk, and the Feloup (Dyola) who wanted to expand towards their fertile and picturesque country').

Dyola invasion caused the disintegration of the Bainuk on the south bank, as these Bainuk lived:

> ... se réduisant à quelques familles de courtiers portugais et tendant a disparaitre . . .[8]
> ('... being reduced to a few families of courtiers to the Portuguese and tending to disappear').

Mandinka invasion also precipitated this Bainuk disintegration, for example, the Bainuk on both banks of the Soungrougrou river:

> Les Bagnouns [Bainuk] de Soungrougrou song déjà mélés aux Mandingues . . .[9]
> ('The Bagnoun [Bainuk] of the Soungrougrou are already mixed with the Mandinkas').

The arrival of the Portuguese had, therefore, found the Bainuk already under Mandinka[10] domination, and perhåps speakers of Mandinka as a second language.

According to the oral traditions, the Bainuk were originally from Guinea Bissau[11] and perhaps even the founders of Ziguinchor (a Portuguese deformation of the Bainuk word *Iziguichos*).[12]

The lack of cohesion amongst the Bainuk, caused by these invasions and conquests, by the other ethnolinguistic groups, left them with a mother tongue in the process of disappearing and Mandinka as a second language. This situation of conflict in which the vanquished had no possibility of using their language in all domains, aided the development of a new language in their new role as courtiers of the Portuguese — Kriul.

Balanta

These were the 'Moors' of the Casamance, who concentrated their lives around the art of war, by using their well constructed boats to attack their neighbours on both banks of the rivers Casamance and Cacheu. Their ability in war helped them resist Mandinka invasion in the Brassou region.[13]

Like the Bainuk, the Balanta are considered to be one of the original inhabitants of the Casamance.[14] The cultural similarities between the Balanta and the Bainuk could have been developed due to the inclusion of the Bainuk and the Balanta in the Kassanke kingdom during the sixteenth century,[15] and due to the conquest of the Bainuk by the Balanta.

Dyola

Like the Balantas, the Dyola have a warrior tradition. They were particularly decentralised:

> ... chaque faction a formé des villages à peu près indépendents les uns des autres ... et s'entend rarement pour l'attaque ou la défence.[16]
> ('Each faction formed villages more or less independent of one another ... and rarely cooperated in attack or defence').

Their decentralization into Dyola factions probably contributed to the existence of many different Dyola dialects in the Casamance, e.g. Fogny, Kombo, Buluf, Karon, Fulup etc. This fragmentation of the Dyola language into district dialects, aided the adoption of Kriul as a second language by the Dyola.

Cases (Cassangues, Cassangas, Kassanke)

The Casa are linked, from an ethnolinguistic viewpoint to the Bainuk.[17] It is from this ethnic group that the river Casamance got its name: *kasa-mansa*, meaning 'river of the king of *kasa*', *kasa* being the name of the region and *mansa* meaning 'king' in Mandinka:

> ... the chief named Casamanca, who dwelt thirty miles up the river...[18]

Referred to also as Cassanga or Kassanka (meaning inhabitants of the *Kasa*) their presence is mainly mentioned on the south bank of the river Casamance in the sixteenth century.[19]

Under Mandinka domination during the fifteenth and sixteenth centuries, the Casa captured the non-Muslim peoples of the Casamance, like the Bainuk, the Balanta and the Dyola, and sold them to the Portuguese:

> Dans les échanges du Kasa avec les Portugais, les èsclaves tenaient une grande place. Lorqu'ALMADA y vint, en 1570, c'était pour acheter des èsclaves ... Il est probable qu'une partie des èsclaves était obtenue aux depens des peuples voisins.[20]

('During the exchanges between the Kasa and the Portuguese, slaves had a prominent place. When ALMADA came there, in 1570, it was to buy slaves ... It is probable that some of these slaves were obtained at the expense of the neighbouring peoples').

Perhaps due to their role as slave-traders, the Casa and the Portuguese were often attacked by the inhabitants of the coast. Due to the loss of Portuguese vessels during one attack, the Portuguese abandoned, for nearly twenty-five years, their slave-trading association with the Casa.[21]

The Casamance became, as a consequence, a haven for runaway slaves.[22]

Mandinka
The Mandinka descended from the Futa-Djalon and, in their diffusion of Islam among 'the pagans' of the Casamance (Bainuk, Balanta and Dyola), they subjugated 'the pagans' and sold them as slaves during the Atlantic Slave Trade with the aid of the Portuguese and the Afro-Portuguese.

Pulaar Speakers (Fulbe, Fula(ni) or 'Peul')
The Pulaar, also Muslims like the Mandinka, used the non-Muslim ethnic groups as slaves, but mainly as domestic slaves.[23]

Afro-Portuguese (Luso-Africans)

> En 1445 une bulle papale autorisait le Portugal à réduire en esclavage tous les peuples infidèles.[24]
> ('In 1445 a Papal Bull authorised Portugal to reduce all infidel peoples to servitude').

Like the Muslim Mandinka, the Portuguese came to Casamance with a religious justification for their development of the slave trade:

> Pendant longtemps les Portugais ont fait la traite des noirs à Ziguinchor.[25]
> ('The Portuguese, for a long period, had traded in black slaves at Ziguinchor').

The Portuguese married with Mandinka women and lived amongst the Bainuk of Ziguinchor since 1645. The Portuguese traded with the Bainuk and the Dyola for the rice that these African ethnic groups produced.[26]

The mulatto descendents of the Portuguese and their African women, ie. the Afro-Portuguese, continued the economic system they inherited from their fathers. They developed Kriul from Portuguese vocabulary with the syntax, morphology and semantics of the African languages of the Casamance.

They adopted Catholicism, the religion of their fathers. They

were also developed by the Casamance ethnic groups who wanted
to mix with them (for example the Bainuk). With their economic
advantages, developed during the seventeenth and eighteenth
centuries, they became the high prestige ethnic group of the
Casamance.

French
Although Ziguinchor was part of Portuguese Guinea (Guinea
Bissau), and under Portuguese domination, the French and their
representatives the Wolof, wanted an economic and political base
in Ziguinchor:

> as Francezes do Senegal tinaham continuado no seu sistema de
> invasão das nosas Possessões da Costa da Guiné.
> ('the French of Senegal have continued to systematically invade our
> possessions on the coast of Guinea).

as described by H.P. Barreto, military commander of Portuguese
Guinea (1839-1859).[27]

Due to a lack of support from Portugal, Barreto could not defend
Ziguinchor from French 'invasion' which began with the establish-
ment of French trading posts at Ziguinchor, but culminated in the
Franco-Portuguese Treaty of 12th May 1886, when Ziguinchor was
ceded to France, despite the 'Portuguese' affiliations of the Afro-
Portuguese of Ziguinchor.[28]

Ethnolinguistic Conflicts

These historical and political conflicts had ethnolinguistic influences:

Ethnic Groups	Ethnolinguistic Conflicts	Ethnolinguistic Resultants
Bainuk	Disintegration of the Bainuk. Mandinka adopted by the Bainuk as a second language.	Creation of Kriul as a new Bainuk language.
Balata	Conquest of the Bainuk by the Balanta.	Integration of Bainuk and Balanta culture in Kriul.
Dyola	Many different dialects. Lack of integration amongst the various Dyola ethnic groups.	Use of Kriul as a language of integration amongst the Dyola ethno-linguistic groups.

Casas	Integration with the Mandinka. Mandinka used increasingly as a first language. Loss of the Casa language. Disassociation from Mandinka, language of the former slave traders.	Adoption of Kriul after disassociation from Mandinka.
Mandinka	Selling of the 'pagan' ethnic groups of the Casamance with the cooperation of the Afro-Portuguese as trading partners.	Kriul used in association with Mandinka as the important languages of this slave trade.
Pula	Use of the 'pagan' ethnic groups as domestic slaves.	Lack of apparent results.
Afro-Portuguese	African languages of their mothers in conflict with the Portuguese language of their fathers.	Creation of Kriul.
French	A minority in the face of a hostile Kriul-speaking majority.	Adoption of Kriul as a second language.

Linguistic Conflicts

The purely linguistic aspect of these conflicts is evident in the choices of words, phonemes and morphemes which have been adopted by Kriul from amongst these languages in conflict. The choices of such items in Kriul indicate, therefore, a resolution of conflicts within the languages in contact, and characterise the language competence of Creole speakers.

We will consider some examples of such conflicts and their resolution in Kriul, mainly from the point of view of Kriul and French, in analysing the lexicon, phonology, morphology, syntax and semantics of Kriul, within which these conflicts have been resolved, or are well on the way to being resolved.

Lexicon

Kriul's lexical base is formed, mainly from Portuguese lexical items. Modern loan words from French have caused a conflict between Portuguese and French lexical items in Kriul, as well as the formation of lexical items of French origin, which have been pidginized in accordance with Kriul phonology and morphology, for example:

Kriul/Portuguese	Kriul/French	Pidginized French[29]
diritu	bon (– 'good')	—
sòng	sèl	—
brutu	stupidu (– 'stupid')	—
dimas	tòròp (– 'too much')	—
mal la	—	valiz la (– 'this suitcase')
baldokai la	—	so la (– 'this bucket')

Phonology

i) [r] or [ř] or [R] in word-initial and word-medial positions, for example:

[rapa] or [řapa] or [Rapa] — rapa — 'razor'
[kore] or [koře] or [koRe] — kore — 'to run'

[R], is indicative of the influences of French phonology which is in conflict with the phomeme [r] of Kriul/Portuguese origin. [R] is used more often by younger and more 'educated' speakers.

ii) v/b for example, vai <Port. bai. Although Port. v becomes b in Kriul, amongst speakers who want to underline their 'Portuguese' sentiments, v is used, eg. vindidòr instead of bindidòr — 'salesman'.

iii) s/z, for example, kwisinya – kwizinya — 'to cook'. z is often used in such French loans, and is in conflict with s from Kriul/Portuguese.[30]

Morphology

Conjunction: di <Fr. de or Wol. ak, for example:

Jean di Eric — 'Jean and Eric'
Jean uk Eric — 'Jean and Eric'

The conjunction di is used more frequently, and is in conflict with the Wolof conjunction ak — 'and'.

i) The relative ki <Fr. qui or ke <Port. que or ku or kə <Fr. que, for example:

bajuda ki sinta — 'The girl who sits'
"girl Rel. sit"

wòmi	ke	yèntra	kasa	— 'The man who enters the house'
"man	Rel.	enter	house"	
kachur	kə	kore		— 'The dog who runs'
"dog	Rel.	run"		
wòmi	ku	bing		— 'The man who comes'
"man	Rel.	come"		

In Kriul, the conflict within which *ki* <*Fr. qui* is implied, is not yet resolved, although *ki* is used more often. Older speakers (of 42 years and over) use *ku* (cf. Dyola *ku – pl.* prefix) with nouns which refer to human and non-human items. Younger speakers, and consequently the more 'Frenchified' or 'educated', (of less than 21 years and more than 22 years old), use *ki* more frequently with nouns that refer to human beings, and *ku* with nouns refering to things non-human.

ii) Specifier: *ki* or *ke* or *kèl* or *kal* or *kè*, for example:

èsli	ki	bajuda	ki	bing		— 'This is the
"this	Specif.	girl	Rel.	come"		girl who comes'
èsli	ke	bajuda	ki	bai		— 'This is the
"this	Specif.	girl	Rel.	go"		girl who goes'
èsli	kèl	wòmi	ki	kuri		— 'This is the
"this	Specif.	man	Rel.	run"		man who runs'
èsli	kal	kasa	ki	wòmi	misti	— 'This is the
"this	Specif.	house	Rel.	man	want"	house the man wants'

The conflict in usage is between *ki* <*Fr. qui*, *ke* <*Port.* and *kèl* <*Fr. quel(le)*. French influences are the most dominant as *kèl* is used the most frequently.

Semantics

The semantic categories [HUMAN] and [NON-HUMAN]:

In the African languages in contact with Kriul, with the exception of Mandinka, there is a system of noun classes in which differences of meaning are implied, for example:

	Singular		Plural	
Bainuk:				
Human	u —	digen	in —	digen
	"*sing.*	man"	"*pl.*	man"
Non-human	bu —	xund	i —	xund
	"*sing.*	pestle"	"*pl.* —	pestle"
	'(the)	pestle'	'(the)	pestles'
Balanta:				
Human	hə	raasa	bə —	raasa
	"*sing.*	Balanta"	"*pl.*	Balanta"
	'(the)	Balanta'	'the	Balantas'

Non-human	f —	mònkè	k —	mònkè
	"sing.	mango"	"pl.	mango"
	'(the)	mango'	'(the)	mangoes'

This distinction is also evident in the use of the marker of specification, for example:

Dyola:
Human	ume — 'this one (here)' eg.
	anyine òmu
	"man Specif.
	'that man (there)'
	òmu — 'that one (there)'
Non-human	kune — 'this one (here)'
	kunyè — 'that one (there)' eg.
	kalakuma kuyè
	"chair Specif."
	'that chair (there)'

In Kriul this distinction is also in the process of being developed, for example:

Kriul:
Human	ki or ke or kèl
Non-human	kal or kè, for example:
	kè trupèsa
	"Specif. chair"
	'this chair (here)'
	kal balèi
	"Specif. basket"
	'this basket (here)'.

However, this distinction is not evident in the Guinea-Bissau dialect, possibly due to the separation of Casamance Kriul from Guinea-Bissau Kriul (by the Frano-Portuguese Convention of 1886) which has left Casamance Kriul more susceptible to the influences of its local African languages of contact. The political maxim of divide and rule, has therefore resulted (above) in dialect divisions between Guinea-Bissau and Casamance Kriul varieties, which may facilitate the easier long-term destruction of Kriul. The Creoles of Saint Lucia, Louisiana, Trinidad, Grenada, the Miskito Coast and Gambia, for example, have all suffered due to such divide and rule tactics of more powerful countries. Such historical conflicts have contributed to the linguistic conflicts of Kriul and other Creole languages.

Sociolinguistic Conflicts

Sociolinguistic studies imply a conflict between linguistic alternants, used differently by different linguistic groups. These conflicts will be examined (below) from the point of view of culture, society and education.

Culture
Kriul culture, like that of other Creoles, is a mixture of European and African cultures. For Kriul these two elements of cultural conflict are represented by Portuguese and Bainuk respectively. The relative dominance of each element in this dichotomy has changed in accordance with historical circumstances. The dominance of the Portuguese and Afro-Portuguese was marked by the desire of Casamance ethnic groups, for example the Bainuk and Balanta, to assimilate themselves to 'Portuguese' culture. When Guinea-Bissau was the metropolitan centre for Casamance, this assimilation was marked by a Kriul with fewer African influences. With the inclusion of Casamance in Senegal, Dakar became the political centre of gravity as well as the centre for the diffusion of Francophone culture for the Casamance and the rest of Senegal. Kriul speakers, nevertheless, do not want to be assimilated into Francophone culture but have some secessionist sentiments indicated by the wish of some Kriul speakers to be politically reunited with their Kriul speaking relatives in Guinea-Bissau. This wish for cultural marronage in the face of French culture is partly due to the fact that Kriul culture has become a common culture for all the ethnic groups of the Casamance. This is itself due to the fact that these Casamance ethnic groups had diffused fundamental aspects of their culture(s) within Afro-Portuguese culture during their former domination by the Portuguese and, subsequently, the Afro-Portuguese.

Kumpo is the 'male' spirit of the Casamance forests and is of Bainuk origin, although *Kumpo* has been diffused into Kriul and amongst the other ethnic groups of the Casamance. *Kumpo* appears on festive occasions in the Casamance, e.g. weddings: the *Kumpo* mask is followed by its 'priests' and by its entourage of singers and its initiated followers, as well as by the non-initiated population. The appearance of *Kumpo* at the Catholic marriages of Kriul speakers is also symbolic of the larger unity of Creole culture within which elements of European (Portuguese) culture are in close association with elements of African (Casamance) culture.

This unification of elements from the past cultures above underlines, nevertheless, new cultural conflicts in which the French elements in Casamance Kriul, which differentiate the latter from Guinea-Bissau Kriul, are not viewed by Casamance Kriul speakers as elements of common culture with the Francophone northern regions of Senegal.

The cutting off of Casamance Kriul speakers from their 'Portuguese' associations in Guinea-Bissau, with the more far-reaching influences from African languages of contact in Casamance, indicate also the possibility of cultural reassimilation of Afro-Portuguese cultures within the African cultures of Casamance. For example, the majority of present day Kriul speakers have adopted the (African) ethnic group of one, or both, of their parents. They do not identify themselves as 'Creole'.

Society

If cultures are the result of history, then societies are the results of culture. This possible interpretation is evident in the analysis below, of Casamance Creole society.

Due to the reassimilation of the former Afro-Portuguese into the African culture of the Casamance, there is no longer a distinctively Afro-Portuguese society in the Casamance. There is in Casamance a 'Creole' society, formed by the group of Casamance societies which have Afro-Portuguese influences.

In 'Creole' societies, Afro-Portuguese influences are now no longer the markers for feelings of superiority, although economic and political power still remains mainly in the hands of individuals of Afro-Portuguese ancestry and, therefore, of the Catholic faith. These local influences, in the rural milieu of the Casamance, are in contrast with the urban and centralist influences of nothern Senegal, dominated by the Muslim Wolof and the capital city Dakar. These differences in development underline the attitude of Creole societies that only the northern Wolof are the real Senegalese.

Most of the youth of Casamance society of 21 years and below have links with Guinea-Bissau. These links were reinforced by refugees from the war of national liberation from Portugal in Guinea-Bissau (1960-74) and have influenced a recent political movement: Movement for a New Casamance, which had/has as its goal the secession of the Casamance from Senegal and its reattachment to Guinea-Bissau.

These sentiments are aided by the fact that although in Senegal Kriul is only a regional language, in Guinea-Bissau Kriul functions at a national level, as the common language of communication between diverse ethnolinguistic groups.

Education

Only young people of 21 years and under have a modern/French education at primary and secondary levels.

It is above all amongst this 'educated' youth of Kriul speakers that cultural and linguistic ambiguity is at its most profound. Due to their 'French' education, they use alternants of French origin in their Kriul, but, due to their links with young Kriul speakers from Guinea-Bissau, of the same age range, they are even more conscious of the cultural and linguistic differences between themselves and the northern 'Senegalese'.

Conclusion

Studies in physics show that forces in conflict produce a resultant. Koestler[31] adopted this fact in literary studies, in suggesting that the 'act of creation' in literature/art is the result of conflicts.

It seems to me that the choice of French lexical items and of pidginized French by Kriul speakers in Casamance are the results of conflicts in the choice between French and Kriul/(Portuguese) lexical items. This modern conflict may be contrasted with the past conflict between the choice of Portuguese and African lexical items in the creation of Kriul's lexical base.

Synchronic Kriul also suggests the presence of similar conflicts in the phonological, morphological, syntactic and semantic system of Kriul under the influences of French and the African languages of the Casamance.

Such conflicts are also evident in the history, culture, society and education of Kriul speakers.

If such conflicts are part of productive creativity of Kriul, and other Creole languages, they would seem to me to occupy a central position in the competence of all Creole speakers.

Notes

1. Dalphinis, M., 1979(a).
2. Weinreich, U., 1968.
3. Chomsky, N., 1965, pp.10-15.
4. Fernandes, V (1506-1510), in Monod, Th., Teixeira da Mota, A., and Mauny, R., 1951, p.59.
5. Vallon, A., 1862, p.457.
6. Dalphinis, M., 1981, p.55.
7. Vallon, A., 1862, pp.457-458.
8. Idem.
9. Vallon, A., 1862, p.458; Touze, R.L., 1963, p.77; Roche, C., 1976, p.24 & p.63.
10. Fernandes, V. (1506-1510), in Monod, Th., Teixeira da Mota, A., and Mauny, R., 1951, pp.71-75 & Roche, C., 1976, p.25.
11. Roche, C., 1976, p.13.
12. Ibid., p.37.
13. Vallon, A., 1862, p.460.
14. Roche, C., 1976, p.13.
15. Ibid., p.2.
16. Fernandes, V (1506-1510), in Monod, Th., Teixeira da Mota, A., et Mauny, R., 1951, p.61 & Vallon, A., 1862, p.457.
17. Teixeira da Mota, A., in Monod, Th., Teixeira da Mota, A., and Mauny, R., 1951, p.163; Hair, P.E., 1967, p.251. Roche, C., 1973, p.36 indicates that this was also the opinion of Almada (1595).
18. Cadamosto (1455-1475) in Crone, G.R. (translator and editor) 1937, p.75; Vallon, A., 1862, p.458.
19. D'Almada, A.A. (1594), in Köpke, D., 1841, pp.39-42.
20. Boulègue, J., 1972(b), p.11.
21. Ibid., pp.12-13, a translation of Almada, A.A. (1594) in Köpke, D., 1841, p.38.
22. Coelho, F., (1668) in Peres, D. (ed), 1953, p.31 and translated in Boulègue, J., 1972(b), p.13.
23. Vallon, A., 1862, p.462.
24. Andrade, E., 1973, p.13.
25. Vallon, A., 1862, p.467.
26. Fernandes, V., (1506-1510), in Monod, Th., Teixeira da Mota, A., and Mauny, R., 1951, p.59; Vallon, A., 1862, p.467 & p.764.
27. Barreto, H.P. in Walter, J., 1947, document no.12, p.77.
28. National Archives, Dakar, document no.2F4, piece no.13; Roche, C., 1976, p.101.
29. Dalphinis, M., 1979(a).
30. Dalphinis, M., 1981, pp.86-87.
31. Koestler, A., 1959.

Part II.
Language.

1. Introduction.

Language

Of the many world languages, the Creole languages of the Caribbean have fascinated scholars world-wide, because of the rich diversity of their cultural heritage and the opportunities they offer for theoretical development and debate about the nature of human language. For example, is Patwa *té* — completive marker, for example in:
mwen té li — 'I have read'
"I Complet. read"
a descendant of Yoruba *ti* — completive marker, or French *été* — past participle of *être* — 'to be'? This is as much a question of the plural possibilities in the genetic stock of Caribbean peoples and languages, as well as a theoretical question as to how languages change their forms and meanings, coupled with the wish of linguists to see if there are any rules governing these changes.

'Various Approaches to the Study of Creole Languages: the case for African influences', suggests that African languages are the main sources of structure and meaning in Creole languages.

In 'Lexical Expansion in Casamance Kriul, Gambian Krio and St. Lucian Patwa', the theme of African influences is expanded by examining the methods by which three Creoles, each within different European language camps, i.e. Portuguese, English and French respectively, remain very similar from the point of view of common African grammatical structures, nevertheless, all used similar processes to develop from restricted trade languages, i.e. pidgins, into full languages having a wider voculabury, i.e. Creoles.

'A Synchronic Comparison of the Verbal Systems of St. Lucian Patwa and Guinean Crioulo' makes a closer analysis of the nature of the similar structure between two Creoles having vocabularies from different European languages, i.e. French in the case of Patwa and Portuguese in the case of Crioulo.

Unlike the African Creoles in Gambia and Senegal, St. Lucian and other Caribbean Creoles also have the added dimension of influences from the early Arawak and Carib peoples of the Caribbean and the Americas. The nature of these influences is described in 'Island Carib Influences in St. Lucian Patwa'.

2. Various Approaches to the Study of Creole Languages: the case for African influences.

What is a 'Creole Language'? Creole languages in the Caribbean and to a limited extent in West Africa can possibly be described as the resultant linguistic index of the Euro-African miscegenation that was part and parcel of the history of African slavery within the Caribbean.

To deny the racial angle is to deny reality; in the island of Martinique for example there was an institutionalization of such a caste-colour system: at the bottom of the ascending scale was the 'black'; above was the 'brown', above the 'brown' the 'quadroon', above the 'quadroon' the 'octaroon' — until we arrived finally to the desired social product, the *sang mêlé* (mixed-blood), who for all intents and purposes had the position of the white man in past Caribbean society.[1]

Such Euro-African miscegenation has only been successfully denied by the language policy of the Union of South Africa, which emphatically denies that the Coloureds were in any way associated with the development of Afrikaans and that Afrikaans is in any way a Creole Language with black-African links; in short they believe that their past white ancestors, unlike other human beings, had no human intercourse with others.[2]

Creole Languages have also been defined as the languages of the slave trying, unsuccessfully, to speak the language of the master; in linguistic terms the 'target language' is seen to be the language of the dominant European colonizer while the 'source language' is seen to be the native language of the slave which interfers for ever and ever with his/her attempts to speak the language of the master perfectly. In short:

> *i de wan tak Inglish bot i de brek am smol smol*[3]
> ('He/She wants to speak Standard English but he/she talks non-Standard/broken English')

For the literally sophisticated this is the language of Caliban trying to speak like Prospero in language that defines more that "the isle is full of noises".[4]

Creole languages have also been defined as the languages of the mentally subnormal; the (negro) writer Broussard, for example, writing on the French Creole of Louisiana USA, says: "The negro manages to express his thoughts with a present, and a future with an occasional conditional and pluperfect".[5] In short, the black man's brain needs no sophisticated conditional logic such as: if X, then Y logically follows; he lives only in the present, wanting only (and I quote one of ex-President Ford's supporters) "large shoes, a fast car and a tight pussy".

The counter-argument to what is possibly regarded as a chip on my shoulder (it's no chip by the way — it's the log of five hundred years of slavery) is that many Creole languages and West African languages may seem to work in this manner syntactically speaking. However, I would reply that no defination is so innocent that it gives no index of its internal prejudices. If the writer had wanted to make an unprejudiced statement he would possibly have left out the words "the negro" and "manages" and possibly have said: In X language, Z, M and N linguistic phenomena are evident. As with all such 'innocent' writing I can only say that "It is only the snake who innocently warns us that he has no poison".[6]

As far as the linguistic term 'dialect' is concerned, Creole languages have sometimes been defined as quaint Negro 'dialects' of various European languages; for example, my language is called Patwa by St. Lucians, but the former meaning of this near-obsolete[7] French word is 'dialect'. This word shows therefore the past definition of the language as far as French-dominated St. Lucian plantation society was concerned.

However, as is fitting to our quasi-scientific methodology, we linguists are not supposed to have any such prejudice towards any phenomenon definable as human language; to us what is defined as 'dialect', whether because it is a regional variety or otherwise, is no more and no less a language to be respected than what is the 'standard language', which is after all nothing more than a dialect which has been adopted by a given society as the language of prestige, government and education. In linguistic terms the Cockney is as correct as the queen.[8]

Ideally, I suppose, a linguist is like a doctor who sterilises his prejudices before analysing any language so that the 'body'[9] can be laid bare for analysis; and possibly sterilisation is most difficult when the language (or body) concerned is one's own. Nevertheless I would like to give a comparative view of the possible links between Caribbean Creole languages in terms of Possessive Constructions, Aspect Markers and the Zero Copula[10] (i.e. the absence of an overt marker for the verb 'to be').

In the possessive constructions of the following Caribbean languages we note the similar structure:

Noun + *possessive suffix marking the possessor*
Beni:

    èra mè — 'my father'
    òwa mè — 'my house'

Hausa:

    dokin mu — 'our horse'
    abokin mu — 'our friend'

Yoruba:

    eyawò *mi* — 'my wife'
    òrè *mi* — 'my friend'

Central Igbo

    enyi m — 'my friend'
    ehi anyi — 'our cow'

and 'lo and behold' the same structure is repeated in all the French Creole languages of the Caribbean. For example in St. Lucia we

    chat mwen — 'my cat'
    Noun + *marker indicating possessor*
    kabwit mwen — 'my goat'

This similarity in possessive constructions is not echoed in the Anglophone Caribbean,[11] for example Jamaican:

    mi daag — 'my dog'
    mi kaw — 'my cow'

In their emphasis upon an aspect, rather than a time-based yardstick of concepts such as past, present and future, however, both the Francaphone and Anglophone Creole languages show a great similarity to West African languages. The term 'aspect', by the way, is used to measure parameters such as completed action versus uncompleted action, progressive versus non-progressive action and futuritive versus non-futuritive action. It is consequently a different yardstick to that of time.[12] We have for example the following exemplifcation of progressive aspect in West African languages:

Yoruba:

    eni mu lo si òja — 'Today I'm going to market,' i.e. literally:
        "today I'm in the process of going to market."
    òla mu lo si òja — 'Tomorrow I'll go to market,' i.e. literally
        "tomorrow I'm in the process of going to market."
    anō mu lo si òja — 'Yesterday I went to market,' i.e. literally:
        "yesterday I'm in the process of going to market."

Central Igbo:

    tâ: agam aga ahya — 'Today I'm going to market', i.e.
        literally: "today I'm in the process of going to market.
    tâ: ta: agam agaahya –'Now I,m going to market,' i.e.
        literally:"now I'm in the process of going to market."
etshi garaga agaram ahya[13] –'Yesterday I went to market,', i.e.
    literally: "yesterday I'm in the process of going to market."
etshi na bjamò agam agaahya—'Tomorrow I'll go to market, i.e.
    literally: "tomorrow I'm in the process of going to market."

The important similarity in the above examples is that it is progressive aspect rather than time which is the standard by which the 'action' of the verb is judged; it could be 'today, yesterday or tomorrow', and in Igbo and Yoruba one can say: "I'm in the process of going to market" — the verb does not change its form nor the personal pronoun its shape with any change along a time-scale.[14]

'Lo and behold' we have similar behaviour both in the Anglophone and Francophone Caribbean Creole languages; in St.. Lucian Patwa for example, one has the following examples:

    jòdi a mwen ka manjé chat— 'Today I'm eating cat,' i.e.
        literally:"today I'm in the process of eating cat."
    demen mwen ka manjé chat— 'Tomorrow I'll eat cat," i.e.
        'iterally:"tomorrow I'm in the process of eating cat."
jè mwen té ka manjé chat-"Yesterday I was eating cat," i.e. literally:
"yesterday I was in the process of eating cat, but I have already completed this action."

In Jamaican Creole, we have the following examples:

    nau mi a go makit — 'Now I' going to market,' i.e. literally:
        "I'm in the process of going to market."
    yestide mi a go makit —'Yesterday I went to market, i.e. literally:

yesterday I'm in the process of going to market.
tumoro mi a go makit — tomorrow I'll go to market, i.e. literally: tomorrow I'm in the process of going to market.

In the deletion of the 'copula', we again find extreme similarity between the Caribbean Creole languages and African languages of West Africa, for example:

Jamaican creole:
    im dred – 'He/She is a Rasta/He/She is frightening.'

St. Lucian Patwa:
    i fou – 'He/She is mad'

Yoruba:
    omi tutu – 'The water is cold'
    eyawo mi atata – 'My wife is beautiful'

Twi:
    o bòdam – 'He/She is mad'
    insyo awò – 'The water is cold'
    èyè fèfèfè – She is beautiful / He is handsome'

Central Igbo:
    wāgnyim maramma – 'My wife is beautiful'
    mmiri òji – 'The water is cold'
    ò baraba – 'He/She/It is rich'

It is therefore not surprising that a literal word-to-word translation of many Caribbean languages would give close approximations to Caribbean Creole languages. For example:

    eyawò mi atata — "wife me beautiful"

Compare St. Lucian Patwa:

    madam mwen bèl — "wife me beautiful"

in which both the position of the possessive pronoun and copula deletion is the same; or Jamaican creole:

    mi wuman nais — "my wife beautiful"

in which only copula deletion is the same.

Despite the importance of a linguistic viewpoint, however, other scholastic viewpoints are of paramount importance to the study of creole languages; for example, Bynon's[15] viewpoint that oral literature entails its own literary criticism is important, as only oral items judged by the given speech-community to be of special value will be remembered by them, and by means of memory be perpetuated for successive generations. It is consequently of no surprise that the victims of the Atlantic slave-trade found that the sociological comment of the wily spider Ananse on human craftiness, treachery, cruelty and vindictiveness were comments to be valued and perpetuated by telling these tales to their children; after all, were not their very lives in the 'New World' the summary of all the above human attributes?

Johnson[16] in fact indicates that the perpetuation of the Ananse and the Brer Rabbit stories are a means of classifying the general geographical origin of Caribbeans and Afro-Americans: those having the Ananse story would most likely come from the Southern Forest Zone of the West Coast of Africa, while those having Brer Rabbit stories would most likely originate from the Savannah Belt of the West Coast.

On the more divine plane, we see the importance of the gods and religions of various West African cultures in the perpetuation of the names[17] of these gods in the Caribbean Creole languages: Ogun, the Dahomean and Yoruba god of warfare, and Legba, the god of the pathway leading to the Supreme God; both have their home in Haiti. The incantation to Legba:

Attibon Legba
Attibon Legba
Ovum bayi pou' moi....[18]

as well as the attached sacrifices of chicken's blood, are all a living part of the language and culture of Haiti. In Trinidad, on the other hand, the god whose name and practices have been perpetuated is Shango. In St. Lucia, the name of the Dahomean religion *Voudou* and its herbalists, among them the deceased *Djòlif*[19] have been perpetuated, as well as the Ghanaian mythical god-figure *Mami Wata*, whom we call *maman glo*. Where the actual West African names have not been perpetuated in St. Lucian Patwa the West African religious concepts have been, for example, a *Bolonm*, which is an invisible dwarf under the command of a witchdoctor who sends the *Bolonm* on any mission he wants (unfortunately the missions are usually malevolent) — the *Soukouyè*, a bat-like creature which screams through the trees at night, and if the creature is lucky enough to find a lone human at night, it will suck the human's blood dry; and the *Adjablès*, a woman who will entice you in the wood (where she lives disguised by day), cause you to lose all sesne of physical reality and kill you by getting you to walk over a precipice — what we do if we find a man in such a demented state in the wood is to turn his shirt inside-out and put it back on him; he is then supposed to come back to his senses.

Wars and revolts in the Caribbean have also been a means by which words from African languages in Caribbean Creole languages have been perpetuated; for example it is possibly due to the Marroon wars against the British in Jamaica that sentences of Akan origin such as:

obroni odabra — 'The white man is coming;'

compare Akan:

òburoni oreba — ʼThe white man is coming' as well as many other Akan words such as:

òyarefò— a sick or dead person

compare, for example, Jamaican Creole:

yarefo — a sick person[20]

Another example is the Haitian War of Independence which culminated in the imprisonment of the genius Toussaint Louverture[21] in the Franco-Swiss Jura, one third of Napoleon Bonaparte's army dead or defeated and the factual realization of the Haitian army-leader Dessalines' possible sentiments: 'Tomorrow we will have two battles, one against the settler, one against the French; we shall win both'. This war also ensured the perpetuation of Dahomean words to do with religion, as it is parrtly by means of this that the slaves were motivated to destroy their masters with their bare hands, where other means were not available.

In more immediate times, however, in which education is becoming more and more a means of securing the 'Kingdom of Daily Bread' rather than as an end in itself, the perpetuation or non-perpetuation of these at least African-influenced Caribbean Creole languages have had some important educational implications; in the Caribbean generally, this has been conceptualized in terms of the necessary acquisition of standard European languages by non-Europeans who, despite being "Afro-Greeks",[22] do not for the most part of their lives speak standard European languages — they speak lexically related Creole languages.

Imagine if you can the problem of learning Standard English in the St. Lucian class-room only to go outside the room to speak a Creole language in which many of the syntactic constructions are, as seen previously, extremely different.

In England, the educational implications of the perpetuation of these Creole languages in the Caribbean-British population is that they and their children are classed immediately as Educationally Subnormal,[23] because their language is after all 'Subnormal English', and their speakers educationally destined for the social history of 'first to be sacked and last to be employed'. On a more positive note, some Caribbeans have addressed themselves to this problem, which is essentially one of communication, by creating Supplementary Schools to educate their children in a better fashion than thet of a society which, through its own inherent ignorance and weaknesses, find it expedient to alienate or destroy what it cannot understand.

For me this is important, as my personal definition of education is: 'the perpetuation of man in an image of himself which is good'. It is extremely difficult for me to imagine my children successfully growing through a British Educational System, be it in Britain or in the Caribbean, with a good and creeative image of themselves. Further, if we are all the images of God, it is extremely sad that a good image of Creole languages, let alone of their speakers, cannot be ensured within the British educational system.

The greater tragedy, however, is that such prejudices against Creole languages have been 'mimicked' by the native speakers of these Creole languages themselves; in St. Lucia, for example, among those who had a social prestige to protect, children were immediately rebuked or beaten should they dare to speak a tongue which only brought them closer to those who were poor or 'black'. The situation is explained in linguistic terminology [24] by the term "diglossia" in which a "High" variety of language, which scores positively in terms of social prestige, is distinguished, for example, Standard French in Haiti is opposed to a "Low" variety of language, for example Creole French in Haiti.

However, with increasing nationalism, Africanisation and Caribbeanisation of the Caribbean, these Creole languages are becoming more and more socially acceptable and even seen in their true light as languages indexing the cultural, historical and national identity of the particular Caribbean island; for example, now in St. Lucia we listen to Radio Martinique avidly when they play Creole songs and stories which we also have in St. Lucia.

This new status being given to Creole languages in the Caribbean does have some political implications, as far as Africans and their Caribbean descendants are concerned; it indexes a common culture which becomes more and more important in an era in which Jamaica was once willing to send volunteer freedom-fighters to aid the guerillas fighting in Southern Africa, some Caribbean governments provide more money for the freedom of the African in Southern Africa than some African governments do, while Cubans, many of whose African ancestors came from Angola, decided to 'bring it all back home' and help to free Angola.

From the European view point such political implications are necessarily psychologically far-fetched, and if real, dangerous to the only relationship they are interested in as far as Africans are concerned: *mi massa, yu boi.* You see, if Fanon is right when he says that to speak a language: "means above all to assume a culture, to support the weight of a civilization", then any implication that the Creole languages of the Caribbean show some very West African traits as far as their syntax is concerned is a threat to the belief in the superiority of the European mind as it implies that these Creoles are not a perpetuation of European culture, and if anything, they are a perpetuation of African culture.

This is an important point from two points of view, firstly because lexical items (due to huge inter-language borrowings traditional to all human languages, for example, *tobacco* and *potato* borrowed into English from South American Amerindian languages) are not the crucial factor in distinguishing one language from another. The more important similarity of Creole languages to African languages, as far as the more important level of syntax is concerned, only serves to demonstrate the tenacious survival of African culture.

Secondly, given that the language policy of the past slave-masters in the Caribbean was based on a policy of divide-and-rule, namely they separated the slaves speaking the same language in all cases and prohibited, by severe punishments, the use of any African languages, it is a testimony to the African's tenacious survival that this language policy did not work.

This is of particular importance to the French Caribbean islands in which the French "*/mission civilisatrice* ('civilising mission')", aimed at assimilating any Caribbean person capable of showing signs of 'civilisation', the most important sign being the acquisition of the French language. As Fanon says: "The Negro of the Antilles will be proportionately whiter — that is, he will come closer to being a real human being — in direct proportion to his mastery of the French language".[25] Now if after all the trouble the Frenchman took to assimilate Caribbeans, all that are being perpetueted are really twentieth century African languages, then the promotion of Creole as the national language of Martinique, by political activists who want an independent Martinique, represents the only true solution to a 'civilised' relationship which is essentially false, and 'civilised' aims which, as indicated previously, are doomed to failure, as they cannot be realised even after five hundred years of the most 'barbarian' language policy.

In the Anglophone Caribbean, on the other hand, the Aryan superiority complex of the past British slave-masters, as well as their total lack of any civilisation to which anybody, let alone Caribbeans, could be assimilated, left no room for even the attempt at a mistaken assimilado policy towards the Caribbean Creole languages. It left instead only a racially defined rejection of these languages, as it did in the case of African languages in Anglophone Africa, as the languages of inferior peoples which, if the natives wanted to speak them, was no skin off their backs; what mattered to the British was commerce not the dubious assets of culture and civilisation. This more phlegmatic view of language has possibly characterised the pragmatic language policies of many Anglophone Caribbean governments which in present times have adlopted politically and culturally undefined or 'lassiez faire' views towards Creole languages. In St. Lucia, for example (which as well as being colonised by the French in the past was also colonised by the British), the Creole languages of the Caribbean are not looked at as a possible symbol of national culture or of cultural independence from the British; if you want to speak them that's fine, but if you want to get educated or climb the social ladder, English is a necessary and definite asset.

This 'laissez-faire' view, however, possibly deprives the Anglophone Caribbean of a politically orientated nationalist and culturally defined view of their Creole languages, as is more evident in the Francophone Caribbean. Obviously this is fast changing in the present Caribbeanisation of the Caribbean, and in St. Lucia, for example, younger politicians representing more nationally defined political parties use the Creole language of St. Lucia when trying to win the support of the mass of the people, many of whom may only speak Patwa.

To my mind, however, only a cultural and linguistic point of view which takes into account the African basis of the multi-cultural plurality of the Caribbean is capable of being truly representative; the Caribbean's African customs and African linguistic heritage is obviously more truly African than that of many parts of Africa; we are, after all, the only true Africans, we are not one tribe or one story, we are all the tribes and all the stories. Ironically enough, it is we and not the African who faces the problem of having to advocate de-Africanization for some of our people, for they are too African. What does one do, for example, with a Rastafarian who, even after the physical death of Haile Selassie, proclaims "Jah lives"? What does one do with a Maroon from Surinam who has not changed the African pattern of his/her life because from the end of slavery (s)he has severed all links with a white world justifiably defined by him/her as evil?

Possibly, in restricting myself to an Africanist viewpoint, I may seem to have underplayed the extremely useful cultural and technological inheritance we Caribbeans have acquired from our Amerindian, European, Indian and Chinese ancestors. It is not deliberate; they too are evident and we are equally proud of them. One has to be comfortable in one's skin no matter what its origins. Nevertheless, one has to face the fact that nearly every piece of non-material culture in the Caribbean,[26] from Ska to Reggae, has been the contribution of the 'rejected corner-stone in the temple' — the African. Yes, it is true that from language onward, we Caribbeans must be true to our plural heritage of: "Out of many, one people",[27] yes, especially when the many are Africans.

We note, even in our writers, who have been most exposed to the European literary tradition, the drum echoes of African perpetuation. In the writings of Césaire, for example, acknowledged by De Gaulle as the greatest writer in French of the century, the perpetuation of a literary style that is founded on African oral literature is evident. In the following lines from *Cahier d'un Retour au Pays Natal,* for example:

> voom roh oh
> voom roh oh
> to charm snakes to conjure up
> the dead
> voom roh oh to let my own skies
> open [28]

the use of repetition: "voom roh oh" finds a true parallel only with African oral literature. Compare, for example, the lines:

> By thinking of the Congo
> I have become a Congo noisy with forests
> and rivers [30]
> where the water goes
> likwala likwala [31]

in which the use of the ideophones "likwala likwala" to conjure up the sound of flowing water and only finds its true echo in African languages where these abound. Compare, for example, *"sukukun makakan maki"*, the Hausa epithet of an emir in which the idiophones *"sukukun makakan"* are meant to conjure up the wily slithering movement of a snake.

To sum up then, both in an analysis of the Creole languages of the Caribbean as well as Caribbean culture, it is clear that Europe has affected Africa but equally Africa has affected Europe: the words are European, but the syntax is African. For me, it is only on the basis of such an indigenous view of culture that a truer basis can be given to what is claimed to be 'universal' both in Linguistics and in Anthropology. The postulation of parameters claimed to be universal can only be made from a plural cultural viewpoint; it cannot be a one-way view based on the limited cultural view-points of Europe only. In short, 'All roads lead to Rome'[32] and 'Only the fool points to his ancestors with his left hand'.[33]

Notes

1. Hayot, E., 1971, pp.60-61.
2. Valkoff, M.F., 1966.
3. The phrase is in Nigerian pidgin.
4. Shakespeare, W., *The Tempest*, circa 1611-1612.
5. Broussard, J.F., 1972.
6. Dalphinis, M., 1970.
7. Or a rarely used French word.
8. Eg. in the Queen's Christmas speech of 1975.
9. Murray's "A New English Dictionary", p.964, note 17: "(more loosely) An assemblage of units characterized by some common attribute, and thus regarded as a whole . . . ".
10. Note also the treatment of Zero Copula + Adjective as Adjectival Verb without a copula. See pt.III, ch.2, p.160 & pt.II, ch.3, p.106.
11. . This could, however, be due to the influences of different West African languages having a more predominating influence in Jamaica, for example Twi, in which we have examples such as: *mi kramain* — my dog; *mi jeri* — my wife. This would not be surprising given that many Jamaicans are of Twi/Fante African origins.
12. Lyons, J., 1968, and Hockett, E., 1958.
13. This is a possible counter-example to a purely aspect-orientated point-of-view in that the marker r in *agram* is definable as a marker of past time. See pt.III ch.2 for similar examples from Hausa and Beni. in that the marker [r] in [agaram] is definable as a marker of past time.
14. We note by comparison European languages such as French which do change the form of the verb according to the parameters past, present and future; for example: *j'ai quitté* (past), *je quitte* (present), *je quitterai* (future).
15. Dr. Bynon: lecture on Berber oral literature, School of Oriental and African Studies, Univ. of London, 1976. See also pt.III, ch.4.
16. Johnson, H.A.S., 1966 and pt.111, ch.3.
17. We are aware also of the perpetuation of Ghanaian 'day names' in Jamaica. For example, Kwesi in Ghana has a comparable Jamaican Kwashie.
18. Brathwaite, E. *Islands*, 1969, p.54.
19. St. Lucian herbalist. He died about twelve years ago.
20. Dalby, D., 1971.
21. James, C.L.R., 1963.
22. Walcott, D. *In a Green Night*, 1962.
23. Chord, B., 1971.
24. Fergusson, C.A., 1975.
25. Fanon, F., 1970, p.13.
26. Rodney, W., 1969.
27. The national motto of Jamaica.
28. Césaire, A., 1969, pp.80-81.
29. Dalphinis, M. *Hausa children's games and the West African oral tradition*, unpublished manuscript, 1974.
30. Césaire, A., 1969, pp.58-59.
31. Césaire, A., 1969, p.56.
32. English proverb.
33. Ghanian proverb: see the introduction to E. Brathwaite's *Masks*, 1968.

Lexical Expansion in Casamance in Casamance Kriul, Gambian Krio and St.Lucian Patwa.

Linguistic vocabulary

In view of the complex range of terms which have been introduced into the discussion of pidgins and Creoles, this paper begins with a definition of terms used in the subsequent discussion:

Diachronic/Synchronic — are defined here as mutually exclusive terms. Diachronic refers to the interaction of languages in the past which are no longer in contact. Synchronic refers to the interaction of languages which are still in contact (giving rise to synchronic reinforcement of past influences).

Languages in Diachronic contact — languages in past geographical contact, but now separated.

Languages in Synchronic contact — languages in present geographical contact.

Structural mould — the main African language structure at the phonological, morphological, semantic and syntactic levels which characterises the Creole languages under consideration.

Lexical input — (a) the mainly European lexicon which Creole languages adopted in their formative stages;
(b) the lexicon adopted by established Creole languages from either African or European languages in synchronic contact.

Relexification — the massive input of lexical items from one language into the structural mould of one or more others, involving: (a) the continuance of the phonology, morphology, semantic structure and syntax of the latter; (b) the virtual disappearance of its/their former lexicon. This process may be either gradual or swift

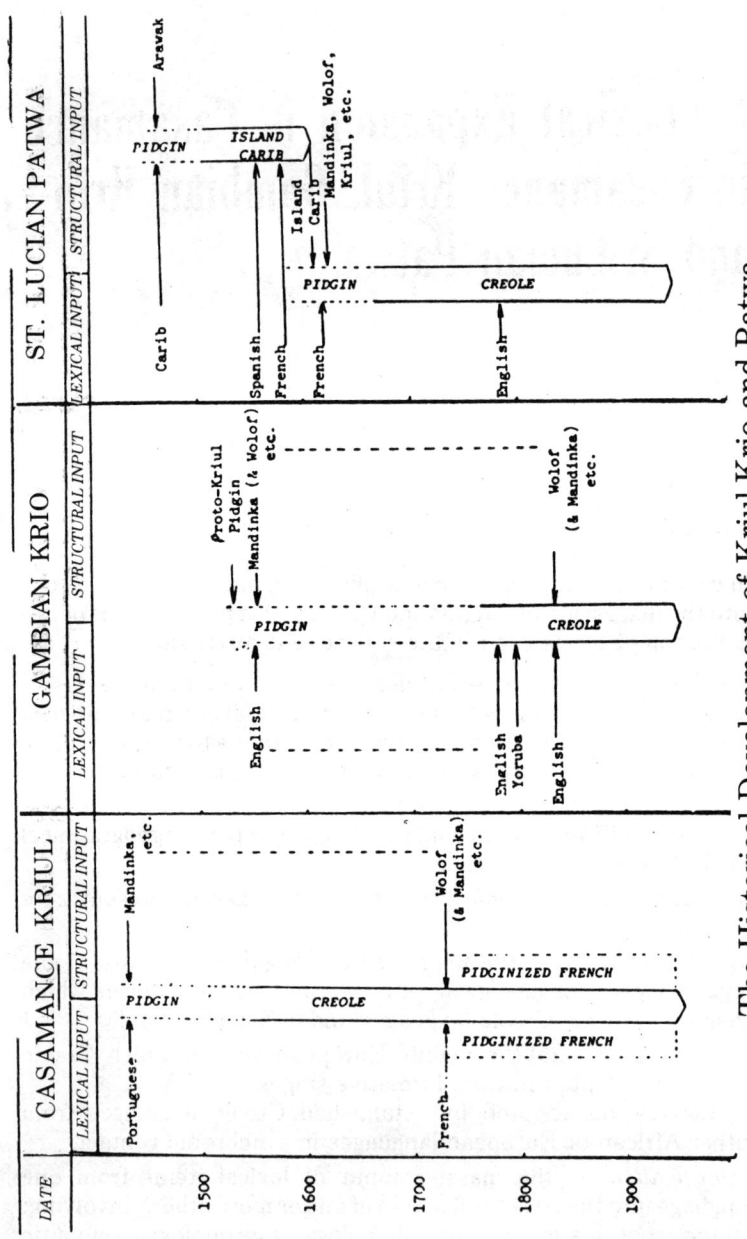

DATE	CASAMANCE KRIUL		GAMBIAN KRIO		ST. LUCIAN PATWA	
	LEXICAL INPUT	STRUCTURAL INPUT	LEXICAL INPUT	STRUCTURAL INPUT	LEXICAL INPUT	STRUCTURAL INPUT

The Historical Development of Kriul, Krio and Patwa.

and may work in different directions at different times, i.e.:

Lexical input	Structural mould
European	African
African	Established Creole
Carib	Arawak
African	African
2nd European language	Established Creole
Established Creole	African
etc.	

Hypercorrection — the adoption of items into a language through deliberate approximation to another language either by relexification or by decreolization.

Decreolization — changes in the phonology, semantic structure, morphology and syntax of an established Creole approximating to the grammatical system of a non-Creole language. Changes in lexicon do not constitute decreolization, but rather relexification.

Domain — semantic field which, in a given language, may have external prestige or influence through superior environmental knowledge.

Prestige — is taken as being directly correlated to domain. Each language is assumed to have one or more domains of internal prestige and may have one or more domains of external prestige.

External prestige — the prestige given to a language by non-native speakers of that language.

Internal prestige — the prestige native speakers give to their own language as a marker of in-group self-esteem.

Pidgin/Creole — a pidgin is a language of limited vocabulary, as spoken by second-language speakers. By lexical expansion the vocabulary becomes a Creole spoken as a home language.

Lexical expansion — a process comprising calques, convergences and loans as a result of the social and psychological interaction of one language on another (subsequently 'suprastrate' and 'substrate, reflecting normally the main lexical and structural sources, respectively).

Introduction

Lexical expansion in African and Caribbean Creoles involved the recasting of European lexical items in an African semantic, phonological, morphological and syntactic mould. In order to examine fully such African influences upon Creole lexical items, comparison is made between Creole languages whose respective lexicons are mainly of Portuguese, English and French origin, thus allowing an evaluation of the common African language mould below their surface lexical differences.

Casamance Kriul, Gambian Krio and St. Lucian Patwa[1] have been selected for this purpose. Patwa has been separated from its African structural sources while all three Creoles have been separated from one or more of their lexical source languages, thus providing a novel opportunity to compare Creoles with and without synchronic contact with their African and European source languages.

Historical background

Casamance Kriul has been separated from Portuguese and Kriul in Ginea Bissau (formerly Portuguese Guinea) due to a Franco-Portuguese treaty in 1886 which made Ziguinchor[2] part of the French colony of Senegal. Kriul and Patwa have both been brought into contact with a European language other than that which formed the basis of their earlier lexical development[3] (i.e. French in the case of Kriul, and English in the case of Patwa). Kriul expanded from a Portuguese pidgin to meet the developing communication needs of the Atlantic Slave Trade, around which early Portuguese settlers, the host African ethnic groups, their Afro-Portuguese descendants as well as other Europeans, cemented profitable commercial activity.

Krio, the next Creole language developed in West Africa, owes, as do other Creoles, some of its lexical expansion to the prior presence of Kriul.[4] Krio became a Gambian language on the arrival of freed-slaves re-shipped from the Freetown area (in Sierra Leone) to Bathurst (now renamed Banjul),[5] where it has been brought into synchronic contact with English and separated from its formative African lexical sources, especially Yoruba (its major diachronic African lexical source and the dominant language of S.W. Nigeria).

Patwa developed from a French lexical input into a Senegambian language mould (Appendix 8)[6] coupled with the general influences of other African languages and of Island Carib, the language of the St. Lucian inhabitants prior to and during the period of African immigration. Patwa has been out of contact with its African language sources for about 500 years; it was mainly exposed to French lexical influences till 1813 when St. Lucia became politically British and the imposition of English began.[7]

Theoretical framework

The complex linguistic situation resulting from the upheaval and crisis which marked 17th and 18th century African and Caribbean history benefits from the Saussurean synchronic/ diachronic framework. Changing lexical influences upon Kriul, Krio and Patwa can be discussed in terms of diachronic languages in contact as opposed to synchronic languages in contact providing varying lexical inputs to the structural mould of these Creoles, with possible reinforcing or decreolizing effects.[8]

Yoruba lexical items in Krio (Appendix 5), for example, partly due to the predominance of Yoruba Creoles (or Aku as they were known by non-Yoruba Freetonian Creoles) are indicative of a diachronic contact with Yoruba. This has since been succeeded by the synchronic contact with Wolof (Appendix 6) (and Mandinka) whose prominent features are: many Wolof loans and the synchronic reinforcement of aspects of the Krio structural mould having origins in Wolof and/or Mandinka (Appendix 7). Diachronic influences upon Kriul lexicon, though varied, have been mainly Mandinka (Appendix 1), spoken by the Mandinka[9] wives of the Portuguese and the many Mandinka-speaking peoples in the Casamance.

Wolof (and Mandinka) have provided the main synchronic reinforcement (Appendix 3) and French the new lexical input, for Kriul. These same African languages, by contrast, were the main diachronic sources of the Patwa structural mould (Appendix 18 & Appendix 20), while English and not French is providing new lexical inputs for Patwa. Both Kriul and Patwa are adapting to European languages different to their formative lexical sources.

Earlier definitions of relexification, i.e. of a Portuguese pidgin becoming a Creole by adopting new European lexicon do not reflect the above exemplification. Relexification viewed as a regular inter-African language feature, involving a change of lexical input between languages of similar structural mould,[10] provides a more suitable framework for the study of Creoles, much of whose structural moulds are African-derived.

Language prestige and other sociolinguistic factors are also relevant. The African Creoles have traditionally had a 'superior' status in relation to African languages while the Caribbean Creoles have had an 'inferior' status. Relexification[11] has been mainly prestige-motivated in Creole societies. For example, Kriul, as the language of economically powerful Afro-Portuguese middlemen,[12] was a language of prestige in the Casamance. This is reflected in the few African language loans in Kriul (Appendix 1) in contrast to the widespread use of Portuguese/Kriul loans in neighbouring African languages (Appendix 2).[13] The few African loans in Kriul are mainly Mandinka. This itself reflects the past prestige of Mandinka as the language of the Manding trade empire extending into the Casamance.[14]

The present semi-official role of Wolof as a language of communication and as an expression of the Dakar-centred[15] state has aided the prestige of Wolof and its spread in Senegambia extending as far as Casamance. Encroaching Wolof influences upon Kriul (Appendix 3) have been on this new background of prestige. The past prestige of Kriul is now expressed in terms of a Casamance regionalism and independence from a 'Wolof' centre of political diffusion. The past external prestige of Kriul has been translated into a present internal prestige in face of the new external prestige of Wolof.[16] Even pidginized French as spoken by Kriul-speakers shows evidence of such increasing Wolof influences (Appendix 3).

The close relationship between prestige and linguistic change as described by Labov suggests the possible adoption of Labov's framework for such African/Creole language situations. However, the latter framework, in its focus on the use/non-use of a single prestige-related language item presupposes the widespread use of a single language, e.g. English in the Euro-American language situation. African/Creole languages by contrast presuppose a varied language background in which the use/non-use of one or more languages of prestige is of Sociolinguistic relevance. The exact domain(s) of such prestige languages would, however, need to be analysed in terms of its/their internal (diachronic) and external (synchronic) prestige.[17]

Diachronic Yoruba lexical influences in the domain of culinary terms, for example, are suggestive of the past external prestige given to Yoruba by non-Yoruba Creoles. It is a prestige which has been translated into the present internal prestige of Yoruba-derived items in Krio as opposed to the external prestige of Wolof in the Senegambia.

In the Krio responses to my Oral Literature Questionnaire,[18] Yoruba loans were more frequent in the song genre related to Christian marriage (in the speech of both younger and older speakers). In the Islamic Senegambia such a selective perpetuation[19] of Christian songs[20] is indicative of the present internal prestige of Yoruba-derived items in Krio.[21] The traditional association of a 'Christian' cultural background with Western European prestige and power suggests that the perpetuation of Yoruba loans in a specifically Christian song genre is related to a probable past role of Yoruba as a language associated with European/Christian power and prestige, at least in the eyes of non-Yoruba Freetonian Creoles.

The synchronic spread of Wolof as a language of external prestige in Senegambia has aided the predominance of Wolof loans in both formal and informal Krio. This contrasts with the more restricted lexical influences of English on modern Krio in the formal domains of education and government where English still enjoys some external prestige. These domains are, however, being encroached upon by Wolof and Mandinka.

Such changes of prestige and domain are motivating factors in relexification and vary with the different languages in contact. French in Senegal, for example, which, like English in Gambia, also enjoyed external prestige in the domains of government and education is also being gradually replaced by Wolof in these domains. It is these new Wolof influences which have partly resulted in the use of a pidginised French by Kriul speakers.

It is not unlikely that the diachronic external prestige of Mandinka, as the language of the Manding empire, encouraged the influence of Mandinka on the proto-Patwa structural mould. The past domains of French in St. Lucia as the language of power, government and education are now being taken over by English, the synchronic language of external prestige. A relexification of Patwa from French to English lexicon is in process. However, as Patwa has internal prestige in informal discourse, such 'English' relexification is mainly in the formal domains of government and education. In fact, English lexical items from these domains are themselves structured in terms of Patwa's mainly Wolof/Mandinka structural mould (Appendix 3, Appendix 8).

Upon such a complex background of varying lexical sources Labov's term 'hypercorrection' can also be usefully reconsidered in terms of Creole/African languages as an approximation towards another language due to its external prestige, involving also relexification as a regular inter-African language feature. For example, the high external prestige of Portuguese, English and French amongst early speakers of Kriul, Krio and Patwa respectively, has made them the target languages for hypercorrecting Creole speakers. The internal prestige of their indigenous African languages, in certain domains, has aided the survival of calques, convergences and loans in the Creoles.

Relexification,[22] therefore, was partly the result of such hypercorrection in which massive borrowing of European lexicon originally became used in what was already an established inter-African language process.[23] It is a process which has continued in synchronic African/Creole language contacts, e.g. the relexification of Krio due to hypercorrection towards a prestigious Wolof.[24] By contrast, due to the strong internal prestige of Kriul,[25] Wolof influences on Kriul are in terms of structural reinforcement alone, coupled with minimal French lexical influences in the domain of education. Patwa, which like Kriul has been politically separated from its formative European language, is showing greater signs of relexification as a result of Patwa speakers hypercorrecting[26] towards an internationally prestigious English.

'Decreolization' within this African/Creole context of varying lines of historical and linguistic force can no longer be viewed in terms of the influences of European languages upon the lexicon of established Creoles, as African languages are having their own 'decreolizing' impacts upon the Creoles, e.g. Wolof is 'decreolizing' Krio. these 'decreolizing' effects are not only in terms of relexification but are also affecting the structural moulds of the Creoles, either by reinforcement or structural replacement, e.g. in the case of Wolof influences upon Kriul and Krio structure respectively.

Such African influences upon Creole structural moulds suggest that changes in a Creole's structural mould constitute decreolization.[27] Changes of lexicon, e.g. the adoption of English lexicon in Patwa (Appendix 20), do not constitute decreolization but a new lexical input into the African structural mould.

The formation of Island Carib from a Carib lexical input into an Arawak structural mould, has, similarly, mainly involved the relexification of Arawak towards the prestigious Carib lexicon of the 18th century Carib (male) invaders of St. Lucia. The Arawak structural mould of their newly conquered women-folk survived. Such historically prior languages have had determining influences upon the structural moulds of subsequent languages; e.g. the Arawakan structural mould has converged with that of African languages (Appendix 9) at certain points in the early development of Patwa.

In all the Creoles, including Island Carib, the earliest recorded language in the Creole's area of original development has often also been the original mother/home languages of the conquered group, e.g. Arawak in Island Carib, Mandinka in Kriul and Krio, Wolof/Mandinka in Patwa and Wolof in Mauritian Creole.[28] It is on their structures that the languages of the conquerors have been moulded.

A model for child-acquistion of language in the African/Creole context would need to emphasise the structural mould of mother/home language as the basis for the African's/Creole's acquisition of lexical items from external/'father' languages. Such impact from historically prior contact languages upon Creoles are frequently convergent with that of the most widespread and prestigious language(s) of the Creole speakers,[29] and are not totally unrelated to lexicon. Island Carib lexical items surviving in Patwa (Appendix 10), for example, are mainly flora and fauna lexical items reflecting the adoption of Island Carib lexicon by Africans in areas outside their former experience.

Given the mainly structural influences of historically prior languages upon the Creoles, the applicability of supposed 'universal' descriptive terms for Creole structural moulds can often be tested by seeing if the 'universal' is applicable to the structural mould of both the Creole and its past structural souce languages.

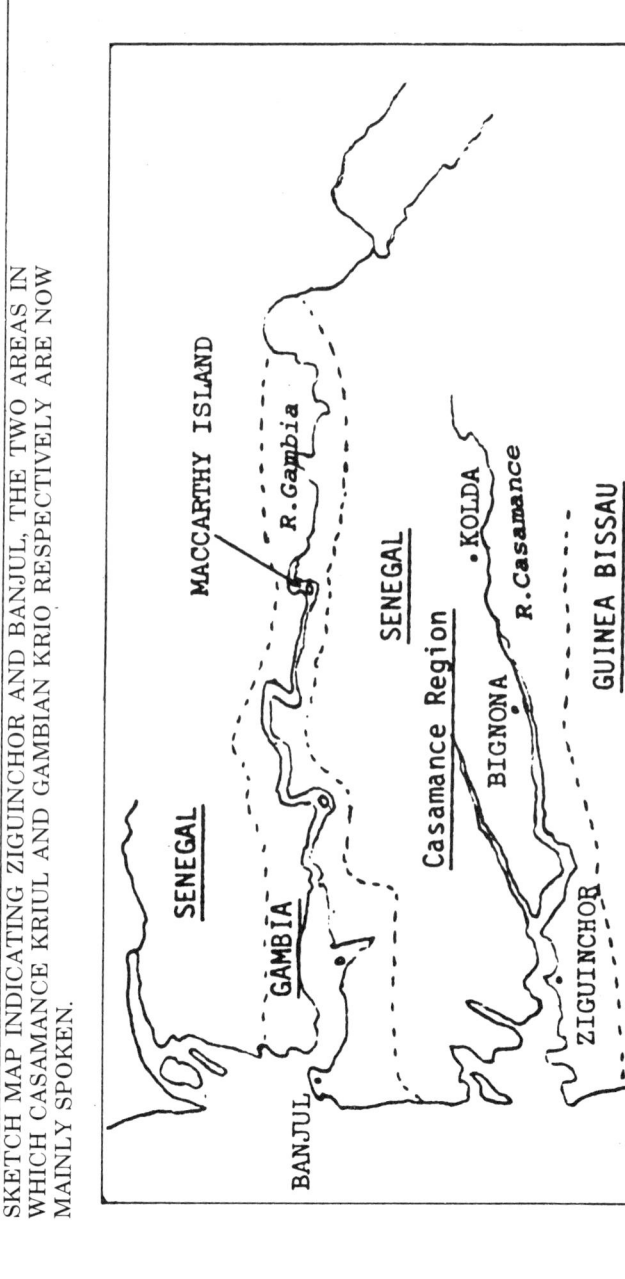

SKETCH MAP INDICATING ZIGUINCHOR AND BANJUL, THE TWO AREAS IN WHICH CASAMANCE KRIUL AND GAMBIAN KRIO RESPECTIVELY ARE NOW MAINLY SPOKEN.

1 Krio was formerly spoken by 18C. Krio settlers in Mc Carthy Island, in the Gambia, but as these settlers have been gradually merged with the surrounding Mandinka ethnic group, Krio is now a dying language spoken by a few older Creoles on the island. 2. Kriul is mainly spoken in the Santiaba quarter of Ziguinchor and in the Greguiss hamlet just outside Ziguinchor by the resident Creoles, and in Bignona and Kolda by Creole families who have moved from Ziguinchor to these towns.

For example, the term 'adjective' adopted from European language descriptions, i.e. as *zero copula + adjective*, has proved to be unsatisfactory on comparison with descriptions of African languages from which the term *adjectival verb* has more relevantly been included in descriptions of Creoles. Similarly, descriptions of the Patwa structure *noun + definite article* can be based on a comparable Mandinka and Wolof structure (Appendix 3). Psycholinguistics are also relevant to this theoretical framework. The slavery-based Creole societies censored the use of African lexical items by various methods, for example, the separation of people from the same ethno-linguistic group,[30] coupled with the general 'inferior' status given to African lexical alternants of European items. Such censorship conflicted with the social need for a language of wider communication as well as with the African need to perpetuate traditional African perceptions by any means necessary. This conflict partly motivated the remoulding of European lexical items as calques (Appendix 12) expressing such African perceptions or the preservation of African items as convergences (Appendix 13) with European lexical items of similar shape (and meaning) in order to by-pass censorship. The few African loans (Appendix 18) which survived reflect the extremity of censorship.

The presence of calques, convergences and loans in the Creoles in both the formative and synchronic stages point to their validity as descriptive terms.

Conclusion

Prior theoretical frameworks based on a Euro-centred view of lexical expansion are inadequate. The terms 'Portuguese-based', 'English-based' and 'French-based' are not representative of the African influences on Creoles which must be viewed en bloc, irrespective of surface differences, in order to delineate the common African lexical (and structural) influences which underlie them all.

Appendix

Kriul

1 Of the relatively few African loans in Kriul, note the following Mandinka-derived items: Kriul *jubé* — 'to look at', Mandinka *jubi* — 'to look at'; Kriul *kaangkara* — 'roof', Mandinka *kangkarang* — 'roof'.
2 Diola (Fogny) *bai* — 'to go', Kriul *bai* — 'to go' cf. Portuguese *vai* — 'goes'; Diola (Fogny) *fèra* — 'market', Kriul *fèra* — 'market', cf. Portuguese *feira* — 'a fair, an open-air market'.
3 Kriul suffixes *li* and *la* indicating proximity and distance respectively, e.g. *omi li* — 'this man', *omi la* — 'that man', are being reinforced by Wolof nominal suffixes of the form Consonant + i and Consonant + a, including *li* and *la*, which also indicate proximity and distance respectively with convergent influences from *ci* and *là* in *celui-ci* and *celui-là*. These Wolof (and Kriul) influences are evident in the pidginized French spoken by Kriul speakers, e.g. *lopital la* — 'the hospital'; *mézon la* 'the house' and also point to the wider influences of singular and plural nominal suffixes in both Wolof and Mandinka, e.g.: Wolof *jangha bi* — 'the girl', *jangha ji* — 'the girls'; Mandinka *sunggut o* — 'the girl', *sunggut olu* — 'the girls'. (Cf. also the similar definite suffix *la* in Patwa and other French Creoles).
4 Kriul *sabi* — 'to know'; Krio *sabi* — 'to know'; Kriul *blai* — 'basket'; Krio *blai* — 'basket'.

Krio

5 Krio *òpolo* — 'frog', cf. Yoruba *òpòlò* — 'frog'; Krio *okoboloto* — 'impotence', cf. Yoruba *okobo* — 'impotence'.
6 Krio a *ndèl misèf* — 'I shaved myself', cf. Wolof *ndèl* — 'to be bald'; Krio *yu na saisai man* — 'you are a profilgate', cf. Wolof *saisai* — 'a profilgate'.
7 Krio *di kau dèm* — 'the cows'. Cf. the use of a separable plural marker corresponding to the 3rd pl. pronoun in Bambara (interintelligible with Mandinka), e.g. *misi* '(the) cow', *misi + u* — '(the) cows'.

Patwa

8 For grammatical structure note Patwa and Mandinka *ka* both = progressive and habitual marker. Also Patwa 1st. sing. *ma, maa, may* 1st. sing. negative progressive/habitual and negative future markers respectively. Cf. Mandinka *mang* — general negative marker.

9 Mandinka *mang* may have converged with Arawak/Island Carib *m* — negative marker. Suffixation of possessive pronouns is a feature of a number of African languages including Yoruba, Edo and Hausa.

10 Patwa *zandoli* — 'lizard', cf. Island Carib *anoli* — 'lizard' (initial z from French *les*); Patwa *mabouya* — 'a grey-coloured lizard', cf. Island Carib *maboya* — 'lizard'.

11 Patwa *obya/obiya* — 'spell'; cf. Twi *obiafò* — 'a sorcerer' in which *fò* is a personal suffix, including probable convergence with Island Carib "Abienra: abiénragoüa, ensorceller".

12 Patwa *achté lamen* — 'to buy from someone' literally "to buy hand (from)". This is a widespread African construction, e.g. Hausa *saya hannu* and Mandinka *sang bulu*, both having the same literal meaning.

13 *Misyé* — 'the man', 'mister', a term of address used for both friends and strangers, e.g. Patwa *sa ka fèt misyé* — "what Prog. do man"; cf. Black American 'What's happ'nin man'. Cf. also Mandinka *cè* and Wolof *gòr-gi* — 'man', similarly used as terms of address. French 'monsieur' has thus been extended to refer to friends.

14 *Manman ou* — "mother your", 'your mother', short for *koukoun manman ou* — 'your mother's vagina'. This is the severest pan-African insult; cf. Hausa *uwarka* — 'your mother!', short for *ka ci uwarka* — '(you) fuck your mother!'. Note also Black American 'mother-fucker'. The fact that women victims of the Atlantic Slave Trade were at the sexual mercy of white men may also have contributed to the force of the latter insult.

15 Patwa *jan mwen* — 'my friend' is a putative convergence of French *gens* and the French name *Jean* with Mandinka/Bambara *jòng* — 'slave'. Like Black American 'John', *jan* was probably influenced by the Mandinka/Bambara *jòng* — 'slave'. Like Black American 'John', *jan* was probably influenced by the Mandinka/Bambara *massa* — 'chief' versus *jòng* — 'slave' tales cycle. Cf. the Patwa *ti jan* tales about a whily youth who defeats his social 'superiors'. Note also similar *ti jan* tales in Martinique and Seychelles French Creoles.

16 Patwa *jabal* — 'prostitute', 'paramour' is a putative meaning shift based on Wolof *jabar* — 'wife'. Note also Patwa *jamèt* — 'loose woman', (a girl behaving like a) 'prostitute', with putative meaning shift from Wolof *jam* — 'slave', plus French nominal suffix — *ette*.

17 *èk* — 'and', cf. Wolof *ak*, probably influenced by French *avec* — 'with' (which exists separately in Patwa: *avèk* — 'with').

18 Patwa *bonda* — 'anus', 'backside'. Cf. Bambara *boda*, i.e. *bo da* "excrement hole", possibly strenthened by Hausa *bood'ad'd'ar* — 'buttocks'.

19 *Mòlòkòi* — 'a lazy person', cf. Kongo *moolo* 'a lazy person'; *m* is a Class 1 prefix referring to human beings, the stem *-olo-* means 'lazy'. *Mòlòkòi* can be analysed putatively as: *mòlòkòi* — "lazy body (French *corps*) his/her". Cf. also Palenquero Creole *mambloyo* — 'useless, lazy

person' also of putative Kongo origin (Lewis, A.R., 1978 p.3, Society for Caribbean Linguistics Conference papers).
20 Patwa *dèsk la* — 'the desk', *bòs la* — 'the bus'. Cf. lexical expansion from English/Krio and French in Gambian Mandinka, e.g. *fiil o* — 'the field', *òòr o* — 'the time' French *l'heure*.

Notes

1. Kriul, Krio and Patwa refer to Casamance 'Portuguese' Creole, Gambian 'English' Creole and St. Lucian 'French' Creole respectively. These are the names used by the speakers themselves to describe their languages. See sketch map below for the geographical position of Kriul and Krio.
2. The Creole centre of the region up to today. See note 2 of sketch map below.
3. See above for the chart of The Historical Development of Kriul, Krio and Patwa.
4. As reflected in Kriul items in Creole English on both sides of the Atlantic (4).
5. See sketch map below.
6. Mainly Mandinka/(Bambara) and Wolof.
7. Alleyne, M., 1961. Dalphinis, M., 1977.
8. See linguistic vocabulary (above).
9. Mahoney, F., 1975, p.20.
10. Dalby, D., 1971, p.285.
11. As defined in the vocabulary, unless otherwise stated.
12. In the Atlantic Slave Trade, see above.
13. Abdoulaye, B., in conversation, London, 1979.
14. The Portuguese choice of Mandinka women as wives was not unrelated to a mutual interest in the profits of the Atlantic Slave Trade.
15. A Wolof centre in the mainly Wolof-speaking Northern Senegal.
16. See linguistic vocabulary.
17. E.g., the varying domains of past and present Kriul prestige.
18. I am grateful to the School of Oriental and African Studies, University of London Central Research Fund and the Cassell Trust for support for my research, and to the Whiteley Fund for making it possible for me to attend the conference on Theoretical Orientations in Creole Studies, St. Thomas, U.S. Virgin Islands, 1979.
19. As opposed to non-Christian Wolof and Mandinka oral literature, also in the communicative competence of most Gambian Krio speakers.
20. A distinction is drawn between the term 'survival' as used in Dalby, D., 1972, where Africanisms in Jamaican Creole are viewed as having 'survived' the censorship of past plantation society. From a synchronic viewpoint where similar African items in the Creoles are being used as markers of internal prestige, the term 'perpetuation' seems preferable.
21. Many 'Aku' Creoles have Yoruba first or middle names in addition to European first and last names, e.g. Ayodele Allen, James Omo Thomas, etc. In Freetown, the Aku even regard themselves as Nigerians in exile.
22. See linguistic vocabulary (above).
23. See Historical Background (above).
24. Ibid.
25. Ibid.
26. Wider interest in the Caribbean Creoles by indigenous educational élites and foreign scholars of international repute is having some modifying effects.
27. Another aspect of hypercorrection.
28. Baker, P., in conversation, London, 1976.
29. Mandinka in the formation of proto-Kriul and proto-Patwa.
30. Gisler, D.B., 1976, pp.59-64.

4. A Syncronic[1] Comparison of the Verbal Systems of St. Lucian Patwa[2] and Guinean Crioulo.

In this preliminary analysis of the Creole languages of French lexical base[3] and the Creole languages with a Portuguese lexical base, I have restricted my study to St. Lucian Patwa and Guinean (Guinea Bissau) Crioulo, respectively, and have dealt with any relevant varieties of either the French-based[4] or Portuguese-based Creole languages in footnotes.

The Crioulo of Guinea (Bissau)[5]

The verbal system can generally be described as follows:

Subject Pronoun (Tense)/Aspect Marker Verb (Object)

Subject Pronoun

Singular:	1	2	3
	ng	bu	i
		polite forms:	
		nyu (m)	
		nya (f)	
Plural:	1	2	3
	nò	bòs	è

The use of the subject pronouns,[6] without any (tense)/aspect markers, is exemplified in the following simple sentences:

    i bing — 'He/She/It comes'
    bu montia — 'You hunt'
    bòs yèntra kaasa — 'You (pl.) enter the house'
    è na kuméél — 'They ate it'

(Tense)/Aspect Markers[7]
The (tense)/aspect markers are as follows:
Progressive Marker: *na*[8]
    i na montia — 'He/She is hunting'
    è na kuméel — 'They are eating'
    no na bing — 'We (pl.) are coming'

Futurative-Immanent Marker: *na*
    i na bin ès dǝ tardi — He/She is coming this afternoon

Futurative-Less Immanent Marker: *ta*[9]
which indicates that a future act or state is less immanent in character than a future act indicated by *na*; for example:
    i ta bing — 'He/She will come'
    nò ta kuméé — 'We will eat'

Habitual Marker: *ta*
    i ta montia — 'He/She hunts'

Past Completive Marker: *ba*
which indicates that the action is completed and that the main verb concerned applies to a time plane previous to that of the main context of the sentence,[10] for example:
    i bing — 'He/She comes'
c.f. *i bing ba* — 'He/She had come/He/She came'
    i ta bing ba — 'He/She will come'
c.f. *i ta bing ba*[11] — 'He/She would have come'

Past[12] Non-Completive Marker: *ja*
which refers to past time and indicates that the action or state concerned still applies to the present, for example:
    i bay — 'He/She has gone, He/She went (on a previous occasion)'
    i bay ja — 'He/She has gone, (recently, and is still gone)'

The Verb
As in many other Creole languages, the basic form of the verb is uninflected and is a simplified form of the verb found in the metropolitan language varieties to which the Creole is related. In Guinean Crioulo, the basic form of the verb is the radical[13] which is in most cases synchronically derivable from the Portuguese infinitive by, amongst other rule, an *r* - final deletion rule, for example:
Crioulo	Portuguese	English
sibi	*saber*	'to know'

An exception to this synchronic derivation rule however, is the possible synchronic derivation of the Crioulo radical from the irregular 3rd person forms of Portuguese monosyllabic verbs:

Crioulo	Portuguese	English
bing	vai (infinitive vair)	'go'
bin	vem (infinitive vir)	'come'
puy	poe (infinitive por)	'put'

Other exceptions are a few verbs which are not regularly derivable from Portuguese:

Crioulo	Portuguese	English
saabi	saber (bem)	'to be nice'

The Crioulo verb can be both monosyllabic, for example *bing* — 'to come', or polysyllabic, for example *durmi* — 'to sleep, to curdle'. All polysyllabic verbs have final stress assigned when they preceed an object pronoun, for example:

i kúnsil kil òòmi — 'He/She knows that man'
+
Stress

c.f. *i kunsii-l* — 'He/She knows him'
+
Stress

and as seen above the final vowel of the verb is also lengthened.[14]

Two important forms of the Crioulo verb are the *imperative* and the *causative*.

The Imperative[15]

The imperative consists of the verbal base only in the case of the 2nd. person singular and of the 2nd. person plural, subject pronoun, followed by the verbal base, in the case of the 2nd. person plural:

bing — come! (2nd. person *sing.*)
bòs bing — come! (2nd. person *pl.* + verbal base)

The Causative[16]

Very typical of Crioulo is the formation of the causative from the verbal base by the addition of either of the following suffixes: *nta* or *nti*, for example from *ciga* — 'arrive, approach', cf. *ciganta* — 'make arrive, put near'.

A type[17] of vowel-harmony is preserved in this suffixation, as the final vowel of the suffix matches the final vowel of the suffix matches the final vowel of the verbal base, for example:

subi — 'go up, come up' cf. *subinti* — 'make go up'

where the root vowel is *i* and the suffix is *nti*. This contrasts with the previous example where the root vowel is *a* and the suffix also ends in *a*.

Where the final consonant of the verbal base is *t*, the *t* of the following suffix is voiced and becomes *d*; for example in:

yentra — 'enter', cf. *yentranda* — 'to make enter'

Objects[18]

Intransitive verbs are followed by objects in the following order: first the indirect object (1) and then the direct object (2):

    da ng   yaagu — 'Give me water!'
    1   2
    Indirect Object pronoun
    1st. person singular (1) + *Direct Object* (2)

As seen in the above examples, pronoun objects are suffixed to the verb, for example:

    i kuméé-l — 'He/She ate it' (Object pronoun)
    si i kuméé-l — 'If he/she eats it' (Object pronoun)
    i ka kuméé-l — 'He/She didn't eat it' (Object pronoun)

Auxiliary[19]

These are verbal radicals which can be followed by another verbal radical in the same verb phrase, for example:

bay	(a)	'go'
	(b)	'go and ... '
baa	—	the auxiliary by-form[20] of *bay* which can only be used with the meaning 'go and ... '
bing	(a)	'come'
	(b)	'come and ... '
	(c)	'and then'
kuma	(a)	'begin (to)'
	(b)	'have just'
misti		'want to'
pudi	(a)	'can, be able to'
	(b)	'may, be allowed to'
	(c)	idiomatic use: *ng ka pudi* — 'I am exhausted'
tardi	(a)	'(be, last, take) a long time'
	(b)	'be old (of a thing)'
tòrna		'again'

When used as auxiliaries some radicals have an idiomatic meaning,[21] for example: *pudi* can, be able to', in the sentence:

    ng ka pudi — 'I am exhausted'.

In the following syntatically defined environment:
when the second verb does not apply to the same subject as the first verb the auxiliary *misti* must be followed by the radical *pa*, for example:

    ng misti bay — 'I want to go'
    ng misti pa i bay — 'I want him to go'
    1   2   1   2
      Subjects are   Not
   not Coreferential   Coreferential
      (i.e. 1 not   (i.e. 1 not
      equal to 2)   equal to 2)

Within the category auxiliary[22] are to be included a set of semi-auxiliaries[23] syntactically defined as requiring a linking particle between them and the main verb; *pa, kə, də* are examples of such particles though *pa* is the most frequently used particle. The behaviour of such particles is exemplified in the following sentences:

i	*sta*	*pa*	*bay*	— 'He/She is about to go'
	Semi-aux.	Linking particle		
i	*tèng*	*kə*	*bay*	— 'He/She has to go'
	Semi-aux.	Linking particle		
i	*dibi*	*də*	*bay*	— 'He/She is to go'
	Semi-aux.	Linking particle		

Negation
Negation of the verbal system in Crioulo is done by placing the negative particle *ka* before the verb, for example:
  i ka bing — he hasn't come.
Where the verb is preceded by a (tense)/aspect marker in its positive form, the negative particle precedes both the marker and the verb, for example:

Positive Sentence	*no*	*na*	*montia*	— 'We're hunting'
		Progressive Marker		
Negative Sentence	*no*	*ka*	*na montia*	— 'We're not hunting'.
		Negative Particle		

As seen in the above examples, the negative particle follows the subject pronoun. Where the subject pronoun is *i* (3rd. per. sing.), *ka*[24] can negate a non-verbal lexical item; for example:

i	*ka*	*bing*	— 'He/She has not come'
	Negative Particle		
i	*ka*	*nòòbu*	— 'He/She is not young/ it is not new'
		Adjective, non-verbal	
i	*ka*	*liibru*	— 'It is not a book'
		Noun, non-verbal	
i	*ka*	*di mi*	— 'It is not mine'
		Possessive construction non-verbal	

Where the 3rd. person subject pronoun *i* is preceded by a noun and
is followed by *ka* + *a non-verbal lexical item*, then, according to
Wilson, *i* 'seems optional'.[25]

Passive Participles
Passive participles are morpholigically derived from transitive[26]
Crioulo verbs by the addition of the particle *du* to these transitive
verbs; for example:

ma — 'to call'	cf. *mạadu* — 'called'
+	+
Stress	Stress
Transitive	Passive
Verb	Particle
fasi — 'to do'	cf. *fasiidu* — 'done'
+	+
Stress	Stress
Transitive	Passive
Verb	Particle

However, these passive participles can also be morphologically
derived from some intransitive verbs, for example:
durmi — 'sleep, curdled' cf. *durmiidu* — 'curdled'
Intransitive   Passive
Verb   Participle

Wilson argues that these particles are used in: "What are, syntactically non-verbal sentences";[27] I would disagree, once again on the basis of the zero copula; in his example:
èè, bu [zero copula] na còmaadu — 'Hey, you (*sing.*) are being called'.
I'd propose that a zero copula at deep-structure[28] provides the
verbal predication in these otherwise non-verbal sentences at
surface structure.

The following phonological rules are associated with the above
morphological derivation for the transitive verbs:
1. The final vowel of the transitive verb is lengthened before *du*,
   for example, *cọma* cf. *cọmaadu*.
               +   +
              Stress   Stress
2. The stress on the first syllable of the transitive verb is replaced
   on the first syllable preceding the suffix in the passive
   participle, as seen in the preceding examples. (Assuming that
   stress is primary, the rule can be rewritten as:
   CV (CV) becomes (CV)CVV + du).
    +   +
   Stress   Stress

The Verbal System of St. Lucian Patwa

As in the case of the Crioulo of Guinea, the verbal system of St. Lucian Patwa can be generally described as follows:

Subject   (Tense)/Aspect   Verb   (Object)
Pronoun   Marker

The Subject Pronoun

Singular:	1	2	3
	mwen	ou	i [30]
	ng[29]		
Plural:	1	2	3
	nou	zòt	yo

for example:

> *mwen vini èk i vini* — 'I came and he/she/it came'
> *yo bwè glo* — 'They drank water'
> *zòt wè glo wouj* — 'You(pl.) saw red water'
> *ou fou* — 'You're mad'
> *nou vini pou palé* — 'We came to talk'

(Tense)/Aspect Markers
Progressive Markers: *ka / ng'a*
These indicate progressive action largely irrespective of the time context of the action; for example:

> *jòdi a mwen ka manjé chat* — 'Today I'm eating cat'
> *denmen mwen ka alé an hòtè* — 'Tomorrow I'm going to the countryside'; literally: "tomorrow I'm in the process of going to the countryside".
> cf. *denmen mwen kay*[31] *alé an hòtè* — 'Tomorrow I will go/I'm going to the countryside'.
> *yè ng'a*[32] *alé bò kay ou lè mwen wè kouzin* — 'Yesterday I was coming to see you when I saw Cousin'; literally: "yesterday I'm in the process of walking to your home when I see Cousin".

Futuritive Markers: kay
Used after all subject pronouns and *'ay* after the 1st. per. sing. subject pronoun; for example:

> *ou kay alé wè'y* — 'You(*sing.*) will go to see him'

but *mwen kay wè'w* — 'I'll see you'
  ng'ay wè'w — 'I'll see you'.

Habitual
There are no clearly separate verbal markers indexing the Habitual in St. Lucian Patwa. The Habitual is marked either by the use of the

markers *ka / ng'a* (which are markers of the progressive) in certain contexts, for example:

i ka manjé ici a	— 'He/She (habitually) eats here'
i ka dòmi la	— 'He/She (habitually) sleeps there'
i ka li twòp	— 'He/She (habitually) reads too much'
i ka katjilé twòp	— 'He/She (habitually) thinks too much'

or by the use of adverbs, particularly the adverb *toujou*:

mwen ka toujou wimen'y	— 'I always stir it'
mwen ka toujou dansé	— 'I always dance'
zòt ka toujou wè'y	— 'You (*pl.*) always see it'.

This use of *toujou* is not tied to use with the above progressive markers only, but can be used with 'habitual' meaning, either by itself:

i toujou sou	— 'He/She is always drunk'
ou toujou sal	— 'You (*sing.*) are always dirty'

or with all the other verbal markers, for example:

ng'ay toujou manjé avèk li — 'I'll always eat with him/her'
yo té toujou enmen tifi-a — 'They had always like the girl'

Completive Markers: *té* or *za* or *ja* or *ay*
Of the above *té* seems to qualify most of all as a verbal marker of completion, for example:

mwen té li'y	— 'I have read it'
zòt té alé	— 'You (*pl.*) have gone'
i té bwè	— 'He/She has drunk';

té[33] seems to be basically an aspect[34] rather than a tense marker as it can be used both in past-tense or future-tense contexts while retaining its completive aspect interpretation; for example in the sentence:

yè zòt té kasé zé poul-la — 'Yesterday you (*pl.*) broke/had broken the chicken's eggs'

denmen ou té kay wè kéchòz! — 'Tomorrow you (*sing.*) would have seen something'.

The latter sentence is an example of the conditional,[35] which is formed by the use of the completive and futuritive markers in combination[36] and has as a basic interpretation the possible completion of a future act; as such this conditional necessarily assumes the retention of the completive interpretation of *té* in a future context.

This completive interpretation of *té* is also evident in present tense contexts: for example, in the sentence:

jòdi a mwen té ka manjé — 'Today I had been eating
lè'y vini when he came'

where present-time is indicated by the adverb *jòdi* and both the completive and the progressive aspects of the act are indexed by *té* and *ka* respectively.

The marker *ja* with it's allomorphic variant *za* also indicate completive aspect, but *ja* is basically an adverbial marker; for example:

i ja vini[37] — 'He/She has already come'
yo té ja manjé — 'They had already eaten'

The marker *ay* also marks completion, for example:

zòt ai tjwé'y en! — 'You (*pl.*) have (gone and) killed him/her yes!'
i ay manjé pen an — 'He/She has (gone and) eaten the bread'.

This marker, however, presents a few problems, because, apart from its morphological similarity to the futurative *ay*, after the 1st. person pronoun, it is also morphologically similar to the imperative forms:

ay mò — '(Go and) die!/Go to hell!'
ay dòmi — '(Go and) sleep!'[38]

The Verb
The verb follows the subject pronoun or both the subject pronoun and the (tense)/aspect marker. Like most morphological forms in the language, verbs are either monosyllabic, as in the case of the following verbs:

vlé — 'to want'
pé — 'to be able to'

or di-syllabic, for example:

kouché — 'to lie down'
dòmi — 'to sleep'
manjé — 'to eat'
pété — 'to burst'.

Tri-syllabic verbs, like tri-syllabic morphological forms, though rare, do exist, for example:

katjilé — 'to think, to ponder'
labouwé— 'to work in mud, to make love'

The verbs which are historically derivable from French verbal forms are derived by, amongst other rules, deletion rules which result in the much simplified and uninflected Patwa verbal base:

French	*Patwa*	*English*
vouloir	*vlé*	'to want'
pouvoir	*pé*	'to be able'
dormir	*dòmi*	'to sleep'
manger	*manjé*	'to eat'
coucher	*kouché*	'to lie down'

which are historically derived from French, in part by means of an *r* - final deletion rule.

The imperative is formed by the use of the verbal base only,
without the use of either the 2nd. person *sing.* or *pl.* pronouns, for
example:
    vini[39] — 'come!'
    alé! — 'go!'
    manjé! — 'eat!'
    kouché![40] — 'sleep!'
The imperative is also formed by placing the form *ay* before the
verbal base, for example:
Intransitive verb   *ay mò!* — '(Go and) die!'
Intransitive verb   *ay dòmi!* — '(Go and) sleep!'
Transitive and   *ay tjwé'y!* — '(Go and) kill him/her/it'
Intransitive verb
Intransitive verb   *ay tonbé!* — '(Go and) fall!'
ai seems to be characteristically used to form the imperative of
verbs which are used only in the intransitive; as indicated in the
above examples, verbs such as *mò* could only be put in the
imperative without a preceeding *ay* in absurd situations such as
commanding someone to drop dead;[41] a verb such as *tjwé:*
(a) 'to kill' — Intransitive
(b) 'to kill someone or something' — Transitive
which has both an intransitive and a transitive use, can be
meaningfully imperative with or without a preceding *ay*; for
example:
    tjwé [42] — 'Kill!'
    tjwé kabwit-la! — 'Kill the goat!'
    An alternative interpretation of the use or non-use of *ay* in the
imperative is that verbs describing acts in which the subject of the
verb is passive to the action of the verb take *ay* in the imperative,
for example, verbs such as *mò* — to die and *dòmi* — to sleep, in which
the subject of the verb is necessarily passive to the action of the
verb; on the other hand verbs such as *vini*, where the subject of the
verb is necessarily active in performing the action of the verb do not
take a preceding *ay;* in **ay vini!* is not a grammatical sentence.[43]

Intensitive
A small sub-class of verbs can be identified in terms of semantic
interpretation and synchronic morphological derivation, as being
the intensitive forms of other verbs; they are derived morphologically by the prefixing of *dé* to certain verb~·

kalé	'to pull back the forskin of the penis'	*dékalé*	(a) 'to dismantle, to destroy a thing' (b) 'to make love vigorously i.e. an intensitive of *kalé*'

kwazé	to crush, to break	*dékwazé*		'to totally crush or destroy a person or thing'
palé	to speak	*dépalé*[44]		'to speak a lot, to speak to much, to say too much'
mòdé	to bite	*démodé*		'to bite to bits'
viwé	to return	*déviwé*		'to go and come back again, but, on coming back, having to go and come back once again, to go up and down (of a person)'
*katjé[45]		*dékatjé*		'to tear from limb to limb of an animal or human by holding each leg and pulling them apart; from this is derived sexual meaning of tearing a female's legs apart in the sexual act.'

Causatives[46]
These are formed by placing the verb *fè* before another verb.[47] *fè* is, however, followed by a direct object which precedes the following verb (the verbs which follow *fè* can be described as the compliments of *fè*. Examples of this 'causative' construction are:

    mwen fè'y vonmi   — 'I made him/her vomit/ I caused him/her to vomit'
    yo fè mwen vini   — 'They made me come/ They caused me to come.'

Auxillaries
These are verbs which can be used before another verb in a verb phrase, for example:
    vlé   — 'to want to'
    pé[48]   — 'to be able to'
    koumansé — 'to begin'
    fini   — 'to have finished (doing something)'
and the following sentences:
    i vlé kouwi   — 'He/she wants to run'
    i koumansé pléwé — 'He/She began to cry'
    i fini bouyi manjé — 'He/She finished cooking (/boiling) food.

ni — 'to have'
sé — 'to be'
do not qualify as auxiliaries; the verb *ni*, for example, is followed immediately by a noun phrase:
    mwen ni chouval — 'I have horses'
and, where it is followed by a verb phrase, this verb phrase is preceded by the complimentizer *pou* ('for . . . to'):
    mwen ni pou twavai — 'I have (for . . . to) work'.
The verb *sé*, one of the two forms of the overt copula, the other being *yé*,[49] also, is not immediately followed by another verb in a verb phrase; it is usually followed by a noun phrase only and, unlike *ni*, it does not use the complimentizer *pou*. For example:

    i sé on nom— 'He's a man'
        Noun
        Phrase
    sé on poul— 'It's a chicken'
        Noun
        phrase

Negation
Usually the negative particle *pa* is placed after the subject pronoun and precedes both the (tense)/aspect markers, the auxiliary and the verb, for example:

Positive sentence	*mwen*	*té kay* (Tense)/ aspect markers	*vlé* + Aux.	*vini* + Verb	'I would have liked to come'
Negative sentence	*mwen*	*pa* Negative Particle	*té kay*	*vlé vini*	'I wouldn't have liked to come.'

· An alternative form of the negative particle, but with the syntactic behaviour is *ma*; *ma*, however, is reserved for the 1st. pers. singular negative only; for example:
    ma té kay alé —'I wouldn't have gone'
but,
    i pa té kay alé — 'He/She wouldn't have gone.'
As seen in the above use of *ma*, it totally replaces the 1st. person *sing.* subject pronoun in the straight negative;[50] where *ma* is preceded by the 1st. person *sing.* subject pronoun in a negative sentence, the sentence is decidedly emphatic with the speaker implying that his/her personal worth is so high that he/she wouldn't perform a certain action, for example:
    mwen! ma vlé palé avèk yo — 'I! I don't want to speak to them.'
A closely related negative particle is *maa*; where the final vowel is

long; this negative form indicates a habitual negative, for example:

maa mandé Mohammed Ali lajan'y	'I'm not in the habit of asking Mohammed Ali for his money'
maa alé bò kay fanm mayé	'I'm not in the habit of going to the houses of married women.'

A negative futuritive exists, but it is for the 1st. person *sing.* only, for example:

    may vini — 'I will not come'

and, as seen in the above example, it's use excludes that of the 1st. person *sing.* except where emphasis upon the self-esteem of the speaker if being made, for example:

    mwen! may vini — 'Me! I won't come!'

Negative Adverbials
These are:
janmen — 'never'
pyès — 'not at all'
mòkò   /pòkò[51]   — 'not yet'
For 1st. sing. For 1st. sing.
subject only and all other
              subject pronoun
              forms

and their interpretations are evident in the following sentences:

mwen pa/ ma janmen alé bò kay yo	'I've not/ I've never been to their house'
yo pa vini pyès	'They didn't come at all'
mòkò[52] wè tifi-a	'I haven't seen the girl (yet)'
mwen pòkò wè tifi-a	'I haven't seen the girl (yet)'
i pòkò vini	'He/She hasn't come (yet)' 'He/She hasn't come (yet).'

As with the pronominal forms, both negative[53] and positive, the use of the first person singular adverb *mòkò* excludes the use of a preceding 1st. per. subject pronoun except where special emphasis is placed upon the self-esteem of the speaker; for example:

mwen! mòkò wè jou-a ki kay	'Me! I haven't seen the day which will bring me round his/her house/
menen mwen bò kay li	Me! I'll never set foot in his/her house'.

Comparative Survey of the Verbal Systems of Saint Lucian Patwa and Guinean Crioulo

The syntactic similarity between the two verbal systems is, in general, very strong;[54] the subject pronouns of the two are identical in places, namely in the 1st. *sing.* and in the 3rd. *sing. i,* or extremely similar, for example: St Lucian Patwa 2nd. *sing. ou* and Guinean *bu*; Patwa 1st. *pl. nou* and Crioulo *n* where the differences are in the presence of a consonant and in vowel quality respectively. The 2nd. and 3rd. plural forms of Patwa, which show the greatest differences, are in the presence of a consonant and in vowel quality respectively.

The 2nd. and 3rd. plural forms of Patwa show the greatest differences to Guinean Crioulo counterparts:

Patwa   Crioulo
zòt   bòs
yo   è

with the only similarity being the vowel in the 2nd. *pl.*

Apart from the morphological differences, the progressive markers in the two languages behave in the same manner with the exception that the progressive marker in Crioulo is not also used as a habitual marker as it is in Patwa. The morphological differences between these two markers are however quite small; merely the difference of a single consonant: *k* in Patwa and *n* in Crioulo.

The futuritive, although basically behaving in the same manner in the two languages are, nevertheless, different in that Crioulo makes a difference between an immanent and a less immanent future whereas Patwa doesn't: *na* marks the immanent future while *ta* marks the less immanent future in Crioulo, whereas *kay* indicates both futures in Patwa.

The sameness of form between the less immanent futuritive marker *ta* and the habitual marker *ta* in Crioulo is echoed in the similarity between the Patwa futuritive *kay* and the Patwa habitual marker *ka*.

As far as syntactic position is concerned, the Patwa completive marker *té* is different from that of equivalent Crioulo *ba*, as the Patwa marker always precedes the verb and any other verbal marker it is used in conjunction with, whereas the Crioulo marker is placed after the verb, and is thus preceded both by the verb and any other verbal marker with which it is used in conjunction. The Crioulo past non-completive marker *ja* as well as in being placed after the verb is different from Patwa *ja*, despite their morphological similarities, as Patwa *ja* defines completed action only.

Despite the differences, mainly morpho-syntactic, between the verbal systems of the two languages, their general use of aspect, rather than tense as the main axis of their descriptions, indicates again general similarity despite their particular differences.

The Verb
Both the Crioulo and the Patwa verb follow the subject pronoun and the verbal markers, and both can be either monosyllabic or polysyllabic.

The Imperative
The basic form of the imperative in both languages is the verb; the Crioulo verb however, differs from the Patwa verb in requiring a preceding subject pronoun in the 2nd. person pl. imperative. An alternative form in Patwa, *ay* + verb — 'go and', like the Crioulo form, is valid for both singular and plural.

The Causative
The Crioulo causative is distinct both as a semantic and a morphologically defined class; the Patwa causative is not a true causative as it is not a clearly defined morphological class.

Intensitives
The class of verbs is evident in Patwa but not in Crioulo.

Auxiliaries
Although having the same syntactic behaviour, namely of preceding another verb within a verb phrase both in Crioulo and in Patwa, there are a few individual differences; firstly, there does not seem to be a Crioulo equivalent to Patwa *pé*, which is the only auxiliary that can stand before a (tense)/aspect marker, or to Patwa *ni* auxiliary which needs a complimentizer between it and the following verb. Secondly, the idiomatic meaning of some Crioulo verbs, when used as auxiliaries, is not echoed in Patwa; and, thirdly, the semi-auxiliaries of Crioulo have no parallels[55] in Patwa; their closest potential parallel is the verb *ni* — 'to have', which has to be followed by a complimentizer *pou* before the following verb; this complimentizer could, under one interpretation be defined as a linking particle parallel to Crioulo *kə* — 'for . . . to'.

Negation
The syntactic accomplishment of negation in both languages is similar, namely the placement of a negative particle: *ka* in Crioulo, and *pa* in Patwa after the subject pronoun and before the following verbal marker and the verb; for example:
Patwa: *i pa vini* — 'He/She didn't come'
Crioulo: *i ka bing* — 'He/She didn't come'.
Morphologically also the negative particles are extremely similar, being differentiated only by different places of articulation: plosive, voiceless *p*, as compared to plosive and voiceless *k*. Patwa *ma*, the 1st. person *sing.* alternant of the negative particle has no comparable Crioulo parallel and, in fact, Patwa's special paradigm for the 1st. person *sing.*, of which *ma* is a part, also has no Crioulo parallel. Patwa's emphatic negative of 1st. person *sing.* subject pronoun + *ma* + verb; its habitual negative *maa*; its negative futuritive 1st. person *sing. may*, also do not have any close Crioulo parallels.

On the other hand, Crioulo's special negation of non-verbal lexical items preceded by 3rd. person *sing.* subject pronoun *i*, has no close Patwa parallel; by contrast, in Patwa, non-verbal lexical items preceded by any subject pronoun can, be negated, for example:

mwen pa blan — 'I'm not white'
i pa wouj — 'He/She is not red'
yo pa nèg — 'They (*pl.*) are not blacks'
zòt pa blé — 'You (*pl.*) are not blue'
ou pa kabwit — 'You (*sing.*) are not a goat'

Crioulo's optional deletion of *i* where *ka* + non-verbal lexical item follows is also not paralleled in Patwa.

Negative Adverbials
I have, so far, found no Crioulo equivalents of these forms in Patwa.

Passive Participles
Crioulo passive participles have no equivalent in Patwa.

Conclusion

It is clear that despite the differences of detail between these two languages, the similarities as far as syntactic behaviour is concerned outweigh these differences. One seems to be viewing the same language twice with different words but the same syntactic categories.

This no doubt gives greater credibility to the Relexification Theory, as well as the theory of a common African origin for all Caribbean and possibly Indian Ocean Creole languages of (mainly) French vocabulary.

Similarities are also apparent between Crioulo morphemes and those of Swahili eg:
Crioulo:
No overt marker for the present indifinite, for example:
    bu montia — 'You (*sing.*) hunt (in general)'
na present progressive eg.
    bu na montia — 'You (*sing.*) are hunting'
ta future eg.
    bu ta montia — 'You (*sing.*) will hunt'
ka negative eg.
    bu ka montia — 'You (*sing.*) hasn't hunted'
ja past non-completive eg.
    bu montia ja — 'You (*sing.*) have hunted'

Swahili:
na present progressive eg.
  u na winda — 'You (*sing.*) are hunting'
ta future eg.
  u ta winda — 'You (*sing.*) will hunt'
ja past (negative) eg.
  ha tu ja winda — 'We didn't hunt'

In the Swahili examples above *ha-* indicates negative and the *ja* form of the past pre-stem marker only occurs in the negative in Swahili. In neighbouring and closely related languages to Swahili, eg. Giryana near Mombasa, *ha* occurs in the positive past. Comparative evidence also suggests that *ha* is historically derived from *(ng) ka,* a morpheme closer in shape to Crioulo *ka.* The absence of an overt marker for the present indefinite also does not occur in Swahili but does also occur in neighbouring languages,eg. Giryana, *u, [zero marker for the present indefinite]* — *gura* — 'you *(sing.)* buy (in general)'.[56]

These morphemes evident in Crioulo and Swahili are also evident in derived or primary forms in Common Bantu. It is likely that wider affinities between African language families have been chosen as core morphemes for Creole languages.

Notes

1. De Saussure, F., 1969, pp.129-143.
2. This represents a spelling of the nearly obsolete French word *patois* meaning dialect and is one closer to the phonetic spelling of the word i.e.: St. Lucian Patwa speakers do not use the word with the French meaning of dialect and, although the pejorative interpretation 'inferior language' is evident both in the St. Lucian and the French use of the word, any equivalence of use stops there. If, as well as this difference in usage we assume the Generative approach that native speaker intuition is one of the most important bases for any definition concerning his/her language, then the term Patwa is an acceptable one. The alternative term 'Creole' although useful to the definitions of non-native speakers would mean to the St. Lucian native speaker: a Negro *Kèòl* or *Kwèòl* as opposed to an Indian St. Lucian *Kouli*. It doesn't mean a very European-coloured person as it does in the Francophone islands of Martinique or Guadeloupe; we would in fact say *milat* (mulatto).
3. Term used at the Études Créoles conference at the University of Nice, 1976.
4. As well as being defined in terms of their lexicon, Creole languages are also described in other terms, for example, Dr. Dalby in his *Language Map of Africa* refers to the Creole languages of Africa and its off-shore islands as follows:
   Krio: having an English lexical base,
   Kreol: having a French lexical base,
   Kriulo: having a Portuguese lexical base,
   and, as previously indicated, Creole languages have also been described in Geographical terms; for example: Sierra Leonean Krio and Guinean Crioulo.
5. The first person singular subject pronoun in Crioulo alters its shape according to the place of articulation of the sound which follows it, for example, the form *ng* (velar nasal) occurs before sounds such as *k* (velar plosive) to which it is hormorganic in terms of place of articulation i.e. both are velar: *ng ka pudi* — 'I'm exhausted'. Where, on the other hand, the sound that follows the vowel *a*, the pronoun changes its form to *m* (a bilabial nasal) in order to be closer to the place of articulation of the following *a*.

   The form *bòs*, 2nd. person plural is the emphatic form and is not normally used for non-emphatic sentences; the form *bòò* is used in such non-emphatic sentences. The Guinean Crioulo sentence *i bing ba* — 'He/She came', would be *i bing bang* — 'He/She came', in Ziguinchor, in Senegal, where the language is known as Kriul.

   D. Diallo and A. Barry, in communication, School of Oriental and African Studies, Univ. of London, January 1977.

   Note that the term Crioulo is used with reference to Guinean variety of Portuguese Creole only, after Wilson, A.A., 1962. Where the Senegambian varieties are discussed the term Kriul is used, e.g. in pt.I, ch.2, p.28.
6. The subject pronoun varieties of:

	SINGULAR			PLURAL		
	1	2	3	1	2	3
Prencipe:	ami/n	bo	e	nõ	inãsé	inẽy
Sao Tome:	"	"	"	"	"	"
Anobones:	"	"	"	"	"	"

   according to Valkhoff, M.F., 1966, p.96; and of the 3rd person singular in Cape Verde according to Barbosa, J.M., 1975, p.143.
7. These verbal markers are basically aspect verbal markers; however, any pure-aspect analysis can be contested by an approach which allows some tense-interpretation to the markers, for example, in the case of St. Lucian Patwa *té*, which will be discussed in the pages that follow. See Lyons, J., 1968, p.313;

Hockett, C.F., 1969, p.237 and Robins, R.H., 1971, for a discussion of aspect as opposed to tense.
8. The marker *ta* has progressive meaning when used after an auxiliary verb; for example: *i kumsa ta còòra* — he began to cry and continued crying (see Wilson, A.A., 1962, p.22). However, this is a semantic interpretation of *ta* and thus not necessarily in contradiction to the purely syntactic interpretation of the marker which I hope to give; that is, unless one wants an argument about Generative versus Interpretive semantics.
9. See Wilson for a description of the markers. Many of my examples are also from Wilson, A.A., 1962 (henceforth Wilson in this chapter).
10. Compare the similar behaviour, as far as completive aspect is concerned at any rate, of the Yoruba completive marker *ti*.
11. Used conditionally *ba* indicates a hypothesis as does a change from Present to Past in English. In such cases *ba* can be repeated (optionally) in the main clause, for example: *si i bing ba, nò ta òjaal (ba)* — 'If he/she came we should see him/her'. See Wilson, p.23.
12. The word "Past" seems quite suitable in the case of the "Past Completive" in that the action specified by the verb does take place in 'time' which is past relative to the time context of the main verb. It however doesn't seem suitable to the "Past Non-Completive" as it is the non-completed aspect of a past event which is being emphasised i.e. an aspect-based rather than a 'time' based criterion seems to be the most important factor.
13. Pei, M., 1966, p.277.
14. Wilson, A.A., 1962. Note that Stress under a vowel indicates stress in the syllable concerned.
15. Ibid., p.21.
16. Ibid., p.20.
17. By "type of" I mean that a total vowel-harmony between all the vowels of the verbal base with the vowels of the suffix is never preserved; for example, in *ciganta* we have both the vowels *i* and *a* in the verbal base.
18. Wilson, p.26.
19. Wilson, p.24.
20. A form of *bay* used only as an auxiliary.
21. Wilson, p.24.
22. Ibid., pp.25-26.
23. Field-work would be necessary for a clearer definition of this category.
24. Wilson, p.29. Although Wilson associates this syntactic behaviour of *ka* with the presence of *i*, I would associate it with a zero copula which can, like all other predicates, be negated; for example:
    i [zero copula] *liibru* — 'It is a book'
    i ka [zero copula] *liibru* — 'It is not a book'.
25. Ibid., p.29. It is possible that in such cases the 3rd person subject pronoun has been preceded by a co-referential noun phrase, thus making the deletion of the pronoun *i* unimportant to sentence-meaning, for example:
    John *i* / [zero copula] *ka nòòbu* — 'John is not young'
       1 2
    co-referential (ie. 1 is equal to 2).
    Note that this potential deletion of *i* supports the idea of a zero copula as a sentence formed by *ka* + *non-verbal lexical item*, for example:
    ka liibru — literally "not book"
necessitates that, if negation is to have some syntactic function in Crioulo, a predicator of some sort be negated, namely zero copula: *ka* [zero copula] *liibru* — 'It is not a book'. The morphemos *ka* and *i* can also be defined as stabilizers in this given syntactic environment as either *i* or *ka* or *i* + *ka* can stabilize the meaning of the sentence.

26. Note that this passive could be argued to be the syntactic equivalent of the intransitive form of these transitive verbs.
27. Wilson, p.27.
28. Chomsky, N, 1965, pp.16-17.
29. *ng* is used with the progressive marker *a* only, for example:
    ng'a vini — 'I'm coming', cf.
    **ng té vini* — 'I came'
    **ng kay vini* — 'I will come'.
30. This non-distinguishing between masculine and feminine in the 3rd. person singular is typical of most African languages.
31. Futuritive marker.
32. The combined markers *té* (completive marker) followed by *ka* could also be used here. Note that though *té ka* is grammatical* *té a* is not.
33. This marker seems similar to the Yoruba completive marker *ti*.
34. It could be argued that there is no clear basis for deciding whether *té* is an aspect or a tense marker; in the above sentence, for example, the action can be described as past and therefore, complete or complete therefore past, but whether the former or the latter description is the first premise for any conclusion about *té* is possibly arguable.
35. To be discussed in the pages that follow.
36. The use of verbal markers in combination will also be discussed.
37. Note that this argues indirectly for the presence of a copula at deep destrure, as we have no other overt predicate apart from *vini*, but the sentence must be translated in English with the copula 'be' as part of the translation.
38. We note that a distinction between actual imperatives, eg. *mò* — 'die', as in *mò nèg mò*, — 'Die nigger die!' and rhetorical imperatives, eg: *ai mò* — 'Go and die/go to hell'; and that the Patwa imperative is possibly tonally distinct from the other uses of the verb base eg. *mánjé!* (Imperative), but *i ka manjé* — 'He/She is eating'.
39. The vowels in the imperative are tenser than the vowels in the corresponding non-imperative forms.
40. The basically CV syllable structure of Patwa is a counter-example to the hypothesis that CVC is the universally prefered structure; *manjé* is CVCV, for example.
41. If as indicated earlier, actual imperatives are differentiated from rhetorical imperatives, then the latter are preceded by *ay* and the former are not.
42. The seeming counter-example *ay tjwé!* — '(Go and) kill!', as it has an understood object 'someone', would make this use of the verb transitive and therefore, not a true counter-example.
43. Compared with the previous morphologically based account of the imperative, this one is inferior in that it is a semantic interpretation divorced from the syntactic and morphological behaviour of the language. Note also that *ay vini* could be excluded on the grounds of meaning only as *ay* is usually used as an imperative for actions carried out at a distance from the speaker. This is a distinction that many Bantu languages in fact make. M. Mann, in communication, School of Oriental and African Studies, Univ. of London, January 1977.
44. Note that this prefixing of *dé* is associated with other than intensitive usage; for example, in the verbs:

    pan — ¹ 'to hang, to hook'   dépan — 'to unhook, to unhang'
    mawé — 'to tie up'   démawé — 'to untie'
    klué — 'to nail'   déklué — 'to unnail'

    where the meaning is equivalent to that of the English prefix 'un'. This use of *dé* can be differentiated from an intensitive use of *dé* by the stress placed on *dé* when used intensitively, for example in:

    déviwé   dékwazé
    +   +
    Stress   Stress

We note further that these intensitive forms are often associated with verbs describing destruction or violent physical action.
We also differentiate a third use of *dé* i.e. as an equivalent to English 're' in morphological paradimes such as 'turn — return, move — remove'; compare for example, Patwa *monté* — 'to mount a horse or donkey', *démonté* — 'to dismount'.

45. This form doesn't exist in synchronic Patwa but it is possibly the past diachronic form from which the synchronic *dèkatjé* is diachronically derived.
46. We note that this is not a true causative, for, though semantically distinct, it is not morphologically distinct.
47. This is similar to the French 'faire + verb' construction.
48. Note that a stress marker of some sort would differentiate this verb from the verb *pé* — to shut up, as in *i pé djòl li* — 'He/She shut his/her mouth (gob)'. There is, I think, a greater stress on the verb *pé* meaning 'to be able to'; how far this is a feature of intonation rather than tone is arguable. We note also that of all the verbs and auxiliary verbs, only *pé* — 'to be able to' — can stand before a (tense)/aspect marker, for example:

    i pé té vini — 'He/She could have come'
    i pé ka dòmi — 'He/She could be sleeping'

    while a similar sentence with *vlé* is ungrammatical: **i vlé ka vini*
49. This form seems linked to question forms:

    sa sa yé — 'What is that?'
    sa ka fèt — 'How are things?/How are you?'
50. By this I mean the unemphatic negative.
51. We note this alternance between the 1st pronoun and the other pronoun forms, in the subject pronoun we have the form, for the 1st. sing. only; in the progressive *ng'a* for the 1st. sing. only *ng'ay* in the futuritive; *ma* in the straight negative; *may* for the corresponding negative futuritive *maa* for the negative habitual; and, as seen above, *mòkò* for the negative adverbial 'not yet'.
52. Paradigmatically, these first person singular forms are interderivable, eg: the morphological rule *ng/m* could relate the following paradigms:

	POSITIVE	NEGATIVE
Subject Pronoun	ng- —	m*
Futuritive	ng'ay	may
Habitual	ng'a	maa
Progressive	ng'a	maa
Completive	té	ma
Adverbs	*ngòkò	mòkò

    The forms with an asterik are what we'd expect of a complete paradigim which the proposed rule was fully productive; however, such forms do not exist in the language. On the basis of internal reconstruction, these forms are hypothetical proto-forms of Patwa and we would wonder whether Haitian *m* 1st. sing. subject pronoun in sentences such as: *ma aap boulé* — 'I'm drunk', is not the historically oldest form of this pronoun in all the Caribbean Creole languages with a French lexical base.
53. We note that what I have so far defined as a "straight negative" may in fact be a negative completive *ma* which contrasts with negative habitual *maa* and negative progressive *maa*. This negative completive *ma* seems to be in syntactic free variation with *ma té*; for example: *ma vini* — 'I didn't come'; *ma té vini* — 'I didn't come'. The only possible difference is that *ma té* is more often translated as 'hadn't' than is *ma*.
54. Indeed this basic similarity of verbal systems is one which all Creole languages share.
55. Forms with similar meaning and similar structure.
56. Nurse, D., in communication, School of Oriental and African Studies, Univ. of London, January 1977.

5. Island Carib Influences in St. Lucian Patwa.

The Island Carib[1] language in Guadaloupe and other parts of the Caribbean was described during the seventeenth century (see below). It is unlikely that the mainly Guadaloupean variety would have been substantially different from that spoken by the St. Lucian Island Carib with whom the Patwa-speaking maroons in St. Lucia (*nèg mawon*) had close social contact. The contact, both linguistic and genetic, has left its influences in St. Lucian Patwa. Contrast is made with modern Central American Island Carib and Surinan Carib using Taylor[2] and Hoff[3], respectively, as sources. As suggested below, 17th century Island Carib shows some similarities with modern Central American Island Carib.[4] Due to Arawak and African influences on Island Carib, the latter has retained relatively fewer similarities with modern Carib.

Outline of the Island Carib Verbal System
(after Breton, 1667)

Pronominal Elements
Singular	Plural
1. n	ou
2. b	h
3. l (*mas.*)	nh
t (*fem.*)	

When used as subject pronouns, the pronominal elements may occur in either verb initial, for example:
Sing. *Niem*, i.e. dis, *biem*, tu dis: *liém,* il dit, *tiem*, elle dit. *Tiem*, se prend aussi pour on dit.
Plur. *Oüagnem*, nous disons, *hiem*, vous dites; *nhànyem*, ils disent;[5]

or verb final position, for example:
tariátina tone, i'ay esté [*sic.*] à elle,
tariátibou, il a esté,
tariátiheu, vous avez esté,
tariánum, ils ont esté.[6]

They may also be used, word finally, as object pronouns, for example:
nacoiroyénli . . . ie le iette[7]
ie le chasse, *nimoúmainroyénli*[8]

These diachronic Island Carib pronominal elements have retained a similar form in synchronic Central American Island Carib in which *1st.pl. u* or *ua* or *ue* and *3rd.pl. h* or *ha* or *he*[9] are the only differences from the diachronic Island Carib personal pronouns (above).[10]

Possessive Pronominal Elements
The pronominal elements used as subject and object pronouns can also be used to mark possession, for example:
Sing. *Nácou*, mon oeil, *bácou*, ton oeil, *lácou*, son oeil
Plur. *Ouácou*, nos yeux, *hácou*, vos yeux, *nhácou*, leurs yeux.
Breton, however, gives the following as the Island Carib, as opposed to Arawak, forms of the *1st.* and *2nd. sing.* subject and possessive pronominal elements:
i et *a*, e.g. '*ichánum*, ma mere, *achánum*, ta mere'.[11]

It is most likely, however, that the Arawakan pronominal alternants were in more frequent usage as nearly all of Breton's examples make use of the Arawak, rather than the corresponding Island Carib *1st.* and *2nd.sing.* elements. Island Carib nominals are never used in isolation, but nearly always in conjunction with the relevant possessive/subject pronominal element:

> . . . ils les prononcent quasi toujours contractez par des lettres qui tiennent lieu de pronoms possessifs.[12]

These pronominal elements are also important in the differentiation of *sing.* and *pl.* in Island Carib nouns having no other formal distinction:

> D'autres n'en ont point, ou au moins la termination ne change point: comme *nitàcobaye*, mon meuble, et mes meubles: pour nos meubles, on dira ouàcobaye: Neantmoins, ce changement n'est pas du nom, mais suelement du pronom qui luy [*sic.*] est joint . . . [13]

Ki and *hu* are also Island Carib alternants to the Arawak *1st.pl.* possessive *ou*, for example:
kitámoulou — nostre [*sic.*] grand père,
kitamcou, ou *huitáncou*, nos grand pères
Huiouma, nostre bouche
ouàcouchili, nostre pere
ouàcouchilium, nos Peres[14]

Verbal Markers[15]

Present
The present indicative forms of the verb are derived from the infinitive by the deletion of the infinitive ending *a* and the suffixation of *òyem* or *ayem*, also accompanied by some vowel deletions from the end of certain verb stems:

> Tous les presents des verbes actifs se forment des infinitifs terminez en *a*, changeant cette derniere voyelle en *òyem* . . . ostant au adioustant *sic.* quelques voyelles suivant l'exigence des verbes, comme *d'apfoùragoüa*, souffler, vous formez *napfouràgoyem*, i.e. souffle, *d'ababárou*, appeler père, *nababároyem*, i' appelle [*sic.*] père . . . [16]

Cf. modern Central American Island Carib *a* — infinitive verbal suffix.[17]

Imperfect
Bouca suffixed to the verb is the marker of the imperfect:

> L'imperfait se distingue du present que par la diction *bouca*, qui se met à la fin de chacune de ses personnes.[18]
> e.g.: *Nièmbouca*, ie disois [*sic.*]; *bièmbouca*, tu disois; *Oüagnémbouca*, nous disions; *nhanyémbouca*, ils disoient.[19]

Cf. modern Central American Island Carib *ba* — imperfective marker.[20]

Perfect
hátina or *tina*, suffixed to the infinitive form of the verb is a marker of the perfective:

> Le parfait se forme de l'infinitif . . . adioustant *hátina*, ou *tina* seulement.
> e.g.: *arámêta*, se cacher [becomes] *arámêtahátina*, i'ai caché; *arámêtahàtibou*, tu as caché; *arámêtáhanum*, ils ont caché.[21]

Cf. Central American Island Carib (*h*) *a* — perfective marker.[22]

Future
The future is indicated by the suffixation of the marker *ba* to the verb. The form of the verb used in association with this marker is derived from the present indicative[23] form of the verb, by the deletion of the characteristic *yem* or *em* suffix of the present indicative verb.

> e.g.: *naramêtoyem* [becomes] *naramêtouba*; ie cacheray;[24] *áiem* [becomes] *nouba*, ou *nóba*, ie diray [*sic.*].[25]

Pluperfect
The pluperfect is formed by the suffixing of either *bouca* or *éleboüe* to the perfective forms of the verb, i.e.:

> Le plus-que-parfait est semblable en tout au parfait, sauf qu'il retient *bouca*, ou *éleboüe* á la fin de toutes ses personnes, comme[:] Sing. *Arametahátina* — *bouca*, ou *éleboüe*, i'avois caché, *arametahàtibou éleboüe*, tu avois caché, *arametáhali éleboüe*, il avoit caché ... ²⁶

Negative — *m*
Breton indicates the probably Carib form of the negative: "Les hommes ostent du nom la pénultième syllabe, et en sa place mettent *pàtina* ..."²⁷ As he mainly makes use of the Arawakan ('female') form of the negative marker in his exemplification the latter is assumed to be the early Island Carib negative marker:

> ... les femmes mettent du commencement du verbe la lettre negative *m*, tout cela assemble fait le verbe *marámètontina*, ie ne caché pas.²⁸

POSITIVE: Arámêtoni ... caché²⁹
NEGATIVE: *Maràmêtóntina*, ie ne cache pas,
   marámêtontibou, tu ne cache pas,
   maramêtóntium, ils ne cachent pas ... ³⁰

Cf. also the following positive and negative forms of the following Arawak verb:
POSITIVE: *regarder*, neupatey, f. i.e. ['female'/Arawak] ari*c*a³¹
NEGATIVE: ... *comme si tu ne regarde pas*, acabo
   mar*i*kini háman, *ie ne l'ay pas veu*,
   *má*riken nómêti.³²
   ne l'as tu pas veu? máriken bómptirae?³³
   Cf. modern Central American Island Carib *ma* — negative marker.³⁴ *Ma* in modern Surinam Carib, however, means 'but'.³⁵

Verb
The Carib verb usually has a single basic form (the verb stem) to which a pronominal element is prefixed or suffixed and any of the preceding tense/aspect markers may be suffixed, e.g., the infinitive verb '*aboüitaca*, ballier', without the infinitive suffix *a*, gives the verb stem *aboüitac* to which the *1st. sing. n* can be prefixed and the present indicative marker *ayem* can be suffixed, giving "*naboüitacayem,* ie ballie[*sic.*]".³⁶ Note also the similar behaviour of the auxiliary verb *áiem*³⁷ in association with the imperfective marker *bouca* and the *2nd.pl.*, *ᵉhiémbouca*, vous disiez'.

As with the noun, the pronominal elements can also be suffixed to the verb, e.g.:"*ereàtibou*, tu as pris ... *ereàtioua*, nous avons pris".³⁸ Where the suffixed pronominal elements are being used in

association with the perfective markers *tina* or *hátina*, *tina* or *ti*, as in the above examples, and *hátina* or *hati*, as in the following examples: *aramêtahàtibou*, tu as caché . . .
Aramêtahátioüa, nous avons caché . . . [39]
Cf. the similar behaviour of the verb in modern Central American Island Carib:

> The minimal sequence constituting an aspectual verb consists of an underlying form together with an aspect marker, and this may be followed by a personal suffix, with or without the interposition of a relational morpheme.[40]

In Surinam Carib, the verb similarly varies according to a set of affixes e.g.:
we — action is not aimed at another person or thing . . .
– po causation . . . [41]

Imperative
An imperative form of the verb can be derived from the present indicative by deletion of the present indicative suffix *yem*:

> Il y a a d'autres imperatifs, dont les secondes et troisiémes personnes se forment des secondes et troisiémes d'indicatif, ostant [sic.] *yem*, comme *baròncayem*, tu dors, *barònca*, dors . . . Sing. *Barónca* dors, *larònca*, qu'il dorme. Plur. *Oüarónca*, dormons, *harónca*, dormez . . .

Another imperative form of the verb is also derived from the infinitive, but to which firstly, the subject pronoun and, secondly, the concordant imperative form of the auxiliary verb *áiem* 'to say', are suffixed, e.g.:

> Sing. *Arámêtaba*, cache, *aramêtala*, qu'il cache. Plur. *Arámêta oüáman*, cachons, *aramêta hóman*, cachez, *aramêta nháman*, qu'ils cachent . . . [42]

The imperative in modern Central American Island Carib is realised by the use of tone:

> When no personal suffix indicating personnal goal is included, only general situation and tone distinguishes *áfara bá núgucu* 'you've killed my mother' from conjunctive *áfara bá núgucu* 'kill my mother!'[43]

Surinam Carib uses the imperative suffix — *ko*.[44]

Noun
Most singular nouns ending in *i* have plural forms ending in *em*: 'Les substantifs terminez en *i*, pour la pluspart un pluriel en *em*, e.g.:

> *oüekélli*, homme; *oüekêliem*, hommes; *nibiri*, mon cadet, *nibiriem*, mes cadets.[45]

The subject pronoun forms *l* (*mas.*) and *t* (*fem.*) are used to mark the masculine and feminine gender forms in the *3rd. sing.*[46] e.g.:

> *lichànum* la, où sa mere [*sic.*] c'est a dire de Pierre, de Iean etc.
> *tichánum*, où *toucouchourou*, la mere de Perrette, de Ieanne, etc.[47]

As nouns are rarely used in isolation in Island Carib, it seems likely that the above markers are in fact important markers of gender in the Island Carib nominal system. Similar behaviour is evident in modern Central American Island Carib:

> Some but not all nouns referring to animate beings take a pluralizing suffix which occurs in the same variants as does the personal suffix of third plural ... e.g.: *iráhǫiq* 'children', from *iráho* 'child' [i.e. *iq* — *pl.* suffix/*3rd. pl.* pronoun]. A nouns grammatical gender is marked only by third singular pronominal reference to it, as masculine or feminine in another word ... [48]

In modern Surinam Carib nouns are also pluralised by a plural suffix related to the semantic category of the noun — *kong* or *gong* or *sang* ... e.g. *wooto* – 'fish', *wootokong* – 'fishes'.[49] Carib nouns similarly, are themselves unmarked for gender.

Adjective
Gender in adjectives is marked by the suffixation of *ou* to feminine adjectives and *i* to masculine adjectives, e.g.:

àparoutou (f) murtriere
aparouti (m) murtrier

This gender rule is, however, related to items other than adjectives: 'Regle generale [*sic.*] pour tous les adjectifs, participes et troisièmes personnes des verbes'.[50]

Adjectives follow their associated nouns and agree with their nouns both in number and gender:

> Example, *iróponti noùcouchili*, mon père est bon:
> *kanichicotou noùcouchourou*, ma mère est sage:
> *cáintium öuacánium*, nos ennemis sont facheux.[51]

As seen in the above examples, the masculine *sing.* noun *iropont* takes the same suffix *i* as the following adjective *noùcouchili*, the feminine *sing.* noun has the same suffix as the adjective, i.e. *ou*, while both the plural noun and its following adjective have the plural suffix *m*. In modern Central American Island Carib:

> Any word which cannot be inflected for person, possession, or number or marked for position of direction without conversation ... into a verb, a noun, or a locator will be called a particle ... Most particles of Island Carib behave syntactically like adjectives, adverbs, or pronouns, or combine the first with one of the latter functions ...

When used as predicative adjectives, particles precede the noun, when used attributively they follow the noun.[52]

In modern Surinam Carib, Hoff recognizes three categories of adjectives on the basis of the form of their suffixes. Adjectives can be pluralised by the use of the *pl.* suffix — *mong* or *nong.*[53]

Island Carib Calques, Convergences and Loans in Patwa

Calques and Convergences
There are no calques and few convergences of definite Island Carib origin in Patwa.

Lexical Loans
agouti
(Latin *dasyprocta aguti*) 'a rabbit-like animal hunted with the aid of dogs and also eaten'. This is a putative Island Carib loan. Du Tertre, also refers to implied similarities with rabbits: 'L'acouty, que quelques-uns voulu assez mal à propos faire passer pour le Lappin des Indes...'.[54]

Alleyne refers to "aguti"[55] as a Carib item in Patwa. The item was in nineteenth century French,[56] and is still present in modern French.[57] Note also: 'Picouli [sic.], Agouti. Les sauvages font la chasse à l'Agouti avec autant d'avidité que les Français au lievre (Dictionnaire Caraibe-Français (DCF))'. 'Agouti, lièvre [sic.] du pays, picouli' (Dictionnaire Français-Caraibe (DFC)).[58]

The item originates from Guarani (an important Amerindian language) *Chamber's Twentieth Century Dictionary* (1952:20). Du Tertre, also refers to the teeth of *agouti* being used in Carib ceremonies: ',.. s'esgratignant la peau avec des dents d'Acouty' (my emphasis), and to *agouti* bones used in invoking 'magical' revenge upon opponents:

> Ils se seruent de ces os parlans pour ensorcer tous ceux contre lesquels ils ont conceu quelque rancune .... [59]

Chardon also refers to *agouti* by allusion[60] to rabbits: "..*agoutis*; il est de la taille d'un levreau moyen..."

bouri
'calabash for carrying water' (Dominican French-based creole) is a putative loan from Dominican Island Carib 'ku'muri (ku'mori)'[61] which has the same meaning. According to Breton the item is of Arawakan origin: "*calabasse, ou callebasse*, mouloútoucou, f. cómmori."[62] Given the $k - c$ alternation (mentioned below), the Arawakan origin of this item as well as of the alternant c, is most likely.

boutou
'a club', 'wooden', e.g.:

yo	ba	li	dé	kout	boutou
"they	give	him/her	some	blow	club"

'They clubbed him/her'

i	ni	boutou	pat
"he/she	have	club	foot"

'he/she has an artificial wooden leg', is a putative loan of Island Carib: 'boútou, iboútoulou, *massuës des Sauvages, elle leur servent d'espèe [sic.], et ... l'aura bien grosse, et bien grande ... L'en ay pourtant veu un qui en ayant esté frappé n'en mourut pas ...* '⁶³
Du Tertre also comments:

> ... de *boutous* (qui est une façon de massuë faite de bresil ou de bois verd, ou de quelqu'autre bois massif pesant comme plomb)... Quoy que ce *boutou* ne soit pas trop en main, il n'y a boeuf qui'il ne terrasse d'un seul coup... ils leurs donnent d'un coup de *Boutou* (qui est une espece de massuë, et leur arme ordinaire).⁶⁴

A deceased grand uncle of mine with an artificial leg was in fact nicknamed *Ãdwé boutou pat* 'Andrew club foot', 'Andrew with the artificial leg'.

kayè
'submerged rock(s)', 'bay comprising the latter' "<cayo 'écueil, mot arawak ... '⁶⁵

tjenbwa
'magic', 'sorcery', 'a spell': "le maniment du magique est désigné par le terme général de *tchembwa*."⁶⁶

A French origin is suggested by Verin who also relates the item to Patwa *tjébé* or *tjenbé* — 'hold', 'seize': "... peut-être en relation avec le mot *tchember* (prendre, attraper) qui viendrait lui-même de tiens bien..." Verin also points to a potential Carib origin: "mais aussi peut-être, du caraibe *acamboué* (R.P. Breton)", as well as indicating the Martiniquan counterpart of this item: "En Martinique, on emploie le mot *quinbois*".⁶⁷

It seems likely, however, that *tchembwa* or *kenbwa* or *kenbwa* has a different source⁶⁸ from *tjenbé*. The latter is a putative loan of Island Carib " 'chaboui' *seize, take, lay, hold on ...* "⁶⁹ or a convergence between Carib Island *'chaboui'* and French 'tiens bien' or 'tiens bon'.

Breton also give the following references: "cheménbaebaé loüagó, *les hommes disent* keménbakê, *accoustume moy'*.⁷⁰ 'chémenbae, *iettelle*" (idem); "*iettele, lancele,* cheménbae, chiboukibae, f. [i.e. 'female' language/Arawak] *coíbae*";⁷¹ "*acàmbouée, acansàncou, esprit*";⁷² "*esprit,* acansáncou, acámbouée, f. ópoyem".⁷³

The last two references above indicate a probable association between '*acàmbouée ... esprit*' and Patwa *tjenbwa* meaning 'black magic'. Breton, as well as indicating that $k <$ Carib and $c <$ Arawak (above), also makes the following comment: "Les Sauvages usent du C et du K au lieu de Q".[74]

This may well account for the k or tj synchronic alternation in Patwa *kenbwa* or *tjenbwa*, as well as Martinique *'quimbois'*, which may also indicate the influences of French orthography, either on Verin or his informants. *tjenbwa* was also perpetuated in the men's language of the St. Vincent Island Carib.[75]

In synchronic Patwa the concept of *tjenbwa* may include the idea of being seized (*tjébé*) by an evil spirit. However, as *tjenbwa* may have other dimensions e.g. ritual cursing, the use of herbs, etc., it is not as closely associated with the item *tjébé* as Verin's comments suggest.

kaban
'bed' Cf. Arawakan ka?ban 'house',[76] with subsequent shift of meaning. The item is not in Island Carib of 1665 but seems to have passed into seventeenth century French.[77]

kako
'cocoa', according to Alleyne[78] is a putative Island Carib loan.

kanawi
'large earthenware pot', said to be from the Canaries area of St. Lucia[79] where 'red'-skinned St. Lucians of Carib descent specialised in making them and other earthenware implements from the local reddish coloured clay.[80] The word is a putative loan from Island Carib: "Canari aurait la même origine que canot (kanoa)... tous deux seraient dérivés d'une racine caraibe qui signifie *qui contient*".[81] Breton gives the seventeenth century meaning of this Island Carib item as:

> *canálli, grands Vaisseaux de terre dans* lesquels les Sauvages font leur vins.[82]
> ... *canaris pour d'autres usages* chamácou, taóloüy, roúara, iáligali. v. la page 107 *de la première partie*.[83]

As seen above, the item also referred to earthenware in general. Its presence amongst the French (italicised) items in the French-Carib Dictionary suggests its probable adoption into Caribbean French in the seventeeth century, at least by Breton.

The Island Carib source of this item is also underlined by the presence of a separate Island Carib item referring to the Island Carib implement and its equivalent in Dominican creole French:

> The canari, or earthenware, and no longer made locally, is the same name given to the 'fait-tout', or 'buck pot' of the Creoles.[84]

The item is also present in Senegalese French, also in reference to large earthenware pots and owes its origin to the Atlantic Slave Trade

terme très répandu aux Antilles et même en Afrique occidentale où il
dut être importé naguère par la voie du commerce triangulaire... [85]

R. Mauny also alludes to the Island Carib source of 'canari' as
well as to its Slave Trade diffusion:

> Canari a donc franchi l'Atlantique entre 1728 et 1757, sans doute
> avec les négriers qui faisaient sans cesse le trajet Europe-Afrique-
> Amérique.

Mauny also alludes to the Island Carib origins of other words used
in Francophone West Africa:

> D'autres mots que nous employons quotidiennement proviennent
> également des langues des Indiens des Antilles: *avocat* (le fruit),
> *caîman, goyave, lamantin, ouragan, papaye, patate, pirogue, savane*,
> et bien d'autres.[86]

Cf. Patwa *avoka* '— 'avocado pear(s)'; *gwiyav* — 'guava(s)'; *papai*
— 'pawpaw(s) and *patat* — 'potato(es); Breton (1665) makes no
reference to *avocat, goyave* or *savane*.

He does, however, refer to the other items:

> caiman, (sont trois syllabes) *allons*. caiman-co, *allons vistement.*
> (DCF); lámati, malámatinoúrna, *i'ay les iambes roides, affamé*es, ie
> *suis las, non* (DCF); *lamantin,* manátoüi.
> Manattoüi, *en Sauvage, et lamantin en François; c'est un grand
> poisson sans ècailles, dont le muflle est semblable à celuy d'une vache,
> et à la queuë large comme une paële à four* (DCF); oüágagan, du
> Oüalloman (DCF) oüallóman, *ionc à faire des paniers, tables, etc.*
> (DCF); *ouragan, orage,* iouallou, bo*i*ntara (DFC); bo*i*ntara, *tempeste,
> orage,* ouragan (DCF); *grosse papaye,* abàbai, *petite,* áleulé (DFC);
> Aabábai, *grosses papayes* (DCF); *patate, racine bonne à manger
> mabi, ma patate,* nimábiri, noule (DFC); Mábi, miti, *ouira, sont des
> racines de patates* (DCF) pirauge, canáoa, oucounni (DFC): Can-
> áoa, *pirauge, sont les gallions des sauvages[;]ils sont longs de
> soixante pieds, plus ou moins* (DCF); oucouri, *canot* (DCF)[87] Breton
> however makes no reference to *savane*.

kayal
'a stork-like bird, frequenting marshland areas in St. Lucia'; this is a
putative loan of Dominican creole/Island Carib *cayali* 'bird'.[88]

mabouya
'a grey coloured lizard'. Breton also refers to *mabouya* as a type of
lizard: "... *autre appellé maboya, qui a un cris effroyeble,* acacámoulou'(DFC)";[89] "acacámoulou, *lezard appellé maboya, des autres,
brochet de terre* (DFC)".[90] Du Tertre gives the following additional
information:

> l'Ay [*sic.*] veu dans toutes les isles deux autres sortes de lezards, que
> les Sauvages appellent *Maboüyas,* qui est un nom qui'ils donnenet
> communément à tout ce qui fait horreur... Les seconds n'arrivent
> iamais à la longueur d'un pied: ils sont gris, vilains, bouffis, et hideux

[sic.] à voir . . . Ils se retirent pour l'ordinaire sur des branches d'arbres . . .[91]

De Tertre in fact also gives a description which exemplifies the use of *Maboüyas* to refer to anything which the Island Carib found fearful:

> . . . il fit mettre le feu à son Canon, qui fit un si estrange carnage de ces Sauvages, que ces pauvres gens croyans [sic.] que tous les *Maboyas* de la France estoient sortis de la gueulle de ce Canon pour les destruire . . . (my emphasis).[92]

manikou
'a rabbit-like animal hunted, usually with the aid of dogs; though not having the long ears of a rabbit, and having a slightly longer body. It tastes similar to rabbit. It is usually brown in colour and long-tailed'. This is a putative loan from Island Carib according to Alleyne.[93]

roukou
'a red dye used in decorating the body during carnival and other local mask ceremonies'.[94]
"*roucou* — 'plant from which red dye is extracted', used by Caribs as war paint".[95] Breton gives the following references to the item *roucou*:

> bichet, *roucou. Les Caraibes plantent cét [sic.] arbre proche leur cases* . . . cabichati nibichet, (*disent-ils) il produit son fruict [sic.] par touffe, il est semblable au noyau de pesche, [sic.] mais il n'est pas dur, ils le font boüillir en l'eau, puis l'eau estant tiede, ils le frottent entre leur mains dans l'eau, la peinture tombe au fond et fait comme un pain de cire, ils mestent de la poussiere de charbon de sandal avec (parce que son éclat trop vif offenseroit la veuë) puis l'ayant détrempé avec l'huille, ils s'en rougissent souvent, et c'est leur chemise blanche: cette peinture ferme les pores, empesche que l'eau de la mer ne fige sur leur corps, fait fuir les maringoins et fait mourir les chiques.*[96]
> rocou, peinture, emátabi, cochéhúe, f. bichet . . . *il a du rocou*, kicouchehuéréti, Kolocámbouleti, f. Kàbicheti.[97]

According to Breton's subscript f., (i.e. 'female language') next to the item 'bichet', *roucou* is the Carib equivalent of an Arawakan term.

However, Breton's italicised references are reserved for French items in his dictionary. This would suggest that *rocou – roucou* was in Caribbean French in the seventeenth century and that it may have entered French via Patwa.

titak
'a little bit' is a putative loan of Island Carib 'titaka, a little bit'.[98]

touloulou
'a red coloured beach crab living on the landward side of the beach'. The item is a putative loan of Carib 'Tourourou'. Breton makes the

following references to 'Tourourou:

> *tourelourou, petite crabe rouge,* itoúrourou (DFC);[99] *petite crabe de jardin,* itoúrourou (DFC).[100]

Du Tertre describes them as:

> ... les *Tourlourous* (qui sont certains petits cancres)[101] ... Il y en a encoire deux autres sortes; sçavoir [sic.] les Crables [sic.] blanches et les *Tourlourous* ...[102]

Chardon adds:

> Le Tourlouroux ressemble à la crabe, à l'exception qui'il est plus petit et que son écaille est rougeâtre.[103]

Littré described them as follows:

> Jeune soldat d'infanterie... Nom vulgaire, aux Antilles, des espèces du genre gécarcin (décapodes)... ou crabe de terre... dit tourlourou par les matelots, qui le comparaient au fantassin de l'armée de terre.[104]

The nautical connection of the Atlantic Slave Trade and therefore of some Patwa lexical items could only have facilitated the entry of this 'sailor's metaphor' into French via Patwa e.g.:

> TOUTLOUTOU [sic.] ... 1834; probabl. [sic.] emploi fig. de tourlourou crabe rouge, 1686; mot antillais, à cause de la couleur de l'uniforme ...[105]

zagaya
Fr. *les* + *agaya* — 'beach crab living closer to the seaward side of the beach, and usually hiding its white-coloured body by burying itself beneath the sand'. Is a putative loan of Dominican Creole/Island Carib "agaya"[106] — 'crab'.

zandoli
'lizard' is a putative Island Carib loan (see also above). Breton makes the following references to: "*Anoli: Auoli v laizard*" (DFC),[107] "*Autre laizard gros comme un baston, et long presque d'une coudée il est gris,* anáoli."[108]

Du Tertre gives the following description:

> Les *Anolis* [sic.] Ils portent un pied ou pied et demy de longueur... Ils ont le ventre de couleur de gris cendré, et le dos tanné tirant sur le roux, et tout rayé de bleu... Ils sont tousiours dans la terre ...[109] (my emphasis).

Anoli may have passed into Caribbean French in the seventeenth century. The item was in nineteenth century French according to Littré:

> Terme de Zoologie. Genre de reptiles qui rassemblent au lézard, et qu'on trouve aux Antilles (*anolis bullaris* [Latin]).[110]

The item does not appear to be in modern French.[111]

Grammatical Convergences

Such convergences are partly due to the early Caribbean influences on pidgins and Creoles in both the old and New World which were 're-imported' into the Caribbean via the Atlantic Slave Trade (see *kanawi* above).

ka[112]
Hab. and *Prog.* marker. Cf. Island Carib *bouca* possible pronounced [*buka*] given the possible *c* or *k* alternation in diachronic Island Carib (see above). Cf. also *ka* — a marker of the "present"[113] in modern Guyanese Arawak (Lokono). Note the possible convergent influences of Mandinka *ka* — progressive and habitual marker.

li
'he/she' (*3rd. sing.*) Cf. Island Carib *l* 3rd. sing. (*mas.*) Cf. the convergent influences of *Fr. lui* — 'he'.

ma, maa
1st. sing. negative past progressive/habitual markers respectively, <Mandinka *mang 1st. sing.* negative marker also. These alternants may have been influenced by Island Carib *ma* — negative marker.

m
a marker of the negative in the Patwa *1st. sing.* only, e.g.:

ma	vini	— 'I did not come'
"I *Neg.*	*Past* come"	
maa	vini	— 'I do not usually come'
"I *Neg. Hab.*	come"	

m is a putative loan from Arawak/Island Carib, (see above), where *m* is also a negative marker, e.g.:

ma'niçiku tibu — false, lying thou art (m, negative; a'niçi, heart; tibu, thou hast).[114]
POSITIVE: niboyeiri, *medecin, prestre de sauvages*
NEGATIVE: Manboyéiriti, *il n'est point boyé, medecin*[115]
POSITIVE: Kanicoüátibou, *tu fais mal*
NEGATIVE: Manicoüátiba, *ne fais pas de mal.*[116]

Note the possible converging effects with Mandinka *mang* — perfective negative (past/present), e.g.:

(n) man	naa	'I have not come'
(I) *Neg.*	come	

Archaisms of Island Carib Origin

A number of items of putative Island Carib origin are rarely used except in the speech of older Patwa speakers:

cali
"Filet monté sur un cercle de bois d'environ un mètre de diamètre".[117] Verin suggests that the item is of a definitely Island Carib, rather than of a French origin:

> Contrairement à une idée fréquemment répandue, le mot ne vient pas due français *calut*, mais d'un mot caraibe attesté par BRETON [*sic.*].[118]

This item is not commonly used in modern Patwa and was not known to the Patwa speakers interviewed.[119]

lébiché
"an instrument used in making cassava flour"..[120] According to Verin the Island Carib prononciation of the item was [lebiʃet], but: "Le t final du mot n'est plus aujourd'hui pronouncé en créole saint-lucien: *lébiché*."[121]

Although Breton[122] gives no references to this item in either volume of his dictionary, Du Tertre gives the following information: "... des Hibichets (qui est une espece de crible pour passer leur farine)".[123]

The item is an archaism in modern Patwa and refers to vegetable matter growing on the sea bed. Because of its many perforations, it was used as a strainer, e.g. in the sifting of manioc pulp to make cassava flour. The modern metal strainer has superseded this implement in all but a few rural homes.

tjè
'heart' is a putative loan of Arawakan/Island Carib. *a'niçi* 'heart';[124] *na'içi* (F) — 'my heart'.[125]

piay[126]
"mot d'origine amérindienne signifiant sorcier. Il est couramment employé en langue créole [i.e. St. Lucian Patwa] (Cf. R.P. Breton: *boyer*, même sens)."[127] "On emploi celui de *piaye* quand l'opération a pour but de nuire à autrui ..."[128]

African Items in Island Carib

A few items of African origin were also loaned into Island Carib, probably via Patwa:

moun (Patwa)
'person'. Cf. Belize (formerly British Honduras) Island Carib *mutu* — 'person'; Congolese —*muntu* and Bantu **Munthu*— both also meaning 'person'.[129]

obya – obiya (Patwa)
'black magic': *i mété obya anlè yo* "(S)He put a spell on them". 'He/She put black magic on them'. Cf. Island Carib "*abiara* 'to bewitch, to work sorcery' ".[130]

Cf. also   *Twiobiya*   *fò*   — 'a sorcerer'
               "sorcery   *personal suffix*
Cf. the earlier Island Carib 'acámbouée' (above).

French Derived Items in Island Carib and Patwa

As some Patwa-speaking maroons in St. Lucia and Martinique may well have extended their maroonage to St. Vincent from about 1698,[131] it is possible that they and not the French were the main contributors of the predominantly French-derived loans present in the language of the St. Vincent Black Carib from 1653 to 1797.

Maroons in St. Lucia and in Martinique in 1698 and earlier, are most likely to have had closer contacts with the Island Carib population of both islands. It is these maroons who were also the probable intermediaries in the borrowing of Island Carib items into Patwa and Martiniquan Creole. [132]

The high frequency of French loans in the language of the Black Carib is in fact commented upon by Taylor:

> French still exceeds all other... loan words put together, although the Black Carib of Central America have been out of contact with that language for over one hundred and fifty years.[133]

Further, given that maroons in the forested interior of St. Lucia did have some contact with the St. Lucian Island Carib, as the Island Carib loans in Patwa in fact suggest, it is likely that any of them carrying out *marronage* in St. Vincent would already have had the familiarity with Island Carib necessary to their contribution to the many French loans in the Black Carib language of St. Vincent.

Notes

1. Term used to differentiate the Caribs in the Windward and other Caribbean islands from the mainland Caribs of the American continent, e.g. in Taylor, D.M., 1951, p.53. Labat, J.B., 1722, p.332 in fact underlines the presence of these two separate Carib groups: "... *il y a une difference infinie entre ceux des petits Isles, et ceux de la Terre ferme la plus proche*..." (... there is an infinite difference between those [Caribs] of the small islands, and those of the nearest mainland ...) (1700).
2. Taylor, D.M., 1977.
3. Hoff, B.J., 1968.
4. As also suggested by Taylor (1977) Mrs. E. Charlette, Amerindian Languages Project, Univ. of Guyana & Dr. W. Edwards, also of the Univ. of Guyana, personal communication, 1979.
5. Breton, R., 1667, p.27. Note that the gender differences between *3rd. sing. l* and *t* is a feature inherited from the Arawakan women's language: "*L* et *t*, contractent les noms à la troisiéme [sic.] personne parmy [sic.] les hommes, et parmy les femmes: *l*, rend le nom masculin, et *t*, feminin..." (*L* and *t*, attached to the nouns in the third person amongst the men, and amongst the women: *l*, makes the noun masculine and *t*, feminine ...). (Breton, R., 1667, p.13.) This Arawakan feature has, however, been inherited as part of the Carib grammatical system: "Toutes les troisiémes personnes du singulier, qui se commencent par un *l*, sont du masculin: comme: (All the third person singulars, which begin with an *l*, are masculine: like: *likia, liketa, likira, libonam, lone*... Celles qui commencent par un *t*, sont du feminin: comme: (Those that begin with a *t*, are feminine: like:) *tokoya, toucoúra, tokéta, tibonam*..." (Breton, R., 1667, p.16.)
6. Breton, R., 1667, p.17. Note that (ˋ), (ˊ) and (ˆ) indicate very long, long and short vowels respectively in Breton's works. See Breton, R., 1667, p.3 & p.6; Taylor, D.M., 1977, pp.29-33. In Taylor's Carib studies however "Stress is phonemic and is indicated by /ˊ/". Taylor, D.M., 1951, p.12; 1977, pp.29-33.
7. Breton, R., 1665, p.174, (Dictionnaire Caraibe-Français).
8. Ibid., p.70 (Dictionnaire Français-Caraibe).
   Breton, R., 1667 gives no separate description of object pronouns and the above note is abstracted from his data.
9. Taylor, D.M., 1977, p.45.
10. Although described as personal pronouns in Breton (1667), Taylor, D.M., 1977 uses the term "personal affixes" to describe the pronominal elements above. Note, however, that Hoff gives different forms for Surinam (mainland) Carib pronominal elements dependent upon a variety of "personal processes", Hoff, B.J., 1968, p.159. Note that in Taylor's writings about Island Carib: "All [Island] Carib words appearing in the text are given in their phonemic transcription..." (Taylor, D.M., 1951, p.12). Such phonemic transcriptions are italicised in Taylor's texts and in this chapter.
11. Breton, R., 1667, p.13. Breton also adds that the *1st.* & *2nd. sing.* 'Carib' possessive pronominal elements are also markers of the *1st.* and *2nd.* possessive in the Arawak women's language: "*n* et *b*, sont les deux premieres personnes au language des femmes" (*n* and *b* are the two first person pronouns in the women's language). The presence of Arawakan *n, b, t* and *l* alternants in the Island Carib grammatical system again suggests the importance of 'mother tongue' upon grammatical structure and of 'father tongue' in the lexicon, where one language has been imposed at the expense of another in such colonial historical contexts.
12. Ibid. p.12.
13. Breton, R., 1667, p.11. Possession in the *1st. sing.* can also be marked by the prefixing of *n*, and the suffixing of *lou* to the noun e.g.: "*mabou*, routte, *nimaboulou*, ma routte" *ácou*, oeil, *nácou*... *nácoulou*, mon oeil" (Ibid, p.12.)

This rule is not however, a general one: "*La regle n'est pas pourtant generale...* (Ibid., p.12.)
14. Ibid., pp.13-14.
15. Although some of the verbal markers below could be described as tense or aspect markers e.g.: "*bouca*" (see below), which could be described as an imperfective aspect marker. However the categories used by Breton, R., 1667 are adopted throughout this outline. Again, given the higher frequency of *1st. pl.* items having the Arawakan affix *ou* in Breton's exemplification, the importance of Arawak in the grammatical structure of Carib is underlined. With the exception of *1st. pl. ki*, Hoff gives different possessive pronominal elements:

SINGULAR   PLURAL
1 zero marker or y   ki
2 a or o
3 t

2nd. pl. and 3rd. pl. pronominal elements are not separately indicated in Hoff's description. See Hoff, B.J., 1968, p.221.
16. Breton, R., 1667, p.39.
17. Taylor, D.M., 1977, p.48. Note that Hoff, B.J., 1968, makes no mention of such an infinitive suffix.
18. Breton, R., 1667, p.40.
19. Ibid., p.27.
20. Taylor, D.M., 1977, 49-50. Cf. Hoff, B.J., 1968, who makes no mention of the above as imperfective forms.
21. Taylor, D.M., 1977, p.41.
22. See Taylor, D.M., 1977, p.50-51.
23. "Le future se forme de l'indicatif present..." (The future is formed from the present indicative...) (Breton, R., 1667, p.41.) Breton also makes reference to what may be described as an indefinite future form of the above verb, which is also derived from a present indicative form of the verb, i.e.: "*naramêtàcayem*" becomes "*naramêtàcaba*"... "semble plustot signifier i.e. vais cacher, que ie cacheray".
24. Ibid., p.54.
25. Ibid., pp.27-28.
26. Breton, R., 1667, p.41.
27. Ibid., p.54.
28. Ibid., p.54.
29. Breton, R., 1665, p.50, "Dictionnaire Caraibe-Français".
30. Breton, R., 1667, p.54.
31. Breton, R., 1665, p.333, "Dictionnaire Français-Caraibe".
32. Ibid., p.257.
33. Ibid., p.278.
34. Taylor, D.M., 1977, p.46. Cf. Patwa *ma* — *1st. sing.* negative (see below).
35. Hoff, B.J., 1968, p.414.
36. Breton, R., 1667, p.26.
37. Ibid., p.27.
38. Breton, R., 1667, p.40.
39. Breton, R., 1667, p.41. Note that in the case of the *3rd. sing.*, further contraction may take place, i.e. *ha* as in "*aramêtàhali* il a caché"; while *tina* is deleted in the *3rd. sing.* of the previous example i.e. "*erèali*, il a pris, ...".
40. Taylor, D.M., 1977, p.49.
41. Hoff, B.J., 1968, pp.112, 127 & 133-155.
42. Breton, R., 1667, p.42: "L'imperatif se forme de l'infinitif, adioustant [sic.] l'imperatif de l'auxiliaire *niem* ..." (The imperative is formed from the infinitive, adding the imperative of the auxiliary *niem* ...).

43. Taylor, D.M., 1977, p.52. Note that (ˊ) only indicates stress in Taylor's orthography.
44. Hoff, B.J., 1968, p.188.
45. Breton, R., 1667, p.11.
46. Breton, R., 1667, p.13.
47. "Les noms ... ne se declinent point ... la variation des cas ... dépend des lettres où des pronoms qui font ce que les articles ont accoustumé de faire..." (The nouns ... are never declined ... the variation of cases ... depends on letters or pronouns which do what these articles are in the habit of doing...) (Breton, R., 1667, p.12). It seems very likely, given this general statement, that the subject pronouns are in fact important markers of gender in the nominal. Note also Breton, R., 1667, p.15: "Les pronoms ont genre, nombre, figure, espece, personne et signification" (The pronouns have gender, number, figure, space, person and meaning).
48. Taylor, D.M., 1977, p.59. See also p.45. This use of a *pl.* marker of the same form to the *3rd. pl.* pronoun is a common feature of African languages also evident in Gambian Krio. Note that in Taylor's writings on Island Carib ... "ṿ... which indicates the nasalised counterpart of the oral vowel"... (Taylor, D.M., 1951, p.12.)
49. Hoff, B.J., 1968, p.228, whose exemplification has been modified by use of the I.A.I. orthography.
50. Breton, R., 1667, p.10.
51. Ibid., p.11.
52. Taylor, D.M., 1977, pp.63-64.
53. Hoff, B.J., 1968, p.269. See also pp.260 & 267.
54. Du Tertre, J.B., 1654, p.340.
55. Alleyne, M., 1961, p.2, fn.2.
56. Littré, E., 1873, p.80.
57. Robert, P., 1967, p.33.
58. Breton, R., 1665, p.430 & 13 respectively.
59. Du Tertre, J.B., 1654, p.406 & 409 respectively. See also pp.340 & 341.
60. Chaudron, D.M.A. 1779, p.38.
61. Taylor, D.M., 1938, p.154.
62. Breton, R., 1665, p.58, Dictionnaire François-Caraibe.
63. Breton, R., 1665, pp.94 & 95 respectively.
64. Du Tertre, J.B., 1654, pp.445 & 421 respectively.
65. Larousse, 1975, p.277.
66. Verin, P., 1959, p.360. Note that the item is not in Mauritian Creole; Baker, P., personal communication, 1980.
67. Ibid., p.360, fn.12.
68. Breton, R., 1665, p.134.
69. Taylor, D.M., 1951, p.52, who points to Breton as his source. See Breton, R., 1665, p.155. "Chaboüibae, nachaboüiroyénli, *prendle* [sic.], *ie le prend.* Cháboüinía lábouli náboüa, ie *l'ay pris, empoigné par le poing*". (Dictionnaire Caraibe-François.) "prendle, erébae," ... (Dictionnaire Francois-Caraibe, p.309.) Note also Taylor's statement about the phonology of the Island Carib language in St. Vincent "/c/ varies freely between the sound of 'ch' in 'church' and that of 'sh' in 'shut', 'hush'..." (Taylor, D.M., 1951, p.12): a likely phonetic representation of '*chaboui*', would therefore be [ʃabui]. Some association did, however, exist between "chaboúibae" and "acámbouée" according to the following references in Breton, 1665: "*sorciere*, ebénnêtou..." (Dictionnaire François-Caraibe, p.367); "Ebénnêtou, *voyez*, chebénéboui" (Dictionnaire Caraibe-François, p.191); "chebéneboüitiatina, *elle m'a ensorcelé*" (Dictionnaire Caraibe-François, p.131.) Such association may well be due to a concept of 'seizing' being a part of the Island Carib image of sorcery or due to the *c* or *k* alternation in Island Carib which may have facilitated existing similarities

between "chebéneboüi" — 'to put a spell on' and "chaboüibae" — 'to hold'. Note however, Taylor, D.M., 1977, p.29, who suggests that the use of c or k in Breton 1667 was due to "a printer's shortage of the letter k".
70. Breton, R., 1667, p.134, DCF.
71. Breton, R., 1667, p.209, DFC.
72. Breton, R., 1667, p.9, DCF.
73. Breton, R., 1667, p.159, DFC.
74. Breton, R., 1667, p.435, DCF.
75. Taylor, D.M., 1951, p.103. The Carib invaders of the Caribbean island homes of the Arawak killed off the Arawak men and took over their women. This left the language dichotomy between a 'women's language' in which lexical items from Carib predominated. It is likely, that Arawak may have had the most dominating role in this encounter as it was the 'mother' language of the Island Carib children. Cf. the dominating role played by the African 'mother' languages in the slave-plantation situation where European 'father' languages of many Caribbean slaves underwent much modification in the direction of African languages. Note also Taylor, D.M., 1951, p.103, who gives "acámbouée" as the source of the following items in the language of the Black Carib of Saint Vincent: "whence áhambue or ágambue of the Black Carib", which are also related to sorcery: "áhambue ... — 'to call down ... spirit helpers on the part of' " a sorcerer (Taylor, D.M., 1951, p.112). On the assumption that "acámbouée" can be phonetically represented as [akãmbwe] [akãbwe], its close similarity to kenbwa in Patwa and in Martiniquan Creole (above) points to kenbwa as being more widespread than tjenbwa.
76. Edwards, W., 1978, p.6.
77. As suggested by its use as a French item alone in both volumes of Breton, R., 1665, p.227, (DFC).
78. Alleyne, M., 1961, p.2, fn.2. The item is in modern French, Robert, P., 1967, p.208. It is of American origin according to Littré, E., 1873, p.447: "Mot américain [sic.] ... ", and specifically of Mexican origin according to Murray, J.A.H., 1893, p.580, "Cacoa was the Spanish adaptation of Cacault ... the Mexican name of the Cacao-seed". Note also the associated nominal compound in Patwa pyé kako — 'cocoa tree', which is itself a calque upon the following structure "foot tree" in French: "Pied, avec le mot arbre ou avec un nom de végétal, signifie un arbre entier, la plante entière". (Littré, E., 1873, p.1111.) No reference to kako was found in either volume of Breton's dictionary.
79. See Dalphinis, M., 1981, pt.III, ch.1.
80. According to Saint Lucian oral tradition, heard by myself, then aged 10 years, in Vieux-Fort, Saint Lucia. See also Dalphinis, M., 1977(b), p.1.
81. Verin, P., 1959, p.356, fn.15, who also adds: "Dans le créole actuel canari (his emphasis) signifie à la fois un object de forme arrondie et toute poterie en général". (In the actual Creole canari signifies both an object of a rounded and all pottery in general.)This is still the case in synchronic Patwa: kanawi — 'earthenware', e.g.: yo pa ni kanawi — 'They have no earthenware', (lit. "they Neg. have pots/earthenware".) Note however, that Taylor, D.M., 1951, p.56 gives guriára as the Black Carib item meaning dugout. This indicates that the item did not have as general a meaning as Verin's footnote suggests, at least in the Black Carib language of Saint Vincent. Further, Breton, R., 1665, p.60 (DFC) does not indicate that "canálli" also refers to "canot": "canot, oucounnihueri f. coulíalla aóuloubali".
Du Tertre, J.B., 1654, p.439, gives the following reference to "Canoüa": "Les plus grands sont ceux que nous appellons Pirogues et en Sauvage Canoüa; et les plus petits nous les appellons Canots, et eux Couliala" (The largest are those we call dug-out canoes in the language of the savages, Canoüa; and the smallest ones are what we call rowing boats, and they Couliala).
82. Breton, R., 1665, p.107, (DCF).

83. Ibid., p.59, (DFC, 1665).
84. Taylor, D.M., 1938, p.140. Note that *kanawi* made in Saint Lucia was being exported to neighbouring islands, probably including Dominica, in 1959; see Verin, P., 1959, p.346.
85. Verin, P., 1959, p.356.
86. Mauny, R., 1948, p.65.
87. Breton, R., 1665, pp. 101, 332, 222, 349-350, 403, 406, 269, 82, 273, 2, 280, 344, 294, 108 & 419 respectively.
88. Taylor, D.M., 1938, p.156, who includes the item in a list headed "Birds, insects". Breton, R., 1665, however, gives no references to this item. The item is not in modern French, according to Robert's dictionary, and was not present in nineteenth century French according to Littré.
89. Breton, R., 1665, p.221.
90. Ibid., p.8.
91. Du Tertre, J.B., 1654, p.354.
92. Ibid., p.72.
93. See Alleyne, M., 1961, p.2, fn.2, who refers to these and other Carib language survivals in Patwa: "... *manicou* (animals); *cacao, caimite* (trees) ... *moipre* — snake". Breton, R., 1665, p.333, gives the following references: "Manicou, *Renard, i'en ay veu un qui venoit de terre ferme, et fut presenté à Monseigneur le Cardinal de Richelieu, il estoit petit et longuet, et avait une trasse noire qui faisoit quatre ou cinq tours autour de son museau & se terminoit aux oreilles*". "*renard,* manícou. aoüàle et mabiritou *en sont encores deux autres especes*" (... Fox, I have seen one which came from the mainland, and was presented to his Eminence Cardinal Richelieu, it was small and longish, and had a black line which went four or five times round its muzzle and ended at its ears. Fox ... there are also two other species. Breton, R., 1665 (DFC, p.336).
A zoological term for the item was not available in the Encyclopedia Britannica.
No references were found in Breton, 1665 (both vols.) for "*cacao*" and "*caimite*". No references were found for "*moipre*" — 'snake' in the Dictionnaire Caraibe-François, while the reference to serpents in general in the Dictionnaire François-Caraibe (p.360) did not include "*moipre*": "*serpent*, héhue, *les especes de serpents venimeux, sont* ahàoüa, alàtalloüata, ioulia, ioulíati, et màcao, *les autres qui ne sont pas venimeuses,* oüanàche, oüallaoúcoule, toubouloüéro".
94. E.g. *papa djab* — 'a ceremony in which men disguised as devils run around "father devil" the town causing mischief'. See Crowley, D.J., 1957.
95. Alleyne, M., 1961, p.2, fn.2.
96. Breton, R., 1665, p.79 (DCF).
97. Breton, R., 1665, p.347 (DFC).
Du Tertre, J.B., 1650, p.399, also refers to this item: "... et se frotter de roucou ..." Littré, E., 1873, gives the following reference: "... cette matière colorante est employée pour teindre en jaune ou en janue orangé la soie et quelques produits. On dit aussi roucou" (... to rub oneself with ... this colouring matter is used to stain silk and other products, yellow, or orange-yellow. Roucou is also said.) The item is in modern French according to Harrap, 1962, but is not mentioned in Robert 1967.
98. Taylor, D.M., 1938, p.157, who also points to "... such Dominican creole patois expressions as 'titac' ... "
Breton, R., gives no reference to his item (1665).
99. Breton, R., 1665, p.384, (DFC).
100. Ibid., p.94, (DFC).
101. Du Tertre, J.B., 1654, 360.
102. Ibid., p.376.
103. Chardon, D.M.A., 1779, p.48.

104. Littré, E., 1873, p.2275.
105. Robert, P., 1967, p.1804.
106. Taylor, D.M., 1938, p.156. No references were found to "agaya" in either volume of Breton's dictionary.
107. Breton, R., 1665, p.20.
108. Ibid., p.221.
109. Du Tertre, J.B., 1654, p.352.
110. Littré, E., 1873, p.152.
111. Robert, P., 1967.
112. Cf. also Mandinka. *ka — Hab.* and *Prog.* marker.
113. Edwards, W., 1978. p.16.
114. Taylor, D.M., 1938, p.155.
    See also Dalphinis, M., 1979(a), p.8.
115. Breton, R., 1665, p.83, (DCF).
116. Ibid., p.40, (DCF).
117. Verin, P., 1959, p.356, fn.17. I am assuming that this and other items grouped by Verin with definitely non-Island Carib Patwa items, e.g. "betché", "bèkè", meaning 'white person', were in Patwa in 1959 and of course not from a separate St. Lucian Island Carib language at so late a date. Verin, P. 1959, p.530; see also Dalphinis, M., 1981, p.510, where the African language origins of *bétjé* — 'White person', are described.
118. Ibid. See also Breton, R., 1665, p.105 (DCF), "*cali, filets, rests*"; & p.174 (DFC), "*filets, truble, cáli*".
119. By the writer during a field-trip in St. Lucia in April 1979.
120. Verin, P., 1959, p.355. [lebiʃe] is a likely phonetic representation of "lébiché" as given by Verin, writing in 1959 about the language of the Saint Lucian Island Carib (in the La Pointe area of Saint Lucia).
121. Ibid., fn.14. Note that items in italics were also in italics in the original.
122. See also Taylor, D.M., 1951, p.56, who gives *hibise*, — 'sifters' in the language of the Black Carib of Sainte Vincent. Note also *hébichet* referred to in Taylor, D.M., 1938, p.155, as one of the "many words of current Creole patois which appear to be of native origin" i.e. originating from the language(s) of the Island Carib.
123. De Tertre, J.B., 1654, p.422.
124. Verin, P., 1959, p.155.
125. Ibid., p.154. In Taylor's orthography . . . "ç, always soft, is intermediate between the s sound, as in the name of the God Siva; ch as in machine . . . " (Taylor, D.M., 1938, p.153), while (F) indicates that the item is in the women's language and as such is of Arawakan origin. Breton, R., 1665, p.40, gives the following references: "*ánichi, coeur, ame. Ce mot mis avec le verbe denote, envie, volonté, desir, comme* chinhacaécoüa clee banichi, *tu as bien envie de rire....*" (DCF). "*coeur, courage,* ioüànni, f. nan*i*chi" (DFC, p.76). As indicated by the symbol "f" this item is of Arawakan origin. Note also Patwa *pwen tjè* —'take courage'; *i ni tjè kanpech* — 'He/She has great courage (endurance)' i.e. 'He/She has a heart as strong as the "heart" of a *kanpesh* — hardwood tree'... Cf. also the following Island Carib phrase "*le coeur du bois*, tabo*ú*li," (Breton, R., 1665, p.77, DFC).
126. Verin, P., 1959, p.360.
127. Ibid., fn.22. I have, however, found no references to either *piaye* or *boyer* in either volume of Breton, 1665.
128. Verin, P., 1959, p.360.
129. Taylor, D.M., 1951, p.168. Breton, R., 1665, makes no reference to *mutu*.
130. Taylor, D.M., 1951, p.133. Note that the subscript ₎ = nasalization in Taylor's orthography. See also Taylor, D.M., 1951, p.103.
    Breton, R., 1665, p.4, gives the following references: "Abiénroni, *sort, sorcellerie*. Abienra: abiénragoüa, ensorceller. Kabienracátiti, *grand sorcier*"

(DCF) "*sorcière*, ebénnêtou, kihénnêtou, (DFC, p.367). It is also possible that convergence with Twi *obiafo* — 'a sorcerer' has occured, or that the Patwa item is a direct loan from Twi. Such convergence would be very likely, given the presence of Black Caribs in St. Vincent and probably St. Lucia in the eighteenth century. Note also Jamaican Creole "OBEAH" (*sic.*) Cassidy and Le Page, 1967, p.326.

131. See Dalphinis, M., 1977(b). Although Maroonage within Martinique alone and within St. Lucia alone is mentioned in the above reference, it is possible that references to maroon slaves from neighbouring islands joining the St. Vincent Caribs, probably refer to Maroons from St. Lucia and possibly also from Martinique.

132. Note Taylor, D.M., 1951, p.50, who points to French creole as the source of some Island Carib items: "Carib *carigi*, 'grapefruit' and *pasai*, 'passage' (conveyance as passenger) appear to have had their parent-forms in Creole French *chadec sadek* and *passay passai*, which have identical meanings!" Note that Breton, R., 1665, makes no references to "chadec" in either volume of his dictionary. The item was not in nineteenth century French according to Littré and is not in modern French according to Larousse's dictionary. Note however "CHARDON [*sic.*] ... Nom usuel de plusieus plantes feuilles et tiges épineuses ... " Larousse, 1975, p.298. St. Vincent is the closest island to St. Lucia; consequently if maroons escaping from Martinique ran to St. Lucia, it is likely that the maroon route also extended to St. Vincent.

Labat, J.B., 1700, pp.166-167, referring to maroons in St. Vincent writes that: "Besides the savages, this island is also inhabited by a great number of fugitive negroes for the most part from Barbados . . . ". However, as Barbados (Bridgetown) is about 110 miles from St. Vincent (Kingstown) while St. Lucia (Vieux-Fort) is only approximately 29 miles from St. Vincent (Porter Point) it is possible that the maroon influx from St. Lucia may have been either underestimated by Labat or that their numbers were not significant in 1700.

133. Taylor, D.M., 1951, p.47.

Part III.
Oral Literature.

1. Introduction.

Oral Literature

Oral literature world-wide has preceded written literature. In many cultures, however, the oral mode remained the dominant mode of communication for the majority of people, even after the advent of writing within those communities.

For Africans, the oral mode has been, and even up to today continues to be, the preferred mode for cultural dissemination. Consequently descendants of Africans in the Caribbean have continued to be affected by an oral tradition imported by them from Africa and readapted under the cultural conditions of the Caribbean.

'Caribbean Creole Languages in Caribbean Literature' outlines the African and Creole language inputs from this oral tradition which are evident in Caribbean literature.

'The African Presence in Caribbean Oral Literature' sets out a theoretical framework for the discussion of this oral tradition within the context of Caribbean oral and written literature.

This framework is expanded in 'The Writer and Audience: influences of the African oral tradition on Nigerian literature (oral and written)' to consider perspectives for linking the behaviour of African and Caribbean languages with the structure and meaning of African and Caribbean literature.

2. Caribbean Creole Languages in Caribbean Literature.

Introduction

The majority of the Caribbean peoples speak one of the following Creole languages: Creole English, Creole French or Creole Dutch. What is a Creole language? Every world language is or was a Creole language. Consider, for example, the Indo-European language-family in the case of the Romance languages: French, Spanish and Portuguese, for example, can be said to have developed from various forms of Creole Latin (see the General Introduction). In the case of the historically more recent Caribbean Creoles, however, both the African and the European language traditions have been brought to bear upon language development.

Consequently, while the vocabulary of Caribbean literature is from European languages, the language structures in which this vocabulary is used is of African origins.

Consider, for example, the equivalent realisations of 'to be' and the use of aspect in Creole English and Creole French:

To Be Or Not To Be?
Jamaican Creole: *i nais yes* — '(s)he *is* beautiful / handsome!'
    "she nice yes"
Caribbean French Creole: *i bèl* — 'Elle/Il *est* très belle/beau'.
    "(s)he beautiful"
In French, English and German, some form of the verb 'to be' would be required. This is not the case in the Creole languages in which *adjectival verbs* are used in situations where the above European languages would make use of the structure be + VERB. *bèl* and *nais* are both verbal and adjectival in function: *bèl* — 'to *be*

beautiful'; *nais* — 'to *be* beautiful'.

Compare this structure in the following African languages:

Yoruba:
    omi tutu — 'The water *is* cold'
    "water cold"
    eyawò mi atata — 'my wife *is* beautiful'
    "wife me beautiful"

Twi:
    ò fèfè — 'She *is* very beautiful'
    "she beautiful beautiful"
    ò bòni — 'She *is* bad'
    "she bad"

These fecund past influences find potent expression in present-day Caribbean literature, as indicated in the following parts from Brathwaite's poem *The Stone Sermon*:

    Sookey dead
    Sookey dead
    Sookey dead
    God a shark
    God a shark
    God a-bite him[1]

As seen in the above lines, no overt form of 'to be' is needed for the poet's message to be delivered:

Sookey ded — 'Sookey *is* dead'
God a shaak — 'God *is* a shark'

    This construction often typifies the speech of characters in the Caribbean novel, for example, in Selvon's *A Brighter Sun*: 'But Tiger we married now!'[2] — 'But Tiger, we *are* married now!'; as well as actual descriptions often aimed at conveying something typically Caribbean; for example, the description of a dance in Callender's short story *A Reasonable Man*: "Sometimes the dance-floor so crowded that everybody butting into one another . . ."[3]
Cf. English: 'Sometimes the dance floor *is* so crowded that everybody *is* butting into one another . . .'.

Aspect

The use of an aspect based, rather than a time based verbal system in Creole languages is also evident in the aspect based verbal systems of West african languages, for example:

Beni: (a) *iri èki* — 'I *am going* to market'
        Lit.: "I *Prog.* going to market"
        (b) *nodè iri èki* — 'Tomorrow I *will go* to market'
        Lit.: "tomorrow I *Prog.* go to market".

Hausa: (a) *Yau ina gida* — 'Today *I am* at home'
        Lit.: "today I (*Prog.*) home"
        (b) *Gobe ina gida* — 'Tomorrow *I will* be at home'
        Lit.: "tomorrow I (*Prog.*) home"

This use of aspect in the verbal system is again evident in present-day Caribbean literature, for example:
(a) "... Nobody ever help me. I catch me royal from de time Ah small..."
English: "Nobody ever help*ed* me. I ca*ught* my royal from the time I *was* small". (From S. Selvon, *A Brighter Sun*).[4]
(b) "And all the other people gather round and join in like a chorus".
Cf. English: 'And all the other people gather*ed* round and join*ed* in like a chorus'. (From *The Course of True Love* by Callender).[5]

Loan Translations

Although most of the vocabulary used in Caribbean literature is of European language origins, much of this vocabulary consists of loan translations which translated items from African languages into Creole languages, making use of this same European vocabulary:

(a) 'bad-mouth' as in:
yu bad mouth me — 'You slandered me'.
Cf. Hausa *mugun baki* — Lit. 'bad-mouth' as in: *Ka nuna mini mugun baki* — 'You slandered me'.
Lit.: "you show me bad mouth"
Cf. also Mandinka *da jugu*[6] — 'to slander'
Lit.: "mouth bad"
(b) 'big eye' as in:
yu av big ai — 'You are greedy'
Lit.: "You have big eye"
Cf. Igbo *anya uku* — 'greedy'
Lit.: "eye big".

Loans

There exist also in the Caribbean languages concepts and/or vocabulary from Creole languages which are of purely African origin, e.g., *obiya* — 'magic'
Cf. Twi *obiya* — 'magic' and *obiya fò* — 'sorcerer'
Lit. "magic person"
voudou — 'magic'; cf. Dahomean *Fōn vodū* — 'magic', 'religion'..
Both items are in both English and French Creole languages.

Conclusions

Given these differences, both systematic and conceptual, between European and Creole languages, it is important that the two language groups be differentiated, both in the minds of their speakers and the people with whom they communicate.

Ideas related to the supremacy of European language, for example, ideas such as a 'superior' elaborated code as opposed to a non-elaborated code are of little productive value. They have, anyway, been answered by Labov[7] who pointed to the greater succintness inherent in English of the Creole type, as opposed to English of the 'elaborated' type.

The point at issue, however, is not the judgement of one language group by criterion based in another. The yardstick of European languages cannot be used to judge Afro-Caribbean Creole languages or vice versa. Within each language is to be found its own music and its own inherent beauty.

As part of the literary artist's work is to crystalise the historical experience of his/her group, it is essential that the Creole language experience, within Caribbean literature, is appreciated as part of this artistic crystalisation.

Notes

1. Brathwaite, E., 1969. pp. 97 100.
2. Selvon, S., 1976, p.13.
3. Callender, T., 1975, p.90.
4. Selvon, S., 1976, p.175.
5. Callender, T., 1975, p.105.
6. Dalby, D., 1972, p.4.
7. Labov, W., 1970, on p.305 of Giglioli. P., (ed.), 1972.

3. The African Presence in Caribbean Creole Oral Literature.

If a leaf falls from a tree and nobody praises it, the leaf must praise itself — Nupe proverb.

All literature consists of a body of knowledge, past and present, within which a given culture is perpetuated by written and/or oral means. Oral literature in Creole languages spoken by the descendents of African slaves in the Caribbean is no exception. Given its African past, Creole oral literature shares many similarities, in form and content, with African oral literature.

In their content, the *konmpè lapèn* (Brer Rabbit) stories in St. Lucian Patwa have their correlate in Wolof tales about *leuk* and in Hausa tales about *zomo* — a hare who outwits his often physically superior adversaries.[1] The Jamaican Creole Brer Anansi stories, on the other hand, are perpetuations of tales also common to many West African ethnic groups about a spider who also outwits his foes by strategy, for example, Hausa *gizo* the spider and his wife *k'ok'i*, and the Twi/Fante *anansi* stories. It has been suggested that Anansi stories point to a coastal West African origin and Brer Rabbit/*konpè lapèn* stories to a 'savannah' geographical origin for the Caribbean Creole speakers concerned. This guideline, though useful, underestimates the relative nature of the terms 'coastal' and 'non-coastal'. The Twi/Fante ethnic groups are settled both inland and on the coast. This would suggest that diffusion of the 'coastal' spider tales further inland to 'savannah' groups like the Hausa and vice versa via ethnic groups having both an inland and coastal presence.

As far as form is concerned, the use of genres such as song, prose narratives, proverbs and riddles in both Creole and African languages also indicates a link. The high productivity of these genres in both language types, for example, is representative of the

past and present importance of these genres to African peoples.
Creole oral literature is, however, also indicative of the slavery-based social milieu in terms of which these languages developed. Patwa *ti jan* tales of a young man who defeats his social 'superiors' by cunning, for example, is indicative of a slave psychology suitable to a society where cunning was the only possible strategy against socially superior masters. The 'hare' and the 'spider' are famous for their cunning in the face of animals 'superior' in the social hierarchy. It is not unlikely that African societies themselves traditionally based on the institution of slavery fostered the spirit of cunning on the part of their slave castes, e.g. the *jòng* 'slave' versus *mansa* 'king' cycle of Bambara tales where *jòng* can only use cunning to defeat *mansa*.

It is this spirit of cunning welded to the will to survive under any circumstances and by any means necessary which typifies the African archetypal hero in both Creole and African languages.

The calypso is the song-form most studied in the light of African links. Hill suggests a tentative derivation of the word 'calypso' itself from Hausa *kaito*, when used in the phrase *Ba kaito*[2] — 'Without a (human) care', 'Don't give a damn (attitude)', via Trinidadian French Creole *kaiso*, and becoming Trinidadian English 'calypso'.[3]

Whatever the origin of the term, however, it, like all the other Creole oral genres, show similarities to their African sources in terms of i) archival function, ii) the use of praise and abuse, iii) their political function, iv) their social function and v) audience participation.

Archival function
Oral literature in Africa is a means by which items of historical value are stored. The classic example is that of the Mandinka singers *(girots)* who traditionally spent their lives reciting and memorising the history of the Manding Empire within the framework of their founder-emperor Sunjata. When Sparrow[4] sings

> *Melda woi yu mekin wedding belz*
> *Carrying mi nem to obiya man*

it is perhaps not an accident that this Twi/Fante item *obiya* 'magic', 'religion' has been perpetuated in song. When Sparrow sings *"Ah envi di Kongo man"* and regrets that *"Ah neva it a wayt mit yet"* ('I never ate a white person yet'), the history of Belgian-Congolese relations are perpetuated in the present for future memory.

The use of praise and abuse
Typical of African oral literature is the use of praise epithets, e.g. *izibongo* in Zulu and *rok'o* in Hausa as well as abuse, as in Hausa *habaici*. Individuals are praised or abused as rewards or penalties

for conforming or not conforming to the societies' values.
Calypso has perpetuated this tradition well, e.g. the following calypso in English Creole which is critical of past favouritism towards Castries (the capital of St. Lucia) but praises the singer's home-town (Vieux-Fort):

> *Dey centralaiz*
> *Everyting in Castries*
> *To reprizent St. Lucia . . .*
> *Well I from Vieux-Fort*
> *Vieux-Fort got di lot . . .*

Political function
Given the popularity of oral literature amongst Africans both inside and outside Africa, it is a device which even once totally Eurocentred African artists, poets, priests and politicians are coming to terms with. In more traditional African societies, e.g. the Hausa, musicians were often part of a socially distinct group who advertised the qualities of the rulers to the ruled and reminded the rulers of their shortcomings as discussed by the ruled.

The Hausa song in praise of a traditional ruler as "*Bajimin gidan Bello . . .*" 'Bull of the house of Bello'[5] is not unsimilar in its political purpose to Creole songs promoting national pride, e.g.

boyo-a mwen sé létiyo   'my intestines are the (water) pipes
. . . a la Gwadlup . . .   . . . of Guadeloupe . . .'

Social function
Unlike mechanical forms of communication, e.g. radio and television, nearly all individuals have access to the means of production in oral literature. Traditionally the songs attached to important festivals and rites of passage are known to all members of the African society concerned, e.g. Akan dirge songs are known by every functional member of Akan societies. Carnival in Trinidad is the occasion for relatively little-known individuals to perform their calypsoes before a large audience. This socially non-selective production has, therefore, allowed a creative safety-valve for at times anti-social feelings in Creole-speaking societies, as it traditionally has done in African societies.

Audience participation
Given its wide accessibility to all social groups, audience participation in African and Creole oral literature is a natural extension of this mode of communication itself. Hand-clapping as a means of emphasising the rhythm, the singing of the chorus, the sudden exclamations are part of the very essence of audience-participation in Afro-Caribbean oral literatuve as reflected within

the chorus/lead-singer structure of most Afro-Caribbean songs, as well as the 'toastings'[6] of the sound-system operator.

This past and present importance of Afro-Caribbean oral literature points to an even more productive future.

The Influences of Afro-Caribbean Oral Literature in Caribbean Written Literature

This productivity of Afro-Caribbean oral literature has been in some cases enhanced rather than hindered by written literature. In Selvon's 'A Brighter Sun' the hero, like "Man" in K. Armah's 'The Beautiful Ones Are Not Yet Born', is an illiterate: "He must hurry up and learn to read. He couldn't go around asking people questions all the time . . . ".[7] Central to the life of the novel, therefore, is the allusion to the oral tradition in terms of an extensive use of dialogue. This dialogue illustrates audience-participation in oral literature at its basest level where gossip is the equivalent to the 'News at Ten': "Like you know all my business... Ah know...! Everybody does know everybody else business in dis village. You ain't nobody special now,Yeah just like one ah we".[8] The hostility and fears of peoples used to an oral tradition in the face of a written tradition is exposed: "Yuh know why yuh mind turning nasty? Because yuh reading all dem book..."[9] as well as their jealousy: "Don't mind Sookdeo always drunk, he could read though, it have plenty people who does laugh at him, but they couldn't read! Read the news, Sookdeo . . . "[10]

Items preserved formerly only within the archives of oral literature are evident in both dialogue and in reported speech, e.g. items from Indian languages and from French Creole within the novel echo the oral mode within which these 'past' languages now function in Trinidad:

"Never seem you *bap* and mai when dey sleeping in de nnight?"[11]

"Later they ate roti and *bigan* in silence".[12]

"Mango *veh* . . . mango *do-dous...* "[13]

Even Selvon's style reflects an oral background, e.g. the use of drama for emphsis and repetition below find their highest peak in oral literature:

"As for the house he go be living in. Jees and ages!
. . . he giving feast for the poor. Jees and ages!"[14]

In Braithwaite's poetry[15] the oral tradition has found an even more suggestive vehicle. Drum-beat, one of the important non-verbal aspects of African oral literature, forms part of the life of his poems, e.g. in the poem *Tano*:

> dam
> dam
> damirifa due
> damirifa due
> damirifa due
> due
> due
> whom does death overlook?[16]

Audience-participation which characterises Afro-Caribbean oral literature is invited on the part of readers, e.g. in the poem *Bosompra*:

> can you hear
> can you hear me?[17]

and reflected in the frequent use of question forms, e.g. in the poem *Sunsum*:

> in our white teeth
> of praises?
> too rich?
> too external
> too ready
> with old ceremonial?[18]

Repetition as a marker of emphasis in African oral literature, reflected in the use of chorus and refrain, is a stylistic device which finds a home in Brathwaite's world. e.g. in the poem *New World A Comin*:

> It will be a long time before we see this land again . . .
> It will be a long time before we see these farms again . . .[19]

For the poet Walcott,[20] the background is that of both French Creole and some English Creole in St. Lucia. Again the oral tradition as the local news medium is blatantly apparent, e.g. in the poem *Sainte Lucie,* PartII:

> O so you is Walcott?
> you is Roddy brother?
> Teacher Alix son?[21]

What the poet means to 'everyman' is St. Lucia is in terms of his genealogy, not his poetic works, which, being mainly for 'educat' literates are too specialised a reference-point for the oral 'r media'. Repetition as a means of emphasis becomes not literary device but a means of explaining the Afro/Creole r non-African and non-Creole English, e.g. in the same p' told in Patwa (French Creole):

> moi c'est gens St. Lucie
> C'est la moi sorti;
> is there that I born.[22]

The last line in Creolized English both emr' lines and pleases foreign readers and, abo.

Note also that Part III of the poem "Iona: Mabouya Valley [A] Saint Lucian *conte* or narrative songs, heard on the back of an open truck travelling to Vieufort . . ." is in Patwa (French Creole):

    Ma Kilman, Bon Dieu punir 'ous,
    Pour qui raison parce qui'ous entrer trop religion,[23]

while Part IV is an English version of Part III:

    Ma Kilman God will punish you,
    for the reason that you've got too much religion. . .[24]

Emphasis is again thus achieved by a device also useful to non-Patwa speakers.

In Linton Kwesi Johnson's *Dread Beat and Blood*[25] (written version), the oral emphasis is also apparent, e.g. the use of repetition as a stylistic device:

    dem a laaf
    dem a talk dread talk
    . . . dem a skank . . .[26]

and the use of allusion to facts known to the audience as a means of increasing participation, e.g. his allusion to "HIP CITY" and "BRIXTON".[27]

Even his use of capital letters is suggestive of a wish to emphasis items in print in the same way they would be orally emphasised by loudness in voice quality. It is not surprising that, given these oral influences in Johnson's poetry, that he has returned to the oral mode by accompanying them with music in recorded form. One wonders if he is merely the forerunner, and if the other technological forms now available to Afro-Caribbean oral literature (i.e. tape, film and record) will not also be used by other members of our tradition.

Notes

1. The 'hare' stories are found in the languages of the 'savannah' geographical zone of West Africa as well as in most Bantu languages.
2. Hill, E., 1972, pp.55-69.
3. Ibid., pp.61-64.
4. A famous Calypsonean of Grenadian origin, based in Trinidad.
5. Sarkin Gobir na Isa (District Head of Sokoto) was so eulogised by the Hausa singer Narambad'a and his entourage.
6. A 'disc-jockey' or similar sound-system operator may add to a record being played by singing, talking or even clapping along with the music and/or song, usually making use of a connected microphone. 'Toastings' are at times available on the B-sides of certain Caribbean records.
7. Selvon, S., 1971, p.98.
8. Ibid., p.142.
9. Ibid., p.143.
10. Ibid., p.153.
11. Ibid., p.7.
12. Ibid., p.9.
13. Ibid., p.37.
14. Ibid., p.97.
15. Braithwaite, E., 1973.
16. Ibid., p.151.
17. Ibid., p.136.
18. Ibid., p.150.
19. Ibid., p.11.
20. Walcott, D., 1976.
21. Ibid., p.46.
22. Ibid., p.47.
23. Ibid., pp.48-49.
24. Ibid., pp.50-52.
25. Johnson, L.K., 1975.
26. Johnson, L.K., 1975, in the poem *Yout Scene*.
27. Idem.

4. The Writer and Audience: influences of the African oral tradition on Nigerian literature (oral and written).

Oral Literature

All literature consists of a body of knowledge, past and present, within which a given culture is perpetuated by written and/or oral means. Nigerian literature is no exception. All human literature was firstly passed on by word of mouth (i.e. orally) before it became written. In the Western Sudan oral literature was disseminated from at least the 14th century in the Mali-centred Mandinka Trade Empire by *griots*, the singers reciting the history of their group. Among the Greeks, it is suggested that the Illiad and Oddessy were circulated by a singer of tales,[1] before being written down by Homer.

With the advent of the Egyptian system of writing — heiroglyphics and their invention of paper (papyrus), the circulation of written literature began to take the place of oral literature. The advent of a wide circulation of written literature in Nigeria itself began with the use of *ajumi* (a script using Arabic characters) after the *Jihad* (Holy War) of Usman d'an Fodiyo in the writing of Hausa and Yoruba and was followed by the use of a Roman script for all Nigerian languages during and after the colonial period.

Literary Genres

Oral literature in Nigeria is usually in the following forms: riddle, proverb, song, tongue twister, poetry and prose narrative, including myth and legend. The popularity of each may differ within each society during different historical periods.

African Literature

Oral Literary Genres
1. riddle
2. proverb
3. song
4. tongue twister
5. poetry
6. prose narrative

Written Literary Genres
1. novel (may include all oral genres)
2. poetry (may include some oral genres)
3. play (may include all oral genres)

Use and Functions in Nigeria
1. Archival
2. Use of Praise and Abuse
3. Political Function
4. Social Function
5. Audience Participation

The Hausa novel may also include genres of oral origin, for example, *K'irare* (Praise Epithets) of *Gand'oki*:

> Bajimi d'an bajimi
> Sai ni gyauro mai ganin bad'i!²
> ('Only I the self-sown plant which
> will survive next year')

or proverbs, for example, in the novel *Shehu Umar*, after the Muslims successfully raided and enslaved the 'pagans'. The defencelessness of the non-Muslims is described in a proverb:

> Kafin su shiriya maharan sun yi nisa ...
> Babu dama su same su, na gaba ya yi gaba,
> na baya sai labari.³
> ('Before they prepared themselves the raiders had left ...
> there was no way of catching up with them, those ahead
> have gone on and of those left behind we only hear their stories').

However the written Hausa genres have also affected the oral genres. Hausa songs were formally a feature of the *Habe* non-Muslim kingdoms, full of reference to *bori* (spirit possession) and other non-Muslim behaviour. Islamic ideas, formerly mainly confined to Islamic verse (before Usman d'an Fodiyo's *Jihad*), are now evident in the song genre, e.g. in Shata's song *Yawon Duniya* (Worldly Wandering) the concept of the indivisibility of God (i.e. *Tawheed*) is evident:

> ... sai na tuna da nufin Allah
> dadai na tuna da nufin Allah ...
> Nas san Allah
> gud'a d'aya ne
> In ya kashe ni shi ke nan
> Kuma in ya bar ni shi ke nan ...
> '... then I remembered the will of God

Exactly, I remembered the will of God
I know that there is no God but God ...
That should he kill me, so be it
And that should be leave me alive, so be it . . .'

Whatever their background, these genres, in whatever Nigerian Society, Nigerian oral literature can also be analysed in terms of the following guidelines: i) archival function, ii) use of praise and abuse, iii) political function, iv) social function and v) audience participation.[4]

Differing popularity thus reflects the different systems of thought within of the cultures concerned at different historical periods. As African literature was primarily oral in origin, Hausa thought reflecting older traditional African beliefs, for example, in *bori* (spirit possession) is reflected in the older Hausa oral literature. On the other hand, Hausa Islamic thought is reflected in the newer Hausa written literature, particularly poetry in which Islamic concepts such as *Tasawwafi* — Sufism, *Tafsere* — 'commentary on the Koran', *Madahu* — 'panagyric or eulogy to the prophet Mohammed' or *Wa'azi* — 'admonitory verse (verse which warns against non-Islamic practices)'. An example of the latter is the poem *Tabban Hak'ik'an* (Be Sure Without a Doubt) by Usman d'an Fodiyo, where d'an Fodiyo warns his followers against using Islam as a disguise to cheat and oppress the people:

In fa ko ka zamo imanun mutane . . .
Wanda yaz zama imamu don cin mutane,
Shi wuta kan ci gobe tabban hak'ik'an . . .
('If you become an Imam (Prayer Leader) of the people . . .
The one who has become an Imam to cheat the people,
He shall burn in hellfire hereafter without a doubt'.)[5]

As previously suggested, literary genres can be separated on the basis of whether they were initially produced in an oral or a written form. This classification, however, is not as clear cut as suggested as the oral genres have obviously affected the written genres, for example, the Hausa novel may be regarded as a written version of Hausa prose narratives (*tatsuniyoyi*). This is evident in both the Hausa novels *Ruwan Bagaja*[6] and *Gand'oki*[7] in which the narrator is famous for his ability in oral literature, for example, in *Ruwan Bagaja*, the hero Alhaji Imam implies that he can tell longer stories than Koje Sarkin Labari (Koje Master Storyteller) before he begins telling his own tale:

To, duk kai labarunka ashe ba su fi a ba da su
daga safe zuwa magariba ba, har a ke kiran ka Koje
Sarkin labarai?[8]
('Really, with all your stories, they can only last from dawn to dusk,
but despite this you are called Koje Master Storyteller?')

while the character *Gand'oki* is praised because of his knowledge of both written and oral literature:

> Ka san irin labarin littattafai, ka kuma san irin
> labarin da mu ke so mu ji[9]
> ('You know written tales and moreoever you know the oral tales we like to hear'.)

Archival Function

Items of historical value are stored in African oral literature. In the Nigerian context,[10] a similar process can be observed. In the Hausa song *Wak'ar Indefenda* (Song of Independence),[11] for example:

> Yakutu na nan a Kogin Kuwara,
> "rubies be here in river Kwara
> jamfari inda Kogin Kuwara,
> garnets where river Kwara
> sulke yana nan a Kogin Kuwara,
> chain-mail armour be here in river Kwara
> takuban jihadi ga Kogin Kuwara . . .
> swords of *jihad* behold river Kwara . . ."
> 'There are rubies in the River Kwara,
> There are garnets in the River Kwara,
> There are suits of chain mail in the River Kwara,
> The swords from Usman 'Dan Fodiyo's
> *jihad* are in the River Kwara'[12]

The singer, in praising the River Kwara (River Niger), preserves an oral reference to the founding of the Hausa/Fulani caliphate by Usman 'Dan Fodiyo's *Jihad* which reached as far south as the river Niger (in the present Kwara state).

In Achebe's *Things Fall Apart*[13] on the other hand, evidence of pre-Christian (and perhaps post-Christian)Igbo beliefs are evident, for example, that there exist a whole range of inferior gods as well as a great God as expressed by the character Akanna to a white missionary (Mr Brown):

> We make sacrifices to the little gods, but when they fail and there is non-one else to turn to we go to Chukwu.[14]
> (i.e. . . . 'we go to the Supreme God').

Among the Yoruba also this archival function of oral literature is also evident, for example, in the following *Ijala Salute to the Olowu Lineage* reference is made to the past rulers of Owu Town:

> Owu Mojàèlè ti Oyèròkùn ti Gbèmsọ'ti
> Pákopii ti baba Afọ̀kọ̀làjà.[15]
> 'Owu whose citizens were skilled in matchet fights,
> Owu at one time ruled by Oyerokun and at another
> time by Gbemso'.

This use of oral literature, as an archive was, in fact, genetically or 'spiritually' emphasised by some African societies. Amongst the Wolof of Senegambia, for example, the daughter of a *griot* must give birth to another *griot* by 'mating' with the son of the *griot's* patron. In this way betrayal by the griot of his 'master's' family was thus genetically avoided. Among the Shona of Southern Africa, on the other hand, the singer inherited his role by the 'spiritual' ability to compose in the style of a dead singer. Once this ritual rite of passage had been accepted by the audience as evident in the singer's performance, the audience began to confirm his position as a singer.

This emphasis upon the role of the singer as the 'memory' of the group emphasises their value in African societies.

In the same way that the importance of a singer was measured by his/her popularity amongst his/her audience, so too the value of the songs were measured by the oral literary criticism of memory; as long as his/her works were valued they would be passed down from generation to generation of oral group memory.

Such group memory was of great importance in the perpetuation of African oral literature in the Caribbean under the conditions of plantation slavery. Under these conditions no specialist groups of singers survived and African oral literature became perpetuated in group performances of songs, riddles, proverbs etc.

Such group memory is evident in the short choral songs of African, Caribbean Creole, and ex-slave, societies. In St. Lucian Patwa, the short *Bèlè*, *Kèlè*, *Katoumba* and *Jout* songs can be sung as single chorus by non-specialists or as longer linked choruses by specialists, for example:

Koutoumba (non-specialist)
é tilolé a kòngo mònima (repeated chorus)
Unknown items the Kongo *Unkown item*
Koutoumba (specialist)
é tilolé a kòngo mònima
unknown items the Kongo unknown item
ndendèlo ti kòngo asou lamè maman
unknown item little Kongo upon sea mother
nou pa nan pèyi nou
we not in country our
nou pa nan lakai nou. . . .
we not in home us"
'. . . the Congolese descendent is on the sea mother
We are not in our country
We are not at home . . . '

In Gambian Krio similar choral songs are called *Gumbe* and in Senegalese Kriul such songs are called *Kumpo*. In both societies these choral songs also range from the few lines of non-specialists to the longer performances of linked choruses by specialists.

It is likely that group memory of similar forms of African oral poetry has perpetuated these songs for their present reintegration after slavery, by present day specialists, for example, the late Bob Marley.

As repetition of items is a linguistic devise to mark emphasis in African languages, it is likely that the repetition implied in the use of chorus is itself an emphatic device in African literature which is also used for marking items of value to former African societies within the Caribbean context. At times, despite such incantory repetition, the items perpetuated in Caribbean and other Creoles are beyond group memory, leaving only 'nonesence words'/'items of unknown origin' as a trace (see above). They are at times often sources of words of traceable African origin as well as oral references to documented history, for example, the reference to *ti Kòngo* — 'Kongo decendent' is correlated to the fact that people of African descent in St. Lucia, Caribbean, claim to be of two descent groups: i) *Jiné* — 'Guinea', or ii) *Kòngo* — 'Congolese'.

As the Congolese were one of the last groups of slaves imported in St. Lucia,[16] it is interesting that the *Katoumba* songs reflecting the historically more recent Congolese presence are more in evidence than songs reflecting the earlier Senegambian slaves (*Jiné*).

Repetition as a device for memorizing items of cultural value is also evident, where different genres exist as different performances of the same literary content (competence). For example the Hausa proverb:

> *Kaunar Bak'in Wake*
> "burning black bean"
> — 'Raw courage'

is also performed as a prose narrative about the reckless courage of the rebel slave Bak'inWake, who, rather than surrendering himself to abuse by his master, burnt himself and his master to death.

Although pointing to the African oral tradition's methodology of cross-referencing between genres, it is suggestive of the wider uses of repetition and incantation as a memory device integral even in the act of creation in a single literary genre, where different performances of the genre may not only 'perfect' the work artistically, but embed it deeper, in both the individual memory of the artist, and the collective memory of his audience. The Hausa singer's perfecting of his/her *bakandamiya (magnum opus)*[17] and Camara Laye's blacksmith forging his "perfect axe" both point to such an archival memory device:

> But what is an axe? I have forged thousands of them, and this will undoubtedly be the first of them all;

the others will have been no more than experiments
I made in order to forge the perfect axe.[18]

In this act of creation, the artist as well as his audience are therefore linked in the process of linking the ancestors with the living. To this extent Bob Marley has been a more effective archival source of African/Caribbean history of slavery and modern oppression than many African/Caribbean historians.

Use of Praise and Abuse

Praise is used in African oral literature to reinforce conformity to the particular society's values.

Amongst the Hausa, for example, *hak'uri* —'patience' linked with the Islamic idea of accepting fate (*tawakkali*) and descent from Usman 'Dan Fodiyo are positive social qualities; so it is for these qualities that the Sarkin Sudan, Ibrahim na Gwanatse, a direct decendant of Usman 'Dan Fodiyo is praised in the Hausa novel *Gand'oki:*

Ga alheri da hak'uri kamar k'asa[19]
"behold kindness and patience like earth"
'Behold his kindness and patience which was like the good earth'.

although from the point of view of the colonial troops fighting against him, he was a rebel and a slave trader.

Lack of generosity, especially to *marok'a* (praise singers), is, on the other hand, viewed as a negative social quality deserving of abuse (*habaici*) by the Hausa, for example:

kana da kamar ka bai wa yaro
"Your are with as if you give to boy
Riga ta wuyansa ka ke nema . . . [20]
Gown of neck his you are looking for"
— 'You pretend you will give a young man a gown,
but you really want the one he is wearing'.

In Igbo society the same use of praises are evident, in Achebe's *Things Fall Apart*, the character Amalinze is praised for his wrestling ability and given the praise name *Amalinze the Cat.*[21] Such praises in any society obviously change when social values change, for example, success at examinations more than wrestling seems to be a quality valued worthy of present Igbo praises:

O degbue madu[22]
"Killed people by his writing"
— 'He wrote excellently (in an examination)'.

Amongst the Yoruba, distinguished individuals are praised for conforming to socially accepted behaviour. For example, the 'Son of Akinlawon', C.C. Jegun, was praised for taking care of his relatives:

> Jagun t'o gb'ọmọ rè lọ́wọ́ ọ̀lẹ²³
> 'Jagun who rescued his child from sloth and shook
> off misery from his relative-in-law, actively
> going up and down like a thrift-club organiser'.

Political Function

Traditionally in Africa musicians often acted as mediators between rulers and their subjects, for example the *griots* (singers) amongst the Wolof and Mandinka and the *marok'a* amongst the Hausa.

In the Hausa song, *Bajimin Gidan Bello* ('Bull of the House of Bello'), Sarkin Gobir na Isa (then District Head of Sokoto) was being praised by the singer Narambad'a and his troupe. His qualities as a ruler of an imposing personality were also advertised by the singer Narambad'a:

> *Babban dutse a hange ka nesa,*
> "great rock one see you from far-off
> *A ishe ka soronka ya tsar ma kowa*
> one meet you palace you it surpasses indeed all others"
> — 'Great rock you can be seen in the distance
> You may be sought for in your palace which surpasses
> all other (palaces)'.

Singers may also hint at the weak qualities in their patron, and due to which their patron may be losing political support, for example in:

> Look not with too friendly eyes upon the world,
> Pass your hands over your face in meditation,
> The bull-elephant is wise and lives long.²⁴

In the above praise epithet, one of the emirs of Zazzau is asked not to be too friendly in his relations with people outside the Hausa/Islamic community, but to copy the silent self-sufficiency of the bull-elephant.

Among societies where no single overt leader is recognised (i.e. aecephalous societies) for example Igbo societies, an oracle, as in *Things Fall Apart* may tell a person how he/she is conforming, or not, to the politics of his/her tribe or clan:

> You Unoka, are known in all the clan for the weakness of you matchet and your hoe. When your neighbours go out . . . to cut down virgin forests, you sow your yams on exhausted farms that take no labour to clear . . . Go home and work like a man.²⁵

Similarly in Yoruba, distinguished personalities and particular lineages are praised for continuing aspects of political behaviour which their ancestors were famous for, for example, the Mode lineage of Iresa are praised for their ability to get cooperation from their subordinates:

Ọmọ Amòdò[26]
'Offspring of he – whom – people – get – to – know – and thereafter – cling – to him'

In voicing the views of the ruled to the rulers, Bob Marley's protest in songs such as *Concrete Jungle* expresses the frustrations of former agricultural peoples in concrete jungles to the international rulers of these concrete jungles. Marley further extended his role as a singer/politician in his Jamaican Peace Concert to urge peace between the violent political supporters of Manley and Seaga as well as his songs to encourage African political independence in general and Zimbabwe's independence in particular.

Social Function

African literature was, and to a large extent still is, closely tied to acts of social participation. Among the Hausa prose narratives (*tatsuniyoyi*) are a method of analysing social behaviour in terms of Islamic norms. In the tale *Munafunci Dodo, ya kan ci Mai shi* (Hypocracy is a Monster Which Kills its Creator),[27] hypocracy is seen to fail in destroying a family. In many African and Caribbean prose narratives, smaller animals outwit animals 'superior' in the animal hierarchy, for example, Hausa *Zaki* 'Lion' and *Giwa* 'Elephant'. It is not unlikely therefore, that these stories function as a safety valve for the anti-social feelings, even though in fantasy, of the people at the bottom of the social pile both in African and Caribbean societies. The common man can identify with *Zomo* (Rabbit), and *Gizo* (Spider), not with *Giwa* (Elephant); with *Jòng* (Slave), not with *Mansa* (King), (characters from African prose narratives).

Among the Igbo Achebe tells us:

> the art of conversation is regarded very highly and proverbs are the palm oil with which words are eaten.[28]

At face value this statement cannot be immediately related to a social function, but if we consider the difficult social circumstances in which such proverbs may be used, we may begin to appreciate this statement. In *Things Fall Apart* Okoye asks *Okonkwo*'s father, *Unoka*, to pay his debt, but, in order not to insult Unoka, in order to respect Unoka as a human being, as part of the community (*umunna*),[29] he uses proverbs to hint at his wish to be repaid:

Okoye said the next half a dozen sentences in proverbs.
... he spoke for a long time, skirting round the subject and then hitting it finally ... he was asking Unoka to return the two hundred cowries ... ³⁰

Amongst the Yoruba Ijala chants are performed at some of the rites of passage, for example, death and marriage. The extreme emotions which may characterize these events are given creative release by the Ijala singer. For example, the relatives and friends of a dead hunter are given some comfort in his possible reincarnation:

Ògúndiji Qyaníyí Apàmòsàsè
Ódi gbéré
Ódi fíró àrínnako³¹
'Ogundiji Qyaniyi, killer of leopard for a feast
He is now a far, far abode.
He is now the occasional ghostly appearance to a traveller on the road!'

Audience Participation

In African oral literature, the gap between the audience and the performer is one that both parties expect to be bridged. Before a story is begun in almost all African and Nigerian cultures the permission of the audience is invoked by the use of a set formulae, for example in Hausa:

Gata nan gata nan ku (Narrator)
(Formula for beginning a prose narrative)
Ta zo mu ji ta (Audience)
"it come we hear it"
— 'Let us hear it'.

In the performance of some oral genres, there may indeed be no difference between the performers and the audience, for example in *Things Fall Apart* when some of the young men of Umuofia decide to sing their criticism of those who captured them; it is a communal song sung by all of them who are both the performers and the audience:

Kotma of ash buttocks,
He is fit to be a slave (chorus)
The white man has no sense,
He is fit to be a slave (chorus)³²

The chorus in many songs may in fact be the traditional outlet for such audience participation in many African and Nigerian cultures. Amongst the Yoruba descent groups in Sierra Leone and Gambia, for example, wedding songs are mainly composed of a single chorus sung by the audience accompanying the bride:

> *Yawo mami don kam,*
> *òkò want yu de . . .*
> 'Yawo's mother has come,
> òkò wants you · ·
> Cf. Yoruba: *yawo* — 'bride', and *òkò* — 'bridegroom'

To the extent that all language acts are cooperative events, presupposing turn-taking, audience participation can be seen as part of the actual artistic event in which both the writer and his audience are participants. As a language based phenomenon, audience participation can, therefore, be structured into an utterance based analysis in which the writer/artist is also included:

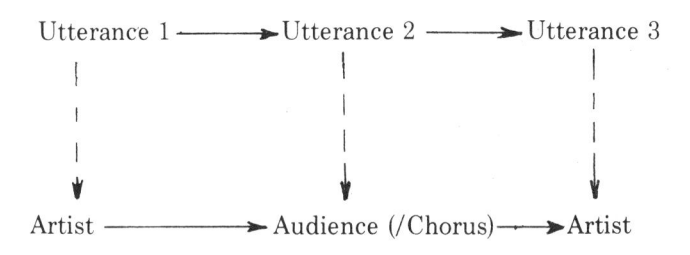

```
Utterance 1 ────────▶ Utterance 2 ────────▶ Utterance 3
    │                      │                      │
    │                      │                      │
    ▼                      ▼                      ▼
Artist ──────────────▶ Audience (/Chorus) ──▶ Artist
```

Although such an analysis would suggest a stimulus/response psychological model, the cybenetic principle involved in when exactly the audience/chorus interpose in the main song, is not clear, although, in the case of Hausa, the type of audience/choral intervention has been well documented (i.e. *amshi, karb'i, karb'eb'eniya* — 'choral responses').[33] It is suggested that the idea of 'official absence may form part of the basis for such a principle of audience/chorus intervention in that the audience/chorus may feel compelled to interpose a chorus, a clap or an exclamation at points of performance breaks where the 'official absence' of audience/choral intervention would be contrary to cultural norms. In the pan-African feature of the use of formulae to begin a narrative, for example, there would be a performance break or 'official absence' if the audience failed to respond to the formulae used by the narrator, e.g.:

> Narrator: *Ga ta nan gata nan ku!*
> (Utterance 1) (Hausa prose narrative beginning formulae)
> Audience: (Official absence)
> (Utterance 2)

In the same way that drumming requires a minimum of two beats, the audience provides the African artist with a 'second beat' which the culture compels them to supply.

Conclusions

Although a functionalist view has been emphasised in this chapter, other philosophical views can be used in the analysis of the writer and his/her audience in the African/Caribbean setting, for example, sociological, psychological, evolutionist, entertainment, historical/geographical and ethnographic.

The functionalist view, however, proved more useful in being able to also include the above perspectives, for example, archival function can be viewed as an aspect of a sociological analysis of African oral literature within which all the other philosophical perspectives above can be seen as processes in the achievement of this archival function of the African artist and his audience.

It has been fashionable to make synchronic and isolated studies of African oral literature, under ethnic terms such as Hausa, Mandinka, Tiv etc. While this reflects an ethnic political base in analysing the African artist and his audience, comparative studies across these ethno-political bases, may suggest larger areas of common ground for theoretical analysis.

Notes

1. Lord, A.B., 1960.
2. Bello, A.M. , 1972, p.1.
3. Balewa, A.T., 1966, p.5.
4. Adopted from Part III, ch.3.
5. *Wak'ok'in Hausa*, 1972, p.32.
6. Imam, .A.A., 1966, pp.1-2.
7. Bello, A.M., 1968, p.2.
8. Imam, A.A., 1966, p.20.
9. Bello, A.M., 1968, p.2.
10. Examples will be from the major Nigerian ethno-linguistic groups only: Hausa, Yoruba and Igbo.
11. By Sarkin Tabshi Alhaji Mamman.
12. Items enclosed in "..." are literal translations and those in '...' are free translations.
13. Achebe, C., 1980.
14. Ibid., p.12.
15. Babalola, S.A., 1976, pp.142-143.
16. See Part I, ch.3, Historical Overview.
17. Muhammed, D. in Abalogu, U.N., Ashiwanju, G. and Amadi Tshiwala, R. (eds), 1981, pp.57-70.
18. Laye, C., 1956, p.236.
19. Bello, A., 1972, p.14.
20. Gidley, C.G.B., 1975, pp.113-114.
21. Achebe, C., 1958, p.3.
22. Egudu, R.N. in Ogbalu, F.C., Emananjo, E.N. (eds), 1975, p.117.
23. Babalola, S.A., 1976, pp.202-203.
24. Finnegan, R., 1975, p.115.
25. Achebe, C., 1980, p.13.
26. Babalola, S.A., 1976, pp.138-139.
27. Imam, A., 1972, vol. 3, pp.74-95.
28. Achebe, C., 1980, p.5.
29. Cf. the above Igbo term with Common Bantu *munthu* — person and Hausa *mutum* — person.
30. Achebe, C., 1980, p.5.
31. Babalola, S.A., 1976, pp.276-277.
32. Achebe, C., 1980, p.123.
33. King, A. and Zurmi, A.I. in Abalogu, U.N., Ashinwaju, G and Amadi-Tshiwala, R. (eds), 1981, pp.98-135.

Part IV.
Creoles and Education.

1. Introduction.

Education

Africans in Africa and their Caribbean descendants have always had a high regard for learning and education. For me this belief is always summed up by St. Lucian peasant women who laboured in the fields so that their children could go to school. Such women would always proudly say to you:

mwen	ka	pòté	ich	mwen	asou	tèt	mwen
I	Prog.	carry	child	me	on	head	me

— 'I (despite my poverty) will protect my children from poverty by sending them to school and pay for the cost through my own suffering.'

On coming to Britain, however, Caribbean respect for education seems to have suffered severe blows in the face of racism and a sad weakening of the strength of such positive ancestral beliefs.

The language issue has often dominated the education debate with respect to Caribbean pupils.

In 'English as a Second Language and the Teaching of English to Pupils of Caribbean Origin in Britain', second-language approaches are suggested to have some useful guidelines which may help in the teaching of Standard English to pupils of Caribbean origin.

'Oral Languages, Power and Education: a comparative survey of English and St. Lucian practices' analyses the different approaches to Creoles in the Caribbean and in Britain, while highlighting the question of political power as a key issue in the development of Creole languages.

'Creoles in Voluntary Adult Education : the Caribbean Communications Project's experience' focusses on how Creole language features affect the written and oral performances of French Creole speakers, learning to read and write, through the efforts of a Caribbean voluntary literacy project in London, the Caribbean Communications Project (CCP).

In 'Recommendations for a Productive Use of Creoles in Teaching' guidelines have been developed, from my own teaching and lecturing experiences, for the inclusion of the use of Creole languages within the British and other educational systems.

2. English as a Second Language (ESL) and the Teaching of English to Pupils of Caribbean Origin in Britain.

Having arrived in England from the Caribbean island of St. Lucia at the age of 11, I have, from the moment I heard English spoken by English people, been very aware of the differences between how they spoke English and the way I did.

I remember practising the word toilet in an effort to change my St. Lucian pronunciation [tɔilɛt] to the working-class English [tɔilaʔ] of my schoolmates. I remember sudden pains in my jaw as my mouth, fed up of practising unfamiliar English sounds, clicked back into positions it found more comfortable.

My shocks with language differences were, however, not restricted to English. I remember doing very badly in a French examination because I had, mistakenly, thought that French was nearly the same thing as my French Creole mother tongue, and thus needed no special effort by me.

The most remembered crisis, however, has been the terrible headaches, related to the psychological trauma that was not explained to me, namely, the reasons why the language going on inside my head was not the same as the Standard English that I used, learned and tried to express myself in, and also, the reasons why the ways in which I wanted to 'play' with English, in any creative work, were not always 'acceptable'.

In examining English as a Second Language, I hoped to deepen my insight into the reasons why the study and use of English are problematic for pupils who, like me, are of Caribbean origin; as well as to consider some solutions to these problems with English, shared also by pupils educated in the Caribbean, e.g.:

> ... I wanted to follow in their footsteps and go to a university. All the black boys were similarly disposed. We all had two major problems — poverty and the *English Language*.[1] (my emphasis)

In this chapter I will, therefore, look at the arguments for and against the use of E.S.L. or E.S.L. approaches, in the teaching of English to pupils of Caribbean origin.

Reasons against E.S.L. approaches with pupils of Caribbean origin

The most evident reason for not using E.S.L. approaches with pupils of Caribbean origin, is the assumption that they all speak a 'dialect' of English, depending upon the Caribbean island concerned, e.g. 'Jamaican dialect', 'Barbadian dialect' etc.

The basis for defining their linguistic background in 'dialect' terms, is that the majority of the lexical items used in these 'dialects' are English, e.g. Cf Jamaican [da:g] with Standard English [dɔg]. Their linguistic background is, therefore, seen as a variant of Standard English (henceforth SE), on the same level as London Cockney, Yorkshire and other English dialects.

Mistakes made by Caribbean pupils in the use of English would, from this perspective, not warrant the extremes of E.S.L. approaches. Some Caribbean adults and parents may also share this perspective that their Caribbean use of English is a variant in the many world uses of English, e.g. Australian and American. As such, an E.S.L. point of view could not be considered, as they could argue that "... in a certain sense English is not a foreign language to West Indians".[2] The latter point of view is often related, in extreme cases, to a Caribbean perspective that true 'development' in language, and in other fields, must be along the axis of 'superior' European culture, which is to be absorbed, and mimiced by Caribbeans in order that the latter become 'civilized' and 'equals' to Europeans. From such a perspective all links to Europe, including the English language, must be heightened, as all other points of view would lead to 'barbarism'.[3] A consideration of E.S.L. would just not be entertained.

However, even when E.S.L. perspectives on teaching English to pupils of Caribbean origin have been considered, it has been suggested that, when they assume that Caribbean language influences upon English are merely interferences in the acquisition of SE by Caribbean pupils, they do not have much success:

> ... Applications of second and foreign language teaching techniques which highlighted the issue of language interference West Indian language-forms, however, did not simply interfere, they OBSTRUCTED[4] (sic).

E.S.L. approaches to teaching SE to pupils in the Caribbean itself, can be opposed on purely economic grounds, as the cost of producing E.S.L. materials for developing Caribbean countries is prohibitive.[5] As most Caribbean countries have, so far, not seen the need to bear the cost of E.S.L. teaching, as a crucial development necessity, it is unlikely that the British taxpayer would back the production of such E.S.L. materials, for pupils of Caribbean origin in Britain.

Experiences in E.S.L. teaching for pupils of Asian origin in Britain have been severely criticised, by some Asian linguists and educationalists, as inefficient and racist, e.g.:

> There are teachers who speak to these children in an idiosyncratic variety of 'pidgin' English all in the name of language teaching. E.S.L. teaching is separate but certainly not equal.[6]
> ... the majority of E.S.L. teachers have not been able to break away from the legacy of paternalism and are quite uncritical and unconscious of their own inherited attitudes towards black pupils other than collusion with the racist assimilationist model.[7]

If Asian educationalists, sensitive to a longer experience of E.S.L. approaches in teaching Asian pupils, are unhappy, it is unlikely that E.S.L. approaches with pupils of Caribbean origin would be welcomed by Caribbean parents, already suspicious of any other 'special treatments', such as E.S.N. Schools (schools for the Educationally Sub-Normal) formerly widely advocated for their children in English schools.[8]

Added to this suspicion, the Caribbean desperation to be carbon copies of Europe, (above), then one can understand the hostilities of Caribbean parents to E.S.L., or any other educational initiatives, which single out pupils of Caribbean origin. For example, two Caribbean parents' associations in the London Borough of Waltham Forest (LBWF), the West Indian Educational Committee and the Caribbean Progressive Association, have complained against the special approaches of the West Indian Supplementary Service (WISS), and of the LBWF, in teaching aspects of Caribbean Culture and language to pupils of Caribbean origin, during school hours, when English pupils are being taught academic subjects. As a consequence of these complaints, the E.S.L. service of the LBWF, the English Language Service (ELS) has deliberately avoided any E.S.L. approaches to pupils of Caribbean origin, although fully aware of some of their possible applications.[9]

The linguistic arguments against E.S.L. approaches with pupils of Caribbean origin

The main linguistic strand of the argument against the use of E.S.L. approaches with pupils of Caribbean origin, is the proposition that the pupils and parents speak a Caribbean dialect of English, and, as such, have no more need for E.S.L. than do the pupils of English dialect-speaking parents.

Another linguistic argument against E.S.L. has been the implications of any special E.S.L. treatment of pupils of Caribbean origin, may place undue emphasis upon the pupils' home linguistic repertoires, when what is needed is a massive immersion of the pupils in Standard English, which is, after all, the language they need for academic achievement and upward social mobility in England.

Another linguistic argument has been that the initial assumptions of E.S.L. for pupils of Caribbean origin, were based upon the idea of teaching various English target structures to pupils, from a structuralist linguistic perspective.[10] As structuralist views have been partly discredited by Chomskean[11] and Communicative[12] linguistic perspectives, all such initial E.S.L. approaches for pupils of Caribbean origin, have been similarly discredited. The West Indian Supplementary Service (WISS), as well as ILEA, had both formerly developed structuralist materials for use with pupils of Caribbean origin, but, with anti-structuralist views, such materials were abandoned. For example, the Dialect Kit, of the ILEA Centre for Urban Educational Studies, as well as former WISS materials, all had a structuralist bias; in the case of the WISS materials, the verb 'to be' and the -ing suffix, which both cause problems to pupils of Caribbean origin,[13] were to be practised in a structuralist manner. Both the ILEA Dialect Kit, and the WISS materials, are now no longer in wide use by both organisations, who also abandoned the E.S.L. initiatives linked to these structuralist materials.

Sociolinguistic theory may also provide arguments against the use of E.S.L. approaches for Caribbean pupils, from the perspectives of appropriacy and usage. From the latter viewpoints, it could be argued that in the home, and during inter-Caribbean communication, Caribbean language forms are more appropriate, but that for communication with the English community, particularly in the formal social context of a school, Standard English, without any input from Caribbean language forms, and thus without any implications for E.S.L., should be used.

Arguments for E.S.L. approaches with pupils of Caribbean origin

It has been argued that pupils of Caribbean origin make use of language forms which are different to those of Standard English. It has been also argued that these language forms are the result of a mixture between African syntactic forms and English vocabulary, which have combined to form new languages i.e. Afro-Caribbean/

Creole languages.[14]

From this perspective, some of the deviant language forms in English, used by pupils of Caribbean origin, may be the result of their bilingual social context: "Children from the Afro-Caribbean background may have a bilingual situation on their hands".[15] As bilinguals, pupils of Caribbean origin could only profit by E.S.L. approaches to English teaching, which would, by their nature, take their bilingualism into account in teaching them English.

E.S.L. could form the context within which Afro-Caribbean languages and cultures could be integrated in British schools:

> ... the need now is not for more experiments on the effects of bilingual education but for finding out ways of integrating languages and cultures in British schools.[16]

A recognition of Creoles as languages, rather than dialects would decrease the alienation of pupils of Caribbean origin from the school:

> ... a major reason for the alienation of many children from the ethos of school is that school ... often seeks to denigrate and belittle children's language.[17]

Linguistic arguments for E.S.L. approaches with pupils of Caribbean origin

The main linguistic strand of the argument for E.S.L. approaches with pupils of Caribbean origin, is that they are bilinguals, who speak a different language from English.

From their very origins, however, Creole languages have necessitated an awareness of second language perspectives. Andersen, for example, approaches Creoles: "... from the perspective of the acquisition of a second language as a first language".[18]

All the original speakers of Caribbean Creole languages spoke a European or African mother-tongue and the original pidgins, (from which the Creoles emerged) as a second language. When the pidgins became the first languages of both the Europeans and Africans in the Caribbean, the pidgins thus became Creole languages of the Caribbean.

If this is the case, then E.S.L. methodologies could only complement a language background, like the Caribbean and its diaspora in England, in which second language acquisition is not unfamiliar.

Creole languages have also been viewed as interlangues, generated by speakers who have limited social opportunities for acquiring Standard English.[19] As interlangues, they could only benefit from E.S.L. approaches, which would facilitate learning contexts for the changing of interlangue Caribbean language forms, into their SE targets.

It has been argued that greater awareness of contrasts between the SE target language and the Creole languages, will result in a greater control over both languages.[20] An E.S.L. perspective could only serve to heighten, through contrastive and error analysis, contrasts between the two languages.

Advocates of monoliterate bilingualism for Creole speakers[21] with which SE is the target written language, and Creole languages are recognised as valid oral languages, also imply the usefulness of E.S.L. perspectives. From a monoliterate bilingual perspective, the target language of writing, i.e. English, has a second language status to the learner, who is more familiar to his/her oral Creole mother-tongue. English, as an established and recognised second language, could only benefit from being taught via E.S.L. methods.

Conclusions

The arguments for and against the use of E.S.L. teaching for Caribbean pupils all gravitate around questions about the status of the home language of these pupils. Where viewed as dialects of English, E.S.L. views are not considered useful; where viewed as languages, E.S.L. is considered useful.

The arguments for the Creole to be considered a dialect, are more popular in England than in the Caribbean, where the case for Creoles as separate languages has greater currency, e.g. as suggested by the members of the Society for Caribbean Linguistics and the Folk Research Centre, St. Lucia.

It has been suggested that Creole languages in Britain are mainly the languages of Caribbean parents. It has, however, also been pointed out that many of the supposed non-Creole speaking pupils of Caribbean origin in Britain, do speak Creole as a playground in-group language.[22]

The main problem, to me, seems to have been one of acceptance by both Caribbeans and non-Caribbeans that the Creole languages used by pupils of Caribbean origin, are not Standard English, and that, like all other languages, they can and will be learned across generations, despite any social legislation by parents and/or educational authorities, that they should not be learned; as well as despite any descriptions of them as non-languages.

E.S.L. teaching would have been of even more use to Caribbean parents immediately on their arrival in Britain, but, unlike the case with other immigrant groups, no money was spent by the British community to facilitate the learning of English by the Caribbean immigrants of the 1950s and 1960s.

A generation later, the acquisition of SE still remains problematic for the children of these Caribbean immigrants. E.S.L., or E.S.L. teaching methods, could provide more coherent explanations for the consistent errors in the English used by pupils of Caribbean origin, as well as provide strategies for their eradication. E.S.L. is, however, not considered as applicable to these pupils as their language has been defined, not by them, but by others, as a dialect, while their errors in SE are considered at best inconsistent errors in SE, and, at worst, as evidence of their cognitive deficiency.

Notes

1. Delsol, S., 1984, p.1
2. Figueroa, J.M., 1980, p.9. See also ch.3, West Indian Supplementary Service (WISS), London Borough of Waltham Forest (LBWF).
3. Fanon, F., 1967, p.13.
4. Whittingham, E., 1982, p.9.
5. Craig, D., 1978, pp.16-17.
6. Alladina, S., 1982, p.15.
7. Mukherjee, T. 1983.
8. Coard, B., 1971.
9. Members of WISS and ELS, in conversation in London, 1984. See also ch.3, West Indian Supplementary Service (WISS), London Borough of Waltham Forest (LBWF).
10. Palmer, F., 1971, pp.107-134.
11. Chomsky, N., 1957.
12. Littlewood, W., 1981. See also ch.3, WISS.
13. Trudgill, P., 1974, ch.3.
14. Comhaire-Sylvain, S., 1936.
15. Ngcobo, A.B., 1984.
16. Alladina, S., 1982.
17. Richmond, J., 1966/67.
18. Andersen, R.W., 1978, p.19.
19. Richards, J., 1972, pp.73, 78-79.
20. D'Costa, J., 1981.
21. Craig, D., 1978, p.4.
22. Brandt, G. Lecture and discussions at the University of London, Institute of Education, 1983.

3. Oral Languages, Power and Education: a comparative Survey of St.Lucian and English practices.

The oral use of language historically preceded the written use of language. The written use of language has superceded the oral use of language partly because the written mode is a superior mode, (at least with respect to quantities of information stored) for the surposes of record keeping. The greater influences by the written mode, however, is that of political/military power.

The written mode has often been used by some literate groups to confuse non-literates and as part of the apparatus for oppressing them. The literate Mandinka and Fulani, for example, convinced their largely Bambara slave class (in the 17th Century in the Manding Trade Empire), that writing was some form of magic belonging only to the rulers.[1]

In more recent times, educational achievement has been largely confined to ability at the written mode. Examinations are largely written and the oral memory of the Homeric bard and the Mandinka *griot* are not the basis of an 'educated standard'.[2]

The cleavage between the powerful and the powerless, between the 'developed' and the 'underdeveloped' world may[3] also coincide with the cleavage between the literate and non-literate. In their bid to close the literacy gap, the peoples of the underdeveloped world have embarked on literacy schemes with extreme zeal. In many respects, the underdeveloped and developed peoples have been quite happy with this educational aim. In a number of cases, however, educational activities in both the developed and underdeveloped world suggest a questioning of this aim, or at least of this aim in its crude form.

An example of this questioning has been the use/non-use of Caribbean Creole[4] languages in Britain and in the Caribbean.

As I had studied[5] the oral language of St Lucia i.e. Patwa (a French Creole),[6] I wanted to use this chapter as a means of contrasting sociopolitical and educational developments related to Patwa in St. Lucia with the same developments to Creole languages in England.

In order to make these comparisons, and to highlight some of the issues at stake I, firstly, investigated the following with respect to St. Lucia:

i) The historical experience of oral and written languages in St. Lucia.
ii) The contemporary choices in relation to Patwa, within the previous fourteen years in St. Lucia (1969-1983) as reflected in written material published or presented in St. Lucia.
iii) The Folk Research Centre, in St. Lucia and the Society for Caribbean Linguistics as examples of two Caribbean organisations with aims and objectives with respect to Patwa and other Caribbean creole languages.

I then investigated the following London organisations with respect to their aims and objectives regarding creole languages in England:

i) The West Indian Supplementary Service (WISS), London Borough of Waltham Forest.
ii) The English Language Service, London Borough of Waltham Forest.
iii) The Caribbean Communications Project (CCP), London.

I summarise my comparisons between St. Lucian and English practices in the conclusion of this chapter.

The historical experience of oral and written languages in St. Lucia

St. Lucia is situated in the Windward Island chain of the Caribbean islands known as the West Indies. Although it frequently changed hands between the French and the English between 1600 and 1813, the island was finally ceded to Britain in 1813 although it has remained primarily African and French in culture.[7]

Language has reflected such cultural influences as well as those of the original Arawak and Carib population and the cultural expressions of the imported African slaves, which can be related to the introduction of the languages below, at the approximate dates, and in the following order:

Approximate Dates	Language(s) introduced into St. Lucia
1600	Arawak
	Carib
	Island Carib
	French
1700	Black Carib
	African languages (Wolof, Mandinka, Igbo etc.)
	Patwa (French Creole)
1800	English
	Hindi
1900	English Creole of Patwa structure[8]

Of the above, Patwa, English and English Creole of Patwa structure have remained as living languages of everyday usage. The remainder have remained as perpetuations of past languages in Patwa with the exception of Hindi which has very few speakers and is in the process of 'dying' without leaving many traces of its former more widespread existence amongst the East Indians of St. Lucia.[9]

The Amerindian groups were not literate.[10] Their Black Carib descendants in St. Lucia have continued this oral tradition, in the Black Carib language.[11]

The Africans imported into St. Lucia also came with an oral language inheritance, although some may have arrived in St. Lucia and other parts of the Caribbean with their own writing systems, e.g. the *Ajumi* script of the Hausa of Northern Nigeria.

The French and English of St. Lucia brought with them a written tradition. Although Hindi has its own written tradition, the limited evidence now available suggests that the East Indians who came as indentured labourers to St. Lucia were largely non-literate.[12]

The literacy brought by the French and the English was, however, limited, as literacy was confined to a few clerks, hired by the French and English elite/slave master group, to do the writing for them.[13]

Unlike other colonial territories e.g. Senegal, Sierra Leone, Martinique, Barbados and Jamaica, St. Lucia was never a centre around which the hub of colonial policy in overseas territories turned. It began instead, as a subsequent and smaller colony after the successful French colonisation of Martinique (to the North of St. Lucia); it was from its origin a society of semi-marginalised French peasants, who chose to live away from central authority in Martinique. Such men were unlikely to have been literate.[14] This prior marginal nature of St. Lucian white society was in fact increased when St. Lucia became a haven for runaway slaves.[15]

With the English conquest of St. Lucia, the same French ruling group and their clerks remained despite changes in political control. One British ruler in St. Lucia, Breen, however provides an exception to the presence of mainly non-literate rulers in early St. Lucian society by his own *written* description of a French and Patwa speaking society whose main cultural activities e.g. the singing competitions of the two St. Lucian 'flower societies'[16] are orally performed.

The earliest contexts necessitating the use of writing in St. Lucia included the registration of slaves imported into the island, according to their African origins, age and residence.[17] These documents were initially in French and, with the final British acquisition of the island in 1813, in English.

The next major use of written documents was by the clergy who used writing to keep records of the baptisms, births and deaths in their parishes.

Written documentation was otherwise restricted to the few letters of the St. Lucian slave masters to their relatives in the metropoles. Indeed, writing under English or French control, for both administrative and commercial purposes, was left in the hands of clerks whose linguistic abilities were at times commended.[18]

This division between literate and non-literate suggests the following social divisions in early St. Lucian society:

Powerful	Less Powerful	Powerless
French & English rulers	Clerks & Clergy	Slaves
(Mainly non-literate)	(Literate)	(Mainly non-literate)

Literacy as a fact did not directly coincide with power, but, as previously suggested, literacy was used as part of the apparatus of the powerful St. Lucian rulers for their oppression of their powerless slaves.

There is tentative evidence which suggests that the society was so orally oriented, even in its upper strata, that drums and a town crier were employed in the promulgation of laws.[19]

There are, however, two periods during which writing as an activity increased in the island: i) during the French Revolution and ii) after the final British invasion of St. Lucia. During the first period, St. Lucians in general, both slave and free embraced the ideas of *Liberté et fraternité* both in its 'reign of terror' and the use of the guillotine for killing many of the slave masters.

The non-literate slaves, however, did not share in the written dissemination of the ideas of the French Revolution which were diffused by some of the revolutionary leaders, in written form amongst themselves, and orally to their non-literate black citizens:

> Nous benissons la revolution, nous admirons la constitution qu'elle nous a donée nous la regardons comme la plus belle ouvrage qui soit jamais sorti de la main des hommes, nous jurons, tous de vive, de combattre et de mourir pour la défendre.[20]
> (We bless the revolution, we admire the constitution that it has given to us, we see it as the most beautiful work which has ever come from the hands of man, we swear by our lives to fight and die in its defence).

During the period of final British acquisition, however, the use of writing increased in the British wish to replace the use of French for administrative and commercial purposes by English. For example, the St. Lucian newspapers ceased publishing in French and started publishing in English with the occassional use of French for advertisements and letters to the editor.[21]

In both the French revolutionary and the British period, the expansion of literacy, therefore, remained within the ruling groups.

The Amerindians (Arawak, Carib, Island Carib and Black Carib) and the Africans in St. Lucia, like other orally centered groups, made use of oral literature in order to perpetuate their culture, e.g. songs, proverbs and narratives.[22] These items of oral literature, as well as being literary forms, were also methodoligical structures for the expansion and perpetuation of both Amerindian and African culture in St. Lucia. These items were perpetuated from 1600 to the present-day because they were thought of as valuable to Amerindian and African peoples in St. Lucia. Where they were not thought of as invaluable they have been forgotten. In this way oral memory provides the cultural critique and the methodology for the perpetuation of its forms (songs, proverbs, etc). Oral literature also provides its own cross-referencing devices to aid the perpetuation of its content e.g. a proverb may refer, in its content. to a song and/or a prose narrative.[23]

From its origins then, St. Lucia was a largely oral society. Under the social conditions of slavery and colonialism writing was introduced mainly to serve the interests of its rulers.

The trend has continued to the present day in the large illiteracy or 'orality' of much of the population and the use of written Standard English mainly by the educated elite.[24]

The contemporary experience of oral and written languages in St. Lucia

Despite its low prestige as the oral language of the powerless in past St. Lucian society, Patwa (French Creole) oral culture, has begun to be expressed through the written mode, within the past fourteen years, and has gained some measure of local prestige, largely due to its centrality in the St. Lucian historical experience.

Patwa's recent change of medium has been largely due to the activities of the Folk Research Centre, St. Lucia, in its promotion of Patwa in St. Lucia.

Many of the Centre's members, however, like others who have promoted Patwa in both written and oral modes in St. Lucia, are literates fluent in both English and Patwa. These literates have also developed and mastered the St. Lucian Creole Alphabet for the writing of Patwa, in addition to their previous mastery of English orthography. They are in effect 'superliterates'.[25]

Their social positions and abilities are often very different from the mainly rural, poorer, non-literate and monolingual Patwa speakers. Despite these social differences, the superliterates aim to make the non-literate Patwa speakers literate in Patwa[26] using Freirean principles.

The real test of these Freirean claims of the superliterates, will be their level of inclusion of non-English speaking non-literates, in the decision making processes, related to Patwa and its development through the written medium in St. Lucia.

In order to situate the activities of the superliterates within contemporary ideas in St. Lucia, about the development of Patwa in the written medium, an analysis is made (below) of selected written material published or presented in St. Lucia, in the past fourteen years (1969-1983), on the use of Patwa in St. Lucia, either in a written or an oral form.

The written materials analysed were chosen from those available to me at the time or writing, and were selected because of their **direct relevance to the aims of the superlatives to make St.Lucians literates in Patwa.**

These written materials were analysed in terms of their explicit and implicit aims, and their behavioural and non-behavioural objectives. The judgement of these aims and objectives is my own subjective judgement.

Date: 1969
Item: *A Visitor's Guide to St. Lucian Patwa*, Lithographic Press, Castries, St. Lucia
Author: Toynbee, M.W.
Aims and Objectives: To provide the foreign literate and tourist

with an outline of Patwa, a language which was learned and transmitted orally by St. Lucians. To provide the tourist with a key of understanding St. Lucian culture. To increase communication between St. Lucian hosts and their foreign guests.

This seemingly simple wish to communicate, in fact, underlined one of the greatest problems most foreign literates had with living in St. Lucia, the sudden exposure to an oral culture without having had any oral tools themselves to cope with it. In order to cope, one such foreign visitor, M.W. Toynbee, provided the key most familiar to literates in learning a new language, i.e. a written outline of Patwa.

The subsequent items below, however, underline another aim, i.e. that of St. Lucians wanting to acquire the written mode for their own inter-St. Lucian communication.

Date: 1978
Item: Research Notes, No 1 of the Folk Research Centre, Castries, St. Lucia
Author: Anthony, P.A.B.
Aims and Objectives: To survey St. Lucian Anthropological Data in Repositiories within the United States of America.
To demonstrate that the greater amount of research done on St. Lucia by non-St. Lucians is part of the politics of colonialism: "I do not think this monopoly on culture research in St. Lucia can be explained solely in terms of the higher level of education in metropolitan countries, nor in terms of the rigours of the university system requiring students in certain disciplines to do research outside their own territories. It is the mathematics of control".[27]
Literate and English-speaking St. Lucians will be able to understand what is done with research done on St. Lucia by foreigners and to know where the research can be consulted.
That foreigners having materials written or otherwise recorded after research in St. Lucia, will take steps to make these materials available to St. Lucians.
To make the St. Lucian government aware of the need for its own involvement in the politics of culture.

The above document may have done much to make St. Lucian English-speaking literates aware of the socio-political implications of their oral language and culture.

Date: Feb 1979
Item: St Lucia at Independence, Voice Press, Castries, St Lucia
Aims and Objectives: To make a record of History, Local Government, Development, Tourism, Education, Art, Culture, Music, Sport and Religion in St. Lucia as a document celebrating independence and for reading by literate and English-speaking St. Lucians.

The St. Lucian population will become aware of the concept of independence as a tangible event.

St. Lucians will buy the document as a symbol of the celebration of independence, irrespective of whether they can read the document or not.

The inclusion of Patwa proverbs in the above document is suggestive of greater official and governmental awareness of Patwa in St. Lucia. This may have been due to the effects of *Research Notes, No 1*.

Date: Dec 1979
Item: Bulletin of the Folk Research Centre, vol. 1, no. 2
Aims and Objectives: To inform literate and English speaking St. Lucians about the African historical dimensions of Patwa.

To help validate Patwa as part of the St. Lucian historical experience.

Literate St. Lucians will be better informed about Patwa.

Literate St. Lucians will place a more positive value upon Patwa.

The above item is suggestive of a greater validation and prestige being given to Patwa by St. Lucians.

Date: April 1980
Item: National Consultation on Education Conference, Draft Report, by The Ministry of Education and Culture, St. Lucia
Aims and Objectives: To discuss aspects of St. Lucian education.

To improve the St. Lucian educational system.

To collect information from Caribbean experts, particularly linguists, with respect to finding a method of writing Patwa for educational purposes.

To take initial steps to providing an orthography for Patwa on which the St. Lucian government and linguists can agree.

The above item suggests that from previous general aims to validate and diffuse Patwa in the written mode, practical steps are being take for the achievement of the written diffusion of Patwa.

Date: Nov 1980
Item: Report on the Feasibility of a National Literacy Programme for St. Lucia, prepared by the Caribbean Research Centre, St. Lucia
Aims and Objectives: St. Lucian literacy is to be derived through the medium of Patwa. An oral language is to be made into a written language. Patwa is to be promoted as a vehicle for making more St. Lucians literate.

Date: Jan 1981
Item: Final Report on a Seminar on an Orthography for St. Lucian Creole, organised by the Caribbean Research Centre, St. Lucia and the Folk Research Centre, St. Lucia.
Aims and Objectives: To agree on an Orthography for St. Lucian Creole. St. Lucian non-literates will become literate in Patwa.
Patwa is to be promoted as a written and, therefore respectable language.

The two documents above suggest that the superliterates, having arrived at an agreed orthography, want to impliment it amongst the many non-literates of St. Lucia.

Date: May 1982
Item: International Conference on Creole Studies held in St. Lucia
Aims and Objectives: To give international academic backing to local initiatives on French Creole.
To give recognition to French Creole.
To promote French Creole on an international basis e.g. in Mauritius as well as in Haiti.

Date: 1982 & 1983
Item: Songs in French Creole and the St. Lucian Creole Alphabet published in the Castries Catholic Chronicle, St. Lucia
Aims and Objectives: To diffuse Catholic ideas to St. Lucian literates.
To bring Catholic ideas even closer to the local Creole psyche.

To promote reading material in Patwa for Catholics becoming literate through the medium of Patwa.
The Catholic Church should be a part of local initiatives on cultural developments.

Date: 1983
Item: Batata — a newspaper using both St. Lucian Creole and English, St. Lucia
Aims and Objectives: To provide a written forum for the development and diffusion of St. Lucian culture.
To provide reading material for Patwa-speaking literates.
To promote Patwa through the written medium.
To promote St. Lucian culture through Patwa in a written form.

In the above three items it is evident that the promotion of French Creole in St. Lucia, in the written mode, now has both international, local religious and local journalistic backing.

An analysis of all the items above suggests that the past fourteen years of Patwa in St. Lucia can be described as follows:

YEAR(S)		LOCAL CHOICES IN RELATION TO PATWA
1978-1979	Local discussions	Local superliterates make the population more aware of the importance of Patwa.
1980	Methodology	Linguists, governmental and educational experts discuss the feasibility and methods for making Patwa a written language.
1981	Decision	Local superliterates decide on an orthography for Patwa.
1982-1983	Application	International and local superliterates promote and develop Patwa as a written language useable for making St. Lucian non-literates, literate.

As previously suggested, however, the aim to promote Patwa in the written mode can only be expanded if St. Lucian non-literates do, in fact select, en masse, to join the superliterates and learn the St. Lucian Creole Alphabet.[28] Should the non-literates not join in this superliterate initiative, then, as in the previous historical experiences of literacy in St. Lucia, the superliterates will only be writing for their own consumption, while the oral mode will remain the mode of the powerless and literacy the tool of the powerful.

An example of the potential for social cleavage between non-literates and superliterates is the dual terms Patwa and French Creole The term Patwa was used by St. Lucian non-literates to refer neutrally to their language. The superliterates, however, suggest that as the original French word 'Patois' meant dialect and/or low status language then it should be changed to French Creole, in order to promote positive ideas about the language in St. Lucia. In arriving at the decision the non-literates were not consulted. Should they have been consulted they would have informed the superliterates of their total ignorance of the French term and its meaning, and that any of their own non-literate views on the low status of Patwa, were not due to French derivation, but due to the social stratification between the powerful and the powerless within which Patwa was the language of the powerless.

Consultation and the inclusion of the non-literates in decision-making remains the only real dimension for full literacy in Patwa in St. Lucia.

The aims and objectives of Caribbean organisations

In order to focus upon the activities, aims and objectives of Caribbean superliterates concerned with French Creole and Creole languages in general, a brief analysis is made of the Folk Research Centre, St. Lucia and the Society for Caribbean Linguistics.

Although both Caribbean organisations have identified the need for literacy and the use of Creole languages to be considered within the context of wider developmental aims, neither has addressed the problem of themselves as organisations of the superliterate and the powerful, who have not yet fully included sufficient members of the non-literate and the powerless, whom they wish to represent.

The Folk Research Centre, St. Lucia[29]

Aims and Objectives
Founded in 1973, the organisation aims to collect, analyse and research the oral and written culture of St. Lucia as "a weapon for change and integral development within which Patwa is to be promoted and appreciated as a vital force in the process of liberation".[30]

Through its membership the use of Patwa was seen as part of "a process of critical self-awareness 'involving' a study of the application of Paulo's Freire's conscientization methodology in the St. Lucian context".[31]

The Language Question
St. Lucian Patwa, formerly of low prestige within St. Lucia, is being promoted both orally and in a written form, by the Folk Research Centre, who see the development of Patwa as part of the liberation of St. Lucians as a 'third world' people.

The Folk Research Centre has done much to promote Patwa in St. Lucia through its membership in the Catholic Church, on St. Lucdian educational panels, in other movements for the promotion of Creole languages (e.g. *Mouvman Kwéyòl Sent Lisi* — Creole Movement of St. Lucia) and in newspapers publishing in Patwa e.g. *Balata* — St. Lucia and *'Gwif An Tè* — 'Fingernails in the Earth', Martinique.

The Folk Research Centre's greatest achievement, however, has been to co-ordinate governmental, academic and local expertise in the creation of the St. Lucian Creole Alphabet 1981.

Analysis of the Folk Research Centre's Viewpoints
The integrated aims of language with development provide a more cohesive overview of literacy objectives in a country where lack of literacy is still at approximately 40% island-wide (Report on the Feasibility of a National Literacy Programme for St. Lucia, 1980), than did former perspectives which saw literacy only in terms of English and unrelated to the Creole linguistic heritage of St. Lucians.

Society for Caribbean Languages[32]

Aims and Objectives
Originating from an initial congerence on Creole languages at the University of the West Indies, Jamaica campus, in 1968, the society's aims and objectives, as implied in the conference papers given[33] were mainly academic.

However, with expansions in its membership and the growing prestige of Creole languages within the Caribbean, governmental concerns about education and language planning have resulted in more practical aims being expressed through the society's membership e.g. the production of various dictionaries for the various creoles (e.g. Holm & Shilling's *Dictionary of Bahemian English*, New York, 1982 and the forthcoming *Dictionary of Caribbean English Usage* by R Allsopp, University of the West

Indies, Barbados campus).

Proposals for language planning originating from the society's membership have included plans for the use of Creole languages at the primary level in Caribbean Education.[34]

The Language Issue
Creole languages in the Caribbean have been generally looked down on, even by their speakers (both monolingual and bilingual), who attributed a higher prestige to European languages, for example English and French. The society has increasingly pointed to the equality of Creoles to all other human languages and has attempted, through its membership, to aid their development as part of the general developmental aims of Caribbean peoples.

Analysis of the Society's Viewpoints
Although the above viewpoints would, at a surface analysis, seem straightforward, the general anti-black perspectives of past Caribbean societies have been inherited by present Caribbean societies, within which the backing of Creole languages may be interpreted as 'a loss of the advanced European cultural life'.

The society's membership, being composed of many whites and Caribbeans fluent in both Caribbean and European languages, may be viewed by the mass, as a hypocritical elite, who, having already imbibed 'superior' European culture, may only want to keep the mass in ignorance by advocating a greater prestige for Creole languages.

A greater involvement of the Caribbean peoples within the society's objectives may, however, alleviate this potential for misunderstanding.

Creole languages and the English educational system

With immigration of Caribbean Creole speakers into England, the social divisions between high status literate speakers of metropolitan languages and low status non-literate speakers of Creoles, already formed in the Caribbean were further solidified by racism, as the non-literate Caribbean Creole speakers had immigrated into a mainly literate English society, which, in the main, also viewed the Caribbean immigrants as inferior.

In order to describe the experience of Creole languages within the English Educational System, a questionnaire was designed to obtain sample responses on aims, objectives and attitudes related to the use of Creole languages from organisations within the English Educational System, whose clientele are speakers of Creole languages, as well as similar organisations outside the English Educational System. The organisations chosen were as follows:

Within the English Educational System
1. The West Indian Supplementary Service, London Borough of Waltham Forest
2. The English Language Service, London Borough of Waltham Forest.

Outside the Educational System
The Caribbean Communications Project.

The above organisations were chosen because of convenience, as the writer lives in the London Borough of Waltham Forest, and had contact with both borough organisations during his teaching practice in 1983. The writer has also been a member of the Caribbean Communications Project since 1979.

During the interviews, 1983-1984 I noted the responses of each person in written form. However, in one case, part of the interview was recorded on a cassette.

Responses were obtained from eight people and these have formed the basis for the descriptions of aims, objectives and of the language issue within each organisation concerned.

Questionnaire

1. How long have you worked with this group/organisation?
2. When was this group/organisation set up?
3. What are the general aims of your group/organisation?
4. What orthography/writing system is used for the languages used by people for whom your organisation caters for?
5. What input does your organisation make to the educational system?
6. What publications have been written/published by your organisation?
7. What are the general beliefs of your organisation?
8. What are the long term objectives of your organisation?
9. What materials have been used for teaching purposes by your organisation?
10. What materials have been developed for language teaching using creole languages in your organisation?
11. Who funds your organisation?
12. What are the aims of those who make the funding?
13. How far have your objectives changed with time?
14. Whom does your organisation see itself as serving?
15. What is the respective status of the teachers in your organisation to people learning to read and write?

(January 1984)

West Indian Supplementary Service, (WISS), London Borough of Waltham Forest (LBWF)

Aims and Objectives
The organisation (WISS) was set up in 1971, in response to a book which suggested that many pupils of Caribbean origin were being deliberately sent to schools for the educationally sub-normal, irrespective of their abilities, i.e. *How the West Indian child is made educationally sub-normal in the British school system.*[35]

This book, written by a Caribbean teacher, had widespread influences within the Caribbean Community in London, and elsewhere, who began their own supplementary and/or Saturday schools as a means of diminishing the damage to the education of Caribbean pupils.[36]

WISS may, therefore, well have been a response within the English community to also give supplementary education to Caribbean pupils in the face of Caribbean dissatisfaction and alienation from the British Educational System, as well as to preempt any mass separatist educational moves by the Caribbean community in London, away from the British state educational system.

As well as such traditional methodologies of dealing with protest in Britain, another concern prompted the creation of WISS, i.e. the need to accommodate many pupils arriving straight from the Caribbean who underwent 'culture shock' on being placed in the British classroom.

The ending of major immigration from the Caribbean and Asia in recent times however, led to the contraction in services created especially with large numbers of immigrants in the LBWF's schools. Consequently, WISS's role as a recipient of such 'culture shocked' Caribbean children, has diminished.

As the children of former Caribbean and other immigrants have become more culturally British than their immigrant parents, there has been less of a demand for WISS to withdraw Caribbean pupils from the classroom for special attention.[37]

The creation of WISS had, however, been of particular relevance to the LBWF as a large percentage of its non-white, and particularly Caribbean pupils had been sent to schools for the educationally sub-normal (ESN).

To this problem of the general low social status and intelligence attributed to Caribbeans and their children, had also been added problems in communication between the Caribbean pupil and his/her teacher, due to differences in Caribbean uses of English; as well as problems due to differences in the culture and ethnic identity between Caribbean pupils and their English educational and social setting. WISS saw itself as providing some guidelines, if not solutions, to these problems.

Coard, on analysing some of the reasons for low academic performance of Caribbean pupils, and their resultant placement in ESN schools, suggested that some of the problems lay in the Caribbean pupils themselves. He pointed to the low self-image of Caribbean pupils in Britain, who, if asked to paint their own face, would paint a white[38] face. The writer Edwards,[39] on the other hand, suggested that interferences from Caribbean usage of English, were some of the causes for the lack of communication in Standard English by Caribbean pupils in Britain.

The issue of low acadmic performance was dealt with by WISS, who tried to introduce books with pictures of black people into the borough's schools and to point out to fellow teachers that the Caribbean usage of English was not a sign of cognative deficiency in Caribbean pupils.[40]

WISS, in its initial stages was, therefore, an organisation mainly geared to providing supplementary educational help to Caribbean pupils, as well as to make the schools in which their numbers were high, more sensitive to their special needs as people from a different culture.

This thrust of WISS and the ideas of the period, to locate some or all of the problems within the pupil him/herself, has changed to a location of the problems at least also within the wider British society, due to the society's perspective on race, culture and class.

These implied views of Britain as a culture biased, racist, and a class-ridden society have been related, in WISS, to new perspectives on withdrawal of pupils from the classroom. WISS, like the English Language Service of LBWF,[41] initially withdrew Caribbean pupils from the mainstream classroom to provide inputs of Caribbean culture and history, in the same way that the borough's English Language Service provided inputs of English as a Second Lanuage to mainly Asian pupils.

With new realisations about the racist and culture-biased implications of separating the black pupils from the white pupils, as well as any idea of educating them away from the errors (both cultural and linguistic) of their past or referent homelands, withdrawal has become a dirty word or, dare I say it, a 'bête noir' in the area of the education of immigrants[42] and their descendents in Britain.[43]

The present multicultural[44] directive in education as well as the perspective that bilingualism is a positive resource, rather than a contribution to cognative deficiency,[45] has altered the concerns of WISS. The borough's education office is (at the time of writing, May 1984) considering a plan to amalgamate both WISS and the English Language Service, into a single multicultural unit of teachers, who will be attached to schools, and also visit the proposed multicultural centre periodically, to train non-WISS and non-English Language Service teachers, as part of an in-service training scheme.

The exact outcome of WISS has not been decided, but its in-flux position, reflects well some of the altering educational aims and objectives of the LBWF, as well as British educational thinking with regards to Caribbean pupils.

The link between the actions of state institutions, followed by protest by ethnic minorities, followed by responses by state institutions, seems to be the pattern which can be abstracted, from the relations between WISS as a state institution and its minority clientele from the Caribbean.

Indeed, the link between protest and reaction to protest may be evident in the appointment of Mrs Little, a former co-teacher of ESN pupils with Bernard Coard at the Gurney School, Newham, as the initial Teacher-in-Charge of WISS.

The LBWF's move to create WISS, after protest by the Caribbean minority that too many Caribbean pupils were in LBWF's ESN schools, may, therefore, fit into the pattern of expressed oppression identified by the Caribbean minority, being accommodated by the creation of 'special' enquiries, 'special' projects and 'special' schools e.g. WISS, for that minority.

Recent protest by the Caribbean minority in the LBWF, however, has been from at least two Caribbean parents groups in the borough, who have protested against the withdrawal of their children from the classroom, which they saw as another form of ESN treatment, in which the Caribbean pupil is deliberately diverted from the concentration on academic subjects, necessary to any possible upward mobility within British society.

To this present protest the LBWF has partly reacted by its anti-withdrawal practices.

Permanent consultation between the LBWF and its Caribbean minorities should be established so that more long-term policies can be arrived at, outside this model for inherent conflict, implied by past policies based on protest and reaction.

The Language Question
People of Caribbean origin in Britain have a native speaker competence in, or a receptive competence[46] in a number of Creole languages. They also have a native speaker competence in, or a receptive ability in, Standard English.

Their, at times, poor grasp of Standard English, was initially taken as yet another index of their cognative deficiency.

WISS teachers saw themselves, therefore, as teachers of Standard English who adopted a non-punitive approach when Caribbean pupils produced errors in Standard English, due to the influences of their Creole mother tongues:

> In general that the kids understand that writing Standard English is the aim and they need to master it . . . without stopping them from writing dialect as expression, paying attention to the appropriateness and context of different uses of language.[47]

This non-punitive perspective on error, as advocated in recent educational teaching,[48] was seen by WISS teachers as part of the need to lay a positive emphasis upon all languages brought into the classroom by pupils, whether Asian, Oriental, Caribbean Creole, white working class/Cockney or others. Such a positive approach to the pupils' home languages(s) would, it is argued, also foster positive attitudes toward the learning of Standard English.

This approach would dovetail nicely with the present multicultural directive of the LBWF, which would be seen to be paying some respect to minority cultures, with an associated positive valuation to bilingualism, through this positive emphasis on the pupils mother tongue(s). This approach also correlates to the present emphasis upon Communicative Language Teaching (Littlewood, W. 1981), in which emphasis is placed upon appropriateness and context of different uses of language rather than language structure only.

In the context of this approach to language, the WISS teacher may be seen as teaching the appropriate socialcontexts for Creole languages, in contrast to those for English; for example, using a Caribbean novel or the description of a Caribbean social situation as a stimulus, group work would be done, in which the Caribbean pupil could ɩrespond with Creole language, relevant to that social situation. This social situation could then be followed by group work on an English novel and/or social situation along the same lines. Appropriacy and use would, therefore, have been taught, without a derrogatory approach to the Creole language, while still focussing upon Standard English.

WISS teachers, like other language teachers, had previously followed a more structural approach to language teaching, within which, errors in Standard English would have been seen as language habits in the Caribbean pupil, which were in need of correction. In short, the behaviourist approach to learning[49] reflected in language teaching generally, suggested, in WISS, the use of English as a second language approaches, in order to correct language habits originating from the interferences of Creole mother tongue(s) of Caribbeans.

This approach is reflected in early WISS teaching materials, in which practice is given in the use of the verb 'to be', a frequent source of error for speakers from Creole backgrounds.[50] The materials are graded as to levels of difficulty, e.g. unit 1 materials giving practice in the verb 'to be', are easier than unit 4 materials giving practice in both 'to be' and verbs in the present continuous.

This structured and corrective approach to language, contrasts with that of later WISS materials, which lay greater emphasis upon the appropriacy of Creole usage, in materials which reflect the speech community, and the culture of the child. For example, *Roger's Story*, the autobiographical account of life in Jamaica by a WISS pupil, Roger Davis, was developed as teaching material appropriate for use with Caribbean, and other pupils, irrespective of its Caribbean use of English, as in the use of the Creole item 'licks' (blows):

> Say we had a test of 30 spellings and only got one, we would get 29 *licks* on our hands (my emphasis).

According to one WISS teacher, this more open approach to language use is crucial, as, in WISS's experience, Caribbean pupils who did not come into the infant school speaking any form of Caribbean English, did, by the ages of 8 and 9, learn some variety of Caribbean Englishh, in the junior school. This would suggest that the same pupils would also learn Standard English when and if they so desire, provided that such an open approach to language was kept up by the teachers.

Some WISS teachers saw no need for a separate writing system for Creole languages, which they thought should be written in the same way as Standard English, whenever, according to social appropriacy rules, there was some need for their use within the British educational system.

Other WISS teachers, although aware of the movement by some primary school teachers to allow pupils to use 'native' scripts, the use of mother tongues and their scripts in schools was, in general, disliked by most teachers, and definitely not considered one of the 'rights of man' by Sir Keith Joseph: "State schools cannot offer mother tongue tuition to pupils as a right . . . ".[51]

This present official British perspective on linguistic minorities, differs from that of the Soviet Union, where education in the mother tongue was seen as one of the rights of Soviet citizens, for which the state would try and provide.[52]

Analysis of WISS Viewpoints

Implied in all WISS views, however, is the acceptance that Creole languages are marginal to the concerns of teaching the Caribbean pupil. The Creoles are not viewed as languages in their own right, but as dialects, in the same relation as Cockney to Standard English. As 'dialects', a concern with the question of a separate script is, therefore, seen as even more marginal to the concerns of teaching the Caribbean pupil.

The view that Creole languages are to be analysed in terms of appropriacy and use , further begs the question of what exactly is usefully appropriate, in terms of British society, for Creole languages; for example, are appropriate uses of Creoles only in describing Rastafarianism and conflicts between Caribbean youth and the British police?

The multicultural approach and its relationship to multilingualism may well not be viewed as relating to Caribbeans. Implicit in the use of term 'dialect' is the idea that, unlike the Asians of the LWBF, the Caribbeans have no language and possibly, some would argue, no culture.[53] From this viewpoint, Caribbeans would be seen as a brown and black coloured section of the working class, needing no other culture than Marxist dialectics, while multiculturalism and multilingualism will continue to be Asian concerns. The latter viewpoint was suggested by a Caribbean pupil's comments in a school in the LBWF, when 'Asian Week' was being celebrated. The Caribbean pupils complained to me that they could not understand why "anything multicultural is always Asian".

It could be argued that multiculturalism may not be well understood by its practitioners, and its clients, who may view it as a competitive model for the expression of different minority cultures, in direct relation to their numbers in any borough. In the meantime, the Greek, Cypriot, Jew, English, Scots and others not numerically dominant in the borough concerned, feel alienated.

Some WISS teachers would argue that such multicultural concerns are meaningless outside an analysis of the sexist, racist and class-biased workings of British society, and that the white pupils were as severely, if not more, in need of cultural enlightenment as were the Caribbean pupils. However, WISS has been funded mainly by Section 11 funds aimed at helping ethnic minorities, and WISS teachers have, consequently, not usually been attached to white schools.

Perhaps a more borough-wide application of multicultural education, irrespective of the 'colour' of the particular school's intake, may ameliorate such views. However, WISS teachers would then cease to have Caribbeans as a direct concern, let along marginalised views of their languages.

Criticisms of WISS have been made by black teachers, within WISS, who would like to see WISS take a stronger stand against overt racist treatment of Caribbean pupils, as observed by them, within schools to which they have been attached. However, as all WISS teachers are attached to schools, only if their presence has been asked for by the headteacher, their guest status, like that of ESL teachers in London schools generally, mitigates against any forceful stand by WISS, on cases that the black teachers may describe as glaring racism.

WISS has also, along with the borough's English Language Service, been criticised by Caribbean parent organisations in the borough, who see WISS's identification of self-image problems in the Caribbean pupil, as irrelevant to the needs of their children, whom they thought were falling behind in school/academic subjects by being withdrawn into either WISS or ESL classes.

These organisations also have a hostile attitude towards any use of Creole languages, by their children, in school. They suggest that the only language which should be appropriate is Standard English, and that any reference to Creole languages in any form e.g. literature, would be against the interests of Caribbean pupils.

Although such parental views may typify the negative attitude to Creoles and to Caribbean culture, by Caribbeans themselves, they also imply the belief that the use of Standard English, by Caribbeans, would increase their social mobility. These perspectives of many older Caribbeans are in direct contrast to the perspectives of many Caribbeans, born in Britain, who have a totally negative perspective on any potential for their social mobility within British society, with or without Standard English.

WISS perspectives on appropriacy of languages use may, therefore, have already taken into account the hostilities, not only of white society, but the black burden of self-hatred.

English Language Service, London Borough of Waltham Forest

Aims and Objectives
The service was established in 1965 in order to teach English to immigrant pupils. With ideas that bilingualism was a problem being current during this period, the service's emphasis was on English only.

However, experience, as well as a census carried out by the service (1978/79) suggested that ESL pupils born in England, did worse in the educational system than those who arrived in England between the ages of 11 and 14. These findings were in keeping with the Bullock report which suggested that bilinguals were lower achievers than monolinguals in the British educational system.[54]

However, later more positive assessments of bilingualism, pointed out the dangers of withdrawal in the case of ESL pupils born in Britain, as well as the need for a positive approach to the pupils' mother tongue, as an asset as well as a resource, for multicultural education.

The anti-withdrawal perspective can be related to a de-emphasis upon structural language teaching, and an increasing emphasis upon interactional and communicative language teaching.
From this perspective, the ESL pupils would learn more English by interaction with their English-speaking peers in the playground,

than in structured language teaching in the context of withdrawal.

The more positive valuation of pupil mother-tongues was partly catered for by the attachment of four Urdu teachers in the modern languages section of some of the borough's schools (1984). This was partly the result of recommendations made by the English Language Service, as well as the influences of Asian organisations in the borough, e.g. The Council of British Pakistanis and the Muslim Parents Association.

With present multicultural initiatives in the borough, the service has emphasised the necessity for an understanding of the various cultures, represented by the ESL learners, on the part of teachers in the borough.

In order to facilitate this, the service has made many pamphlets designed to educate teachers about minority languages and cultures. However, like WISS, the service may be dismantled, on similar lines to WISS, and the service's teachers will be expected to help multiculturalise the individual borough school, to which they will become attached.

The Language Issue
Although the teaching of English as a Second Language has been the service's main brief, the service has served, through its materials, as a source of information about some of the borough's minority languages e.g. Chinese, for teacher's with no background of language study.

The service has not had many direct dealings with Caribbeans as ESL learners, as they were catered for by the WISS.

The service has seen itself mainly as a teacher of Standard English to its few Caribbean clients, again in keeping with perspectives which place little importance upon Creole languages, and also as voiced by two Caribbean parents' associations in the borough, namely the Caribbean Progressive Association and the West Indian Education Committee.

Analysis of the English Language Service's Viewpoints
The service's viewpoints have the advantage of being both clear and specific, namely the teaching of English as a Second Language. It has, however, reacted positively to the mother-tongue needs of the largest minority in the borough i.e. the Asians.

The quantitive view of multicultural education implied by its many materials related to Asian languages and culture, is, however, a more limited perspective on multicultural education than the qualitative view implied by its wide variety of self-produced materials, relating to nearly all the minority cultures in the borough.

Amongst its many self-produced materials on minority borough languages, however, none were found which related to Creole languages. Although this could be argued to be the result of Caribbean parent pressure, via their borough parents' associations, it may well be that the general marginalisation of Creole languages in Britain, generally, merely reflects the service's non-attention to these Creole languages.

The Caribbean Communications Project (CCP), London

Aims and Objectives
The organisation began in 1975 and aimed to promote literacy amongst adults of mainly Caribbean origin, and others of similar need. It organised tutors and teachers of Caribbean origin as voluntary workers who taught Caribbean adults, who did not know how to read and write.

CCP also provided inputs into the training schemes of statutory bodies engaged in literacy work, e.g. Further Education Colleges and Adult Education Institutes, such as the Paddington Adult Education Institute.

CCP focused upon the Caribbean education background of Caribbeans needing literacy, through the provision of tutors familiar with this background and with teaching methods popular in the Caribbean e.g. the alphabetic method, popular in the Caribbean, resulted in students who could recognise 'speak' as 's', 'p', 'e', 'a', 'k', but were unfamiliar with the phonic method, more popular amongst teachers in England, and in which students would be taught 'speak' as [s], [p], [i:], [k]. This phonic method also had some unforseen problems for Caribbean Creole speakers for whom phonic [pat], means 'a pot', and not Standard English 'a pat'.

CCP trained tutors also provided training inputs to the language-experience literacy method, practiced within some statutory bodies. Using the above method, pupils initially tell the tutor about their life experiences, which are then taped and written up by the tutor, as a source of items which the tutor would use to introduce the pupil to literacy. The problem occurs in the case of Caribbean pupils whose life experiences are expressed in Creole;for the latter, the English literacy tutor is faced with either attempting to represent an unfamiliar culture as best as he/she can, or with translating the Creole speech into Standard English.

CCP attempts to provide literacy to Caribbean adults who are particularly disadvantaged, due to such incongruencies between the Caribbean and British educational systems, as well as due to the fact that English tutors are unfamiliar with the Caribbean linguistic heritage and because this heritage has low prestige even in the eyes of many of its speakers.

CCP also attempts to counteract the demotivating effects of British racism, within its students, which results in an undervaluing of the educational potential of Caribbeans and their descendants.

CCP attempts to cater for its students by gearing literacy to the students' objectives in wanting literacy, e.g. the student who wants to know how to sign forms better at his/her place of work, has slightly different objectives from a student who would like to read more now that he/she is retired.

CCP hopes to offer its experiences in Caribbean adult literacy and education, as a guide to the education of Caribbean adults in statutory educational establishments.

The Language Question
CCP takes a positive attitude to the Caribbean Creole heritage, and, through its published Occasional papers, attempts to provide psychologically positive introductions to the Creoles both, for Caribbeans and non-Caribbeans.

CCP believes that literacy must ideally start on the basis of the students' positive valuation of his/her linguistic heritage, in order that a general enthusiasm for language can be built up, and extended to literacy in English.

CCP strives to indicate to its teachers that their relationship to their students must be based upon equality and mutual learning as the student who lacks the literacy skills that they have, may have other skills, e.g. be a skilled mechanic, that the teacher may not have.

CCP also develops and makes use of teaching materials which anticipate, in CCP experience and research, language difficulties typical of Creole speakers.

Analysis of CCP Viewpoints
It may be argued that CCP's holistic perspective on the literacy needs of Caribbean adults, may well be too diffused within related developmental and social perspectives, and that aims and objectives more focussed upon the aquisition of literacy in English, may be more in keeping with the immediate needs of their clients. However, as this latter approach by the statutory bodies to the literacy needs of Caribbean adults has proved alienating to the Caribbean adult learners such an interaction of social, developmental and language aims, by CCP, may prove more meaningful to Caribbean adults, as it reflects both their historical experiences and their present-day circumstances.

Conclusions

A dependency hierarchy is evident in considering the evidence discussed, in that the orally based cultures can be seen as dependent upon the written cultures.

A view of education as a methodology for colonial purposes, would indicate that the oral societies, in their search for literacy, are, by definition, involved in the self-destructive practice of placing less importance upon the oral basis of the cultures they hope to represent.

If Piagets' views that a concrete operations stage of psychological development is essential as a base to later abstract operations in the child, it suggests than an oral culture, in which the written medium does not exist, would not provide a concrete operations base in writing to its children, and that (vice versa) a written culture does not provide a concrete operations base in oral structures.

If this is the case, then, in societies like St. Lucia, in which the written mode is, traditionally for the elites in English, and the oral mode is for the non-elites in Patwa (French Creole), cultural conflict may be reflected at psychological levels, in the presence of two types of psychology in the St. Lucian population: i) those whose abstract operations have an oral basis and ii) those whose abstract operations have a written basis.

Both typologies will be shared at different levels for different individuals in the society. Areas for psychological conflict are therefore implied. It may well be that the introduction of the written norm for the oral language — Patwa, implies a destruction of oral structures in the society as well as the setting up of a written standard in which only the superliterates can participate.

Race does have some implications for literacy in this study, in that the oral group were mainly Africans and the written group were Europeans. The conflicts between these two modes reflect, therefore, racial conflicts and racial domination.

The historical role of mulattos in St. Lucian society emphasise a wish by the mulattos to join the European society as full-fledged and literate members. This wish was rejected by the Europeans in St. Lucia, who continued to discriminate against mulattoes, despite the fact that they were at least as literate as the Europeans in St. Lucia.[55]

It may well be that mulatto society, because of its intermediate racial status, provided an intermediary zone for the written and oral cultures of St. Lucia.

This St. Lucian historical experience of oral languages as the languages of the dominated and enslaved, has led to the persuit of literacy in, and the validation of, Creole languages and culture by, the descendents of the enslaved and dominated in St. Lucia.

The English experience of Creole languages, has, however, been a more complex one, of a literate society trying to meet the literacy needs of one of its many minorities.

Within the English context, the degree of attention given to the needs of any minority seem to be related to the numerical strength of that minority in the borough concerned. Where, as in the LBWF, Asians predominate amongst the minorities, then, more attention is given to the language and other needs of Asians, than, say, the Chinese of the borough. This idea that numerical strength is the most significant axis of a minority's political bargaining power, calls into question the aims of multicultural education which should, ideally, be for all members of British society, irrespective of the numbers in a particular borough.

There are some differences between the more liberal views on language of some WISS and ELS teachers, and those of some Caribbean parent organisations, who believe that Standard English alone should be both the target language, and the language of instruction, for Caribbean pupils. In order to accomodate these views, the Creole language question is avoided by both WISS and ELS.

Both WISS and ELS do not have a Caribbean orientated perspective with respect to Creole languages, which are mainly used in oral work, or referred to in an oral form by both teacher and pupils. The Creole languages are viewed as marginal languages, outside the direct experience of the mainly non-Caribbean teachers in both organisations.

The CCP in Britain has, however, (like the Folk Research Centre and the Society for Caribbean Linguistics), included the diffusion and validation of Creole languages, as part of Caribbean-centred provisions of literacy and education for Caribbean adults in Britain.

The central difference between these Caribbean-centred organisations (both in England and the Caribbean) and the English educational organisations to which they have been compared is that, wheras the English organisations do not see the Creoles as part of overall developmental aims, the Caribbean-centred organisations do.

From the perspective of oral versus written languages, it may well be that speakers of oral languages in St. Lucia are being provided with a means of diffusing their culture, which may supercede its traditional oral mode of diffusion.

The political potential for domination of oral language speakers by literates, however, remains evident, even within the St. Lucian context, as the new literacy leaders for French Creole are mainly superliterates, fluent in the oral and written uses of both English and Patwa, wheras their clients are not. Whether Freirean principles overcome this potential for domination of the traditionally oral language speakers by the superliterates, can only be analysed in the light of future *praxis*.

Recommendations

Given some of the social problems highlighted by the use/non-use of Creoles in the English and St. Lucian educational systems, the following recommendations, at the various educational/age levels, may help to correct the negative social attributes placed upon Creole languages and their speakers:
Primary: The use of Creole oral narratives in the school setting either in the original Creole, or in English reported speech with Creole direct speech, or as translations into English. These narratives can be presented *orally* by the teachers concerned with appropriate mime and drama, or by inviting a Creole-speaking parent or raconteur to do so.
Secondary: The use of Caribbean and African literature as an examination text within which various aspects of Creole language grammatical structure could be presented, e.g. *dem* = *pl.* in a Caribbean poem in which the words *people dem*[56] appear.
Tertiary: Teacher training must begin to include a basic knowledge of Sociolinguistics within which Creole and non-standard English forms can be discussed. Allied to this training an awareness of racial/tribal oppression within which language has a function should also be included. At university, first degree and masters levels, courses about, and on Creole languages should be developed.
Further, Adult and Voluntary: The recommendations of CCP and the Folk Research Centre, St. Lucia within which Creoles are accepted as part of the culture of Caribbeans, and feature in any developmental aims for Caribbean peoples, should become part of 'mainstream' education in Britain and St. Lucia, and not become marginalised at times even by the very cultures they try to represent. A house divided against itself cannot stand. Cultures divided against themselves will cease to be productive. *Chébé'y wèd, pa mòli* ('Hold on hard to life, do not soften').

Notes

1. Jobson, R., 1623, and Moore, F., 1738.
2. Lord, A.B., 1965, and Innes, G., 1974.
3. Cf. Brazil and the USSR which although 'developed', also had problems of high illiteracy.
4. Hymes, D.H. (ed), 1971.
5. See bibliography.
6. The terms Patwa and French Creole are used synonymously throughout this chapter.
7. Dalphinis, M., 1979, 1981 & pt.I, ch.2.
8. Dalphinis, M., 1981, pt. III, ch. 1.
9. Idem.
10. Breton, R., 1665, 1667. The Caribs, however, did communicate through rock carvings. Insufficient data at the time of writing, does not allow me to conclude whether these rock carvings were, in fact, a form of literacy. Y. Collymore, in conversation, London, 1984.
11. Taylor, D.M., 1951; Dalphinis, M., 1981.
12. Dalphinis, M., 1981, pt. III, ch. 1.
13. Pt.I, ch. 2.
14. Dalphinis, M., 1981, pt. III, ch. 1.
15. Pt.I, ch. 2.
16. Breen, H.H., 1884.
17. Public Records Office, London, reference no. CO256, piece no. 2.
18. Pt.I, ch.2.
19. Idem.
20. *Address des Planteurs et Citoyens de l'Isle Sainte-Lucie à M. de Damas, Gouverneur et a l'Assemblée Coloniale de la Martinique*, 1791, p.2.
21. Public Records Office, London, reference no. CO256, piece no. 2, piece no. 3, piece no. 16, and piece no. 36.
22. Dalphinis, M., 1981, pt. III, ch. 6.
23. See also pt. III, ch. 3. Archival Function.
24. Alleyne, M.C., 1961; Carrington, L.D., 1967; Dalphinis, M., 1981, pt. III, ch. 1 and Dalphinis, L.B., 1981.
25. Word coined by myself to describe people who have mastered more than one orthography for the writing of one or more languages.
26. A Report on the Feasibility of a National Literacy Programme for St. Lucia, 1980, pp.16-17.
27. Anthony, P.A.B., 1978, p.vi.
28. Final Report on a Seminar on an Orthography for St. Lucian Creole, 1981.
29. Dalphinis, L.B., M.Phil (in preparation), University of London, Institute of Education, describes the activities of the Folk Research Centre in greater detail.
30. Research Notes 1, Folk Research Centre, 1978.
31. Bulletin of the Folk Research Centre, Vol. 1, no. 2, 1979.
32. The writer has been a member of the above, since 1977.
33. Hymes, D. (ed), 1971.
34. Craig, D., 1979.
35. Coard, B., 1971.
36. The writer was a voluntary teacher at the Marcus Garvey and Kwame Nkrumah Supplementary Schools, London (1971-1972).
37. See below for other views against the withdrawal of Caribbean and Asian pupils from the classroom.
38. This symbol is used to mean pink coloured people of mainly European ancestry. The symbol 'black' is used to mean mainly brown and black coloured people, not of European ancestry. See Cohen, A., 1974 on the question of "Power and Symbolism in Complex Society".

39. Edwards, V., 1979.
40. A widely held perspective, even up to today, and expressed by Eysenck, H.J., 1971.
41. See below.
42. Wilkes, S., 1983, in a lecture on English as a Second Language at Bonar School, London (20th. September 1983).
43. It would, however, be politically naive not to see the present arguments against withdrawal outside the context of government spending cuts, which result in placing burdens of all description, back on the meagre social and educational services presently available. The teacher will, therefore, have to find extra time from his/her already restricted time to deal with any special problems of Caribbean pupils which were formerly dealt with by WISS.
Cf. also other 'anti-withdrawal' exercises, also related to cuts in government spending e.g. anti-withdrawal views on the mentally ill, the criminal and the physically handicapped are not unrelated to cuts in social services and consequently greater burdens being placed on the citizen.
44. As characterised by the Centre for Multicultural Studies, University of London, Institute of Education.
45. Wilkes, S., 1983 (see footnote 42).
46. Dalphinis, M., 1984.
47. WISS teacher, interviewed in 1984.
48. Norrish, J., 1983.
49. Sandstrom, C.I., 1981, pp.84-85.
50. Trudgill, P., 1974, p.70.
51. Times Educational Supplement, 30th. March 1984).
52. Isayev, M.I., 1977.
53. See Whorf, B.L., 1956, on the relationship between language and culture.
54. Bullock Report, 1975.
55. Dalphinis, M., 1981, pt. III, ch. 1.
56. Items in English Creole should be written in the orthography of Cassidy and Le Page, and items in French Creole in the St. Lucian creole orthography, 1981. Dr. R. Allsopp, in conversation, London, 1984.

4. Creoles in Voluntary Adult Education: the Caribbean Communications Project's experience.

Introduction

This chapter analyses the language work of fifteen students of the Caribbean Communications Project (CCP)[1] who, in the research data, are identified by number rather than name. The research presents a statistical analysis of the sex, age, residence, country of origin of student, date of arrival in the United Kingdom and current occupation. The information was obtained from the CCP's own records and, from these, an attempt was made to establish the length, frequency and type of relationship with the CCP. Four of the students were interviewed for an analysis of the Creole features in their language, and supplementary information about their relationship with CCP was obtained.

From an analysis of the Creole features, in both oral and written work of the students in the sample, implications are drawn for the education of Caribbean adults, teaching materials, student recruitment and adult provision in CCP specifically, as well as, generally, in other adult education institutions in England. Examples of students' work on which the analysis was based are to be found in the study.

In carrying out the research, reference was made to the aims of the CCP and recommendations made with a view to furthering these.

This study has been organised mainly as an analysis of CCP student responses to a three part questionnaire:

Part 1 — A Social Data Questionnaire
Part 2 — A Language Questionnaire
Part 3 — A Literature Questionnaire.

The responses of the CCP students interviewed to each part of the questionnaire are analysed in order to assess the use of Creole languages in relation to the acquisition of literacy in Standard English in voluntary adult education, using CCP as an example.

A definition of French Creole and English Creole features is also made in order to have a clear standpoint as to exactly which elements of the students' written and oral responses fell into each of the following categories: English, Creolized English and Creole.

On the basis of the use of the above languages/language varieties, by the students, in their oral and written responses, observations, recommendations and evaluations were made for CCP's aims, objectives and practices, in order to give improved guidelines for the acquisition of literacy in Standard English by CCP's Creole speaking students.

Social Data Questionnaire (Part 1)

Students were asked for the data (below) and their responses were noted.

Speaker Data
 1. Age
 2. Sex
 3. Island/Country of origin
 4. Town/Area of origin
 5. Island/Country of origin of parents
 6. Town/Area of origin of parents
 7. Area of residence of island/country reference group in Britain
 8. Frequency of visits to the Caribbean
 9. Present address
10. Previous addresses/areas of residence in Britain
11. Present occupation
12. Previous occupations
13. Date started with C.C.P.
14. Date finished with C.C.P.
15. Continuity with C.C.P. with dates, if discontinuous
16. Like or disliked C.C.P. service
17. Anything the student would like to see improve in the C.C.P. service
18. Written work done for C.C.P. with dates (approximate)
19. Name(s) of C.C.P. tutor(s) with whom the student worked (/works) with approximate dates
20. Education (both in island/country of origin and in England)

Social Data Analysis of CCP Students

Of the total 15 CCP pupils analysed in this report, 14 have their origins or that of their parents in the French Creole (Patwa) speaking islands of Dominica or St. Lucia.

In order to interpret the language behaviour of these 15 students, their social status is analysed in terms of categories relevant to this report: sex, age, residence, year of arrival in the UK, occupation and country of origin. These categories were based, in the case of the four students interviewed, on their responses to the Social Data Questionnaire (above). In the case of the other students, the data was obtained from CCP files.

Social Categories of Students

Student No.	Sex	Age	Residence	Approx Year arrived in UK	Occupation	Caribbean Island of Origin
1	F	23	W2	1973	Computer Operator (S)	Dominica
2	F	37	W11	1969	Kitchen Assistant (U)	St. Lucia
3	F	29	W11	1980	Unemployed (UE)	Dominica
4	F	60	NW6	1965	Machinist (S)	St. Lucia
5	F	60	NW8	1971	Cleaner (U)	Dominica
6	M	40	SE22	1966	Building Trade (U)	St. Lucia
7	F	58	E9	1976	Unemployed (UE)	Dominica
8	F	64	W9	1958	Cleaner (U)	Dominica
9	M	38	NW8	1976	Factory Worker (U)	Dominica
10	M	21	NW10	?	Machine Operator (S)	Parents from Dominica
11	F	62	W9	1958	Porter (U)	Dominica
12	M	20	NW8	1981	Fur Trade (S)	Dominica
13	M	20	E5	1979	Factory worker (U)	St. Lucia
14	F	48	W9	?	Housewife (UE)	Dominica
15	F	30	E11	1965	Housewife (UE)	Jamaica

Key: S = Skilled; U = Unskilled; UE = Unemployed; ? = Not known
The data for the above social categories was obtained from CCP student registration forms and from interviews with some of the students.

Analysis of Social Categories and Interrelationships in Response to Social Data Questionnaire (Part 1) for the 14 Students of French Creole Origin

In order to ascertain generalizations evident in the social categories to which these students belong, the interrelationships between these social categories were noted.

The following symbols are used in the grid of interrelationships below:

Sex: M – Male
            F – Female
Age: <21 – 21 years and below
            22> – 22 years and above
            42> – 42 years and above
Residence: NW – North Western Boroughs of London
            S – Southern Boroughs of London
            E – Eastern Boroughs of London
            W – Western Boroughs of London
Year of arrival
in the UK   '50 – 1950s
            '60 – 1960s
            '70 – 1970s
            '80 – 1980s
            u – date of arrival unknown
Occupation: S – Skilled employment
            U – Unskilled employment
            UE – Unemployed
Island of
Origin: SL – St. Lucia
            D – Dominica

GRID OF INTERRELATIONSHIPS

Sex	<22	22>	42>		NW	S	E	W		'50	'60	'70	'80	u	S	U	UE	S.L.	D
M	3	2	0	M	3	1	0	4	F	0	1	2	1	1	2	3	0	2	3
F	0	3	6	F	2	0	6			2	2	3	1	1	2	4	3	2	7

Age																		
<21	2	0	1	0		0	0	1	1	1	2	1	0	1	2			
22>	1	1	0	3		0	2	2	1	0	1	3	1	2	3			
42>	2	0	1	3		2	1	2	0	1	1	3	2	1	5			

Residence									
NW	0	1	2	1	1	3	2	0	1	4
S	0	1	0	0	0	0	1	0	1	0
E	0	0	2	0	0	0	1	1	1	1
W	2	1	1	1	1	3	2	1	5	

Year of Arrival in the U.K.					
'50	0	2	0	0	2
'60	1	2	0	3	0
'70	1	3	1	1	4
'80	1	0	1	0	2
U	1	0	1	0	2

Occupation	S.L.	D
S	1	3
U	3	4
UE	0	3

The level of formal education of the students was not analysed as most of the students had, quite clearly, little or no formal education. Education was therefore taken as a self-evident social category relating nearly uniformly to almost all the students.

The following generalizations are evident in the grid of interrelationships above:

Sex
1. Most of the men are <21 while most of the women are 42>
2. Most of the men live in the NW area of London while most of the women live in the W area of London
3. Most of the men and women arrived in Britain in the 1970s
4. Most of the men and women hold unskilled and low status occupations
5. There are more Dominicans, especially women, than St. Lucians in the sample.

Age
1. Most of the students are 22> and 42>
2. Most of the students of 22> and 42> are unskilled and/or unemployed in contrast to most of the students of <21 who are skilled.

Residence
1. Most students live in the western boroughs of London
2. The majority of students live in the western and north-western boroughs of London.
3. All students arriving in the 1950s lived in the western boroughs of London.

Year of Arrival in the UK
1. All the St. Lucian students arrived in the UK in the 1960s, while most of the Dominican students arrived in the 1970s.

The above data suggests that the majority of CCP French Creole students are from the western London boroughs in which CCP is situated, and that few students come to CCP from other more distant London boroughs, for example, the northern and southern London boroughs.

The majority of students are women. This may well reflect the mother/women centred Caribbean culture, the fact that, in the Caribbean some families may have preferred to educate their men rather than their women, as well as the greater conformity of women in general to dominant social norms, including education and literacy.[2]

The majority of students arrived in the UK in the 1960s and 1970s and resided in the western and north-western areas of

London, and have not moved from these areas partly due to the lack of social mobility offered by their mainly low status occupations, as well as the higher degree of solidarity available from other Dominicans and St. Lucians who reside in greater numbers in these London boroughs.

Student Attendance and Relationship with CCP

Of the four students interviewed by the writer, their attendance was generally regular (between about 1981-1983) and they all had a good to very good evaluation of their relationship with CCP. Their 'good' evaluations of CCP, however, contrasts with their views of CCP limitations (see below). Their attendances ranged from two to five years.

Student Relationship with CCP — A Student Perspective
The four students interviewed were all very grateful for the help they received from CCP. They found the tutors friendly and understanding. They appreciated the lessons on Caribbean history and mathematics, which all provided them with new and stimulating educational experiences with which they identified positively.

The students, however, felt that CCP needed more materials than those related only to reading and writing; they felt that CCP needed more publicity within the black community; they felt that CCP needed better financial backing in order to try and ensure that its tutors were paid.

All students were particularly grateful for the initial valuable steps in gaining the confidence to write. For them, their previous non-literacy had been a burden, and an embarrassment to be hidden. CCP staff provided them with both the psychological and material circumstances to make the effort to move from an oral Creole culture, to the written English culture.

Some students were grateful to particular tutors, whose absences often retarded their learning. Given the psychological traumas involved in acquiring writing skills late in life, students had, necessarily, become attached to certain tutors. When these tutors left CCP, or became ill, or left for maternity leave, the students in a sense also 'left' CCP, although they came physically. The new tutor allocated to them was always felt to be not as good as the one who first began the first valuable steps with the student concerned.

However, some tutors were felt to be too distant, or to signal an implied superiority to the student, whereas the student, already seething in the anger, frustration and lack of confidence, of those who try to master writing later in life, was in need of reassurance from someone who would treat them as an equal, without question, and without patronage.

The French Creole students were particularly concerned that very little mention was made of their homelands (St. Lucia and Dominica) in contrast to Jamaica which, they felt, was mentioned too frequently.

One student, in fact, suggested that she ceased to go to CCP classes partly because of this disregard for French Creole culture.

A Definition of French Creole and English Creole Features

For the sake of clarity a number of Creole language features defined are described below so that discussions on the use of Creole by the students (below) can be related to specific features rather than generalization alone. The following features are creole features related to both French and English Creoles (FC and EC respectively) at the points of grammatical contrast to English and French, as well as at points of similarity to their African language ancestors (see the general introduction):

1. *Stabiliser*: *sé* — Similar to the use of the verb 'to be' in English, stabilisers 'predicate' non-predicated items, e.g. pronouns: *li* — '(s)he' as in

    sé   *li*
    "Stab. (s)he"

cf English: 'It's him/her, and French: '*C'est lui*'; or the stabiliser *na* as in English Creole:
na   *im*
"Stab. him/her"

2. *Adjectival verb*: Unlike adjectives in English, French Creole and English Creole 'adjectives' are not only descriptive but verbal, e.g. the English adjective 'red', as in 'it is red', necessitates the use of a preceding 'is'. Cf English Creole and French Creole adjectival verbs which, as verbs, do not need predication, e.g.:
F.C.: *i*   *wouj*   E.C.: *i*   *red*
      "it   red"   "it   red"
English: 'It is red'; and French '*Il est rouge*'

3. *Front-focalisation (and focaliser)* — Emphasis in Creole languages can be achieved by placing the item to be emphasised at the beginning of the sentence, e.g.:

F.C.: i twavay pou sèt jou
"(s)he work for seven day"
cf. English: '(S)he worked for seven days': and French *Il/Elle travaillait pendant sept jours*'. In this unemphasised sentence above, *sèt jou* — 'seven days' can be emphasised thus:
sèt jou i twavay
"seven day (s)he work"
'He/She worked for seven days (emphasised)'.

Further emphasis can be achieved by the placement of a focaliser after the front-shifted item e.g. *sèl* — 'only', or *yon* — 'one', e.g. French Creole:
sèt ju sèl i twavay
"seven day (Focal.) (s)he work"
English: 'He/She only worked for seven days (emphasised)' and French: *'Il/Elle travaillait seulement pendant sept jours'*.

4. *Emphatic Repetition*: Unlike English, Creole languages regularly repeat items which are to be emphasised:
F.C.: i wouj wouj   E.C.: i red red
"it red red"   "it red red"
cf. English: 'It is very red'; and French: *'Il/Elle est très rouge'*.

5. *Emphatic Elongation of Vowel*: Unlike English, vowels in Creole languages can be elongated to mark emphasis, e.g.:
F.C.: i wouuuj;   E.C.: i reeeed
"it red(*Emph.*)"   "it red(*Emph.*)"
cf. English: 'It is very red' and French: *'Il/Elle est très rouge'*.

6. *Topicalisation*: In Creole languages, items can be emphasised by being indicated as the topic of the sentence; for example, by referring to the item again in the sentence, through the use of a pronoun referring to the topicalised item, e.g.:
E.C.: di buk a gi yu i red
"the book i give you it red"
    topicalised   pronoun
    item

cf. English 'The book I gave you is red'.
F.C.: liv la mwen ba ou a i wuj
"book the I give you(sing.) the it red"
French: *'Le livre que je vous ai donné est rouge'*.

7. *Catenation*: In Creole languages a series of verbs can be strung together without an intervening 'and' as in English,
F.C.: i lévé kouwi sòti an kay la
"(s)he stand run leave in house the"
E.C.: i get op ron liv di aus
"he get up run leave the house"

Cf. English: 'He got up and ran out of the house';
French: 'Il s'est levé, il a couru et il est sorti de la maison'.

8. *Use of a Separable Plural Marker*: Unlike the use of English -s plural marker attached to the noun, Creole plural markers are separate from the noun, e.g.:

E.C.:	di	boi	dem;	F.C.:	sé	gason	a
	"the	boy	pl."		"pl.	boy	the"

Cf. English: 'the boys'; and French: 'les garçons'.

9. *Grammatical use of 'say' or 'for'*: Unlike English, 'say' and 'for' also have a wider grammatical usage in creoles:

E.C.:	i	tel	mi	se	ron
	"(s)he	tell	me	say	run"
F.C.:	i	di	mwen	pou	kouwi
	"(s)he	tell	me	for	run"

Cf. English: 'He/She told me to run'; and French: '*Il/Elle m'a dit de courir*'.

10. *Non-differentiation of the 3rd Singular Pronoun*: Unlike English, sexual equality in the use of the 3rd singular pronoun is self-evident in Creole languages, e.g. in both English Creole and French Creole *i* = he/she/it. Cf. English: he/she/it; and French: *il/elle*.

The following feature is relevant to French Creoles only:

11. *Suffixation of the Definite Article and the Possessive Pronoun*:

F.C.:	liv	la	E.C.:	di	buk
	"book	the"		"the	book"

English: 'the book'; and French: '*le livre*'

F.C.:	liv	mwen	E.C.:	mi	buk
	"book	my"		"my	book"

English: 'my book' and French: '*mon livre*'.

Creole Features in the Oral and Written Responses of Students

The Language Questionnaire (Part 2) used sentences (read aloud by the interviewer to the student) which, when orally translated into French Creole or English Creole, exemplify all of the Creole features described previously. For example, sentence 33 — "She took the stick and beat them" (see Language Questionnaire below), when translated into French Creole or English Creole, will give the following example of catenation (Creole feature No. 7):

French Creole: *i pwan baton bat li*
French: *Il/Elle a prit le baton et l'a battu.*
English Creole: *i tek di stik bit am*
English: S(he) took the stick and beat him.

The Literature Questionnaire (Part 3) involves the reading aloud, by the interviewer, of two passages in French Creole to which the students respond orally, and then, respond in writing. Students were then asked to give as many examples as possible of Creole oral literature.

Following Labov's assertion that the social setting defined the style of the speech used in that social setting, the use of a Creole in a social setting in which English is also being used, as in the translation exercise of the Language Questionnaire, is a formal setting in terms of Creole culture. The use of Creole in a setting in which Creole alone is used, as in the Creole oral literature of the Literature Questionnaire, is an informal setting for Creole culture. culture.

The informal setting of Creole oral literature is also used for the written responses of the students, who are asked to write down a few sentences in response to the Creole texts read by the interviewer. The Creole features used/not used in both formal and informal speech settings by the four speakers interviewed were noted. So, also, was the sentence in which the feature occurred. For example, in the Analysis of Creole Features in the Language (Formal Speech) Responses of the Speakers (below), 'Lang 5' refers to the sentence no. 5 in the Language Questionnaire (above).

In CCP's own previous language analysis of its students the following language features were adopted by the CCP Resources Officer, Miss J. Burke (1981-1983), in analysing student's errors in their written English:
1. Unmarked plurals
2. Tenses
3. Subjective/verb agreement
4. Possessives.

These reflect areas of known error in the written and oral English of people of African descent in the U.S.A.,[3] England,[4] the Caribbean and Africa.[5] For example, Trudgill comments on the lack of subject/verb agreement in black English Vernacular (BEV).[6] As well as these grammatical features (above), a number of other features were also outlined by the Resources Officer's analysis sheets (below), e.g.:
1. "dropped words/phrases"
2. "aspirant h"
3. "spelling"

These similarly reflect errors in grammar and pronunciation of Standard English by peoples of African and Caribbean descent; for example, the student who "dropped words/phrases" such as "was" in "Sam Sharpe born", does so in accordance with deletion of forms of the verb "to be" (the copula) in the speech of Black Americans[7] and other African-descent groups. Cf. for example, Black American speech "He smart", Black English Vernacular "He smart" and Caribbean English Creole *i smart* all meaning 'He/She is very intelligent' in Standard English.

The "aspirant h" of another (Jamaican) student as in "chatch" reflects the use of vowel initial *h* in the speech of Jamaicans, for example, *hinvolv* (cf. Standard English "involve").

These errors of grammar and pronunciation are often reflected in speeling e.g."I reach Genoa" in which the past-tense suffix *ed* is missing (cf. Standard English "I reached Genoa").

The Resources Officer's list of errors also includes a frequency list of the number of occurrences of each type of error in the student's written work as well as the dates of each analysis of error.

The limitations of the analysis include the lack of an upward limit to each error counted, for example, to know that the pupil made four mistakes on 1.10.80 in the use of tenses is not comparable to his/her 15 "tense" mistakes on 5.11.81 due to a lack of an upward limit by which the performances, at different dates, can be compared.

Other limitations evident are the lack of definition of the errors described, for example, are "did have", cf. Standard English "had", and "people come my shop", cf. Standard English "the people came to my shop", comparable as tense mistakes, or, is the latter example, "come to ... ", better analysed also as an error in the lack of a following "to"?

These limitations, notwithstanding, the Resources Officer's features provide some evidence of the types of errors which frequently occur in the English of Caribbean students, as well as evidence that 'tense' erros are the most frequent in the writing output of the three students, i.e. having a higher 'frequency' of occurences than the other errors analysed.

	SA	SB	SC	Total
1. Unmarked plurals	1	13	2	16
2. Tenses	0	40	4	44
3. Subject/verb agreement	0	6	0	6
4. Possessives	0	1	0	1
5. Dropped words/phrases	4	0	0	4
6. Aspirant h	0	1	0	1
7. Spelling	0	0	14	14

(See appendix for the tables from which the above figures have been extracted. Note that SA = student A, SB = student B, and SC = student C).

These errors reflect features: phonological, grammatical and semantic, of the deep structure of the Creole languages which surface in the written work of the students.

The Creole features above[8] were, therefore, adopted as a reference point for the analysis of these surface errors in English, which are really positive expressions of Creole language features. Although it can be argued that such errors in English represent an intermediate language variety between Creole speech and the targeted learning of English; such a view does not account for the persistence of the same or very similar errors in the use of English by all peoples of African descent.

A perspective of such error as the result of interferences (between languages) is therefore adopted as more explanatorily adequate, in that it explains these errors as the result of consistent conflicts in the competence of people of African descent, who speak various mother tongues, including Creoles, but who have similar problems when they attempt to master the world's most widespread international language — English.

Theoretical considerations apart, the students' errors in Standard English were analysed throughout this report, whether in relation to their written or oral work, with reference to Creole features, as described by the writer (above), and with reference to other Creole features not described above.

The students' use of Creole features were analysed in order to describe their conformity to them (both in their oral and written language).

Language Questionnaire (Part 2)

1. Where are you going?
2. He's wearing a red shirt.
3. They like eating sweet potatoes.
4. He went to market.
5. He told me to go to the fields, chase the dogs away and come back in the house.
6. Our hands are very large.
7. Here is the girl who brought the green dress.
8. This is a stone.
9. You(*pl.*) always take the bus early.
10. The book I gave you, it's red.
11. She took the suitcase down.
12. The boy chopped the tree down.
13. The man is *very* stupid.
14. He alone went to see the governor.
15. She bought them.
16. My grandfather bought me a present.
17. It's *me*!
18. I shaved myself.
19. You (*sing.*) are the man who ran.
20. Whom do you know in the town?
21. I saw this one.
22. I saw a man in my house.
23. I saw that man.
24. Ninety. etc.
25. Third.
26. They each had two each.
27. He ate before coming here.
28. Sit down!
29. Let them sit down!
30. Wherever he goes he laughs.
31. Everyone who comes sits.
32. It wasn't a woman who visited them yesterday.
33. She took the stick and beat them.

The above questionnaire was used, as outlined (above) and the responses of students to this part of the questionnaire were analysed (below).

Analysis of Creole Features in the Language (Formal Speech) Responses of the Speakers

Speaker 4 (Formal Speech)
Creole Features Used and Examples — French Creole

Grammatical tell 'for' (feature 9)
i	di	mwen	pou	alé	an	savan	la	Lang. 5
"(s)he	tell	me	for	go	in	field	the"	

'He/She told me to go to the fields'

Separable plural (feature 8)
..chasé sé chyen la...   Lang. 5
"chase *pl.* dog the"

'chase the dogs'

Topicalisation (feature 6)
liv	la	mwen	ba	ou	a	wouj	Lang. 10
"book	the	I	give	you	the	red"	

'The book I gave you, it's red'

Front focalisation (with focaliser) (feature 3)
li	yon	alé	wè	gouvènè	a	Lang. 14
"(s)he	Focal.	go	see	governor	the"	

'He alone went to see the governor'

Stabiliser (feature 1)
sé   mwen   Lang. 17
"*Stab.* me"

'It's me'

Emphatic Elongation of Vowel (feature 5)
lamen   nou   gwaan   Lang. 6
"hand   us   big"   (*Emph*)

'Our hands are very large'

Adjectival verb (feature 2)
liv   la   wouj   Lang. 10
"book the red"

'The book is red'

Suffixation of the definite article and the possessive pronoun (feature 11)
liv   la   Lang. 10
"book the"

'The book'

lamen nou
"hands us"

'Our hands'

Emphatic repetition (feature 4)
The speaker instead used emphatic elongation of vowel and *byen*
— 'very':

nom	la	byen	kouyoon	Lang. 13
"man	the	very	stupid"	

'The man is very stupid'

Catenation (feature 7)
The speaker instead used the connective *èk* — 'and':

i	pwan	baton	a	èk	i	bat	yo	Lang. 33
"(s)he	take	stick	the	and	(s)he	beat	them"	

'She took the stick and beat them'

Non-differentiation of the 3rd sing. Pronoun (feature 10) as seen in the sentence above (*Lang. 33*) and:

tout	koté	i	ka	alé	i	ka	wi	Lang. 30
"all	place	(s)he	Prog.	go	(s)he	Prog.	laugh"	

The speaker, however, also uses the following in variation with feature 10:
ti fi — '(little) girl' instead of *i* — '(s)he':

i	ti	fi	a	achté	bagay	la		Lang. 15
"(s)he	little	girl	the	buy	thing	the"		

'She bought them'

ch	ch	tifi	a	mété	kés	la	a	tè	Lang. 11
"she	she	little girl	the	put	case	the	on	ground"	

'She took the suitcase down'

Analysis of the Formal Speech of Speaker 4
The speaker made use of eight of the eleven Creole features analysed. Of the other three features analysed, their non-use and variability in usage are all due to the influence of English. Instead of emphatic repetition, the speaker made use of *byen* 'very' reflecting the English emphatic 'very', for example, 'very large'. Instead of catenation, the speaker uses *èk* 'and', reflecting the English use of 'and' as a connective between sentences. Instead of a consistent use of *i* '(s)he/it' the speaker is influenced both by this French Creole (Patwa) influence and by the English 'he/she' differentiation. In order to satisfy the latter influences the speaker uses *ti fi* '(little) girl' to translate 'she'.

Speaker 5 (Formal Speech)
Creole Features Used and Examples — French Creole

Topicalisation (feature 6)

liv	la	mwen	ba	ou	la	i	wouj
"book	the	I	give	you(sing.)	the	it	red"

Lang. 10

'The book I gave you, it's red'

Adjectival verb (feature 2)
... i   wouj   Lang. 10
"(s)he /it   red"
'It is red'

Focalisation (with focaliser) (feature 3)
i   yon   alé   wè   gouvènman la   Lang. 14

"(s)he Focal. go see government the"

'He alone went to see the governor'

Emphatic elongation of vowel (feature 5)
nom   la   sé   yon   sòòòt   Lang. 13
"man   the   Stab. one   stupid (Emph.)"
'The man is very stupid'

sé   mwen   Lang. 17
"Stab. me"
'It's me'

Suffixation of the definite article and possessive pronouns
(feature 11)
nom   la   Lang. 13
"man   the"
'the man'

lamen nou
"hand our"
'our hands'

Creole Features Not Used by Speaker 5 and Examples
Emphatic repetition (feature 4)   Lang. 6 & 13
Catenation (feature 7)   Lang. 33

Grammatical tell 'for' (feature 9)
i   di   mwen   alé   an   fild   la   Lang. 5
"(s)he tell me   go   in   field   the"
'He told me to go to the fields'

Separable plural (feature 8)
shyen la   Lang. 5
"dog   the"
'The dogs'

Analysis of the Formal Speech of Speaker 5
Of the eleven Creole features considered, the speaker made use of seven of them. Of the non-used features, features 4 and 7 were avoided in the same way as in the responses of speaker no.4 (above). Features 8 and 9 were also not used, although in a different manner from speaker no. 4.

In the case of speaker no.5 a number of important items are omitted by the speaker i.e. *pou* — 'to', in the phrase:

di	mwen	pou	alé
"tell	me	for	go"

and *sé* — '*pl.*', in the phrase:

sé	chyen	la
"*pl.*	dog	the"

(cf. the speaker's response above).

Speaker 14 (Formal Speech)
Creole Features Used and Examples — French Creole

Adjectival verb (feature 2)

lamen	'w	épé	Lang. 6
"hand	you	thick"	

'Our hands are very large'

Emphatic Elongation of Vowel (feature 5)

misyé	sòòòt	Lang. 13
"man	stupid	*Emph.*"

'The man is very stupid'

Front-focalisation (with focaliser) (feature 3)

'w	yon	wè	gouvènman	Lang. 14
"you (*sing.*)	Focal.	see	government"	

'You alone went to see the government'

Stabiliser (feature 1)

sé	mwen	Lang. 17
Stab.	me"	

'It's me'

Suffixation of the definite article and the possessive pronoun (feature 11)

kés	la	Lang. 11
"suitcase	the"	

'the suitcase'

lamen   'w   Lang. 6
"hand   you   (sing.)"
'your hands'

Non-differentiation of the 3rd sing. pronoun (feature 10)
i   pwan   Lang. 33
"(s)he   take"
'She took'

Creole Features Not Used and Examples
Emphatic repetition (feature 4)

The speaker instead used emphatic elongation of vowel:
misyé   sòòòt   Lang. 13
"man   stupid   (*Emph*)"
'The man is very stupid'

Catenation (feature 7)
The connective é — 'and' was used instead:
i   pwan   la   baton   é   bat   yo   Lang. 33
"(s)he take   the   stick   and   beat   them"
'She took the stick and beat them'

Separable plural (feature 8)
The plural suffix is simply not used by the speaker:
chaché   la   chyen   Lang. 5
"chase   the   dog"

Grammatical 'tell'/'for' (feature 9)
The speaker omitted this structure and said:
ou   alé   an   bush   Lang. 5
"you (*sing.*) go   in   bush"
(*sing.*)
'go to the fields'

Topicalisation (feature 6)
The speaker omitted this structure and said:
la   liv   lè   wouj   Lang. 10
"the   book   it   red"
'the book is red'

Analysis of the Formal Speech of Speaker 14
The speaker made use of six out of eleven Creole features selected. The speaker's French Creole is affected by French influences especially in the use of the French definite article which precedes the noun, instead of the Creole definite article which follows the noun, for example:

ia   liv
"the   book"
cf. French *le livre* instead of French creole:
liv   la
"book   the"
'the book'

Dominica is in close proximity to French speaking Guadeloupe. Dominicans frequently go to Guadeloupe in search of employment and Guadeloupeans frequently visit Dominica. The French influence is, therefore, not particularly surprising, although it is not an island-wide feature of the Dominican variety of French Creole.

Speaker 15 (Formal Speech)
Creole Features Used and Examples — French Creole

Non-use of the verb 'to be':
i   we   a   red   shaat   Lang. 2
"(s)he see   a   red   shirt"
'He/she is wearing a red shirt'

Non-use of a plural suffix:
da   dog   Lang. 5
"the   dog"
'the dogs'
da   fild   Lang. 5
"the   field"
'the fields'

Non-use of 'ed' plural suffix:
it   wozant a   wuman whu   vizit   dem   yestode
                                                            Lang. 32
"it   wasn't a   woman who   visit   them yesterday"
'It wasn't a woman who visited them yesterday'
shi   bai   dem   Lang. 15
"she   buy   them"
'she bought them'

Stabiliser (feature 1)
na   mi   Lang. 17
"Stab. me"
'It's me'

Separable plural (feature 8)
mi   no   mi   kozin   dem
"me   know   me   cousin pl."
'I know my cousins'

Said in response to Lang. 20 'Whom do you know in the town', instead of translating Lang. 20

Creole Features not Used by Speaker 15
Of the eleven selected Creole features only two were used. However, two other Creole features, possibly more typical of English Creoles, rather than French Creoles were used. The speaker, otherwise, used Standard English.

Analysis of the Formal Speech of Speaker 15
The speaker mainly uses Standard English, influenced by some English Creole features, in her formal speech.

Literature Questionnaire (Part 3)

The Literature Questionnaire was used as outlined (above) in the following sequence:

1. The student listens to the prose passage (A) and the poetry passage (B), below, which I read.
2. The student responds to both passages orally.
3. The student responds to both passages by writing down his/her ideas about the passages.
4. The student is to give examples of his own repertoire of Creole oral literature; a) proverbs, b) stories, c) riddles, d) songs, e) children's songs f) songs for special occasions only eg. funeral and fishing/work songs.

Passage A[9]
Leonard Jones ni swasant an. Èk kon tout lòt mizisyen ki ka jwé mizik twadisyonal, i pa ka bat tanbou tousel. I ka alé lanmè, i ka fè ti jaden'y, èk lè i ni tan, i ka fè nas pou fè an ti lavi. Mé lè pyès sé bagay-sala pa maché, sé asou tanbou i la fè an ti liv sik.
   Leonard lévé adan an fanmi dansé èk chanté. Èk i koumansé jwé tanbou a douz an. Kon pwès tout mizisyen Sent-Lisi, Leonard pa wisouvwè pyès lison an mizik. Manyè i apwann, sé pa kouté épi gadé lot mizisyen ka jwé épi i éséyé bat tanbou-la i menm. Leonard koumansé pa jwé débot, épi asou alé i apwann sa yo ka kwiyé "Afrikann Dans" (sa vlé di dansé kon alé liwon, koutoumba, èk sé diféwan kalité bèlè la kon bèlè anlè, bèlè, èk bèlè *maté*) èk i vini an mapipi an sa. Lè i té ni vent an, i té ja fò an bat tanbou-la èk tout moun té konnèt li an bout péyi-la.

For the benefit of non-Patwa speakers, this is a free translation of Passage A.

'Leonard Jones is sixty years old. And, like all other traditional musicians, he has other occupations apart from the drum. He goes to sea, he does a little gardening and, when he has time, he fishes with large nets to add to his livelihood. But, when none of these occupations are fruitful, it is with the drum that he ekes out a livelihood.

Leonard was brought up in a family of dancers and singers. He began drumming at the age of twelve. Like nearly all St. Lucian musicians, Leonard did not receive a musical education. He learned by watching other musicians play and by trying to play the drum himself. Leonard began by playing *débot*, and other African Dances (for example, dancing in a circle, *koutoumba*, and the different types of *bèlè*, e.g. *bèlè anlè* and *bèlè maté*) and he became an expert in these. When he was twenty years old, he was already quite accomplished in drumming, and was well known in all parts of the island.'

| *Passage B —* | *Passage B Translated —* |
| *Lafwa Poem-La* | *The Faith of Poetry* |

Mwen di Kwik	I say, Crick
Pèsonn pa di Kwak	No one said Crack
Mwen hélé Tim-Tim	I shouted Tim Tim
M'a tann anyen	I heard nothing
Mwen gadé	I looked
tout moun chapé	Everyone had left
kité mwen la mwen yonn	Leaving me there alone
Pa té ni pèsonn pèsonn pèsonn	There was no one, no one, no one
èk an vwa ka chanté:	And a voice said:
mama'w pa la	Your mother is not there
papa'w pa la	Your father is not there
sésé'w pa la	Your sister is not there
fwè'w pa la	Your brother is not there
sa vwé	That was true
tout moun alé . . . mé	Everyone was gone . . . but
mwen fèt pa ko mwen yonn	I was born alone
kay mò pa kò mwen yonn	I will die alone
sé initil pléwé	It is useless to cry
alo, mwen doubout an mitan lavi mwen	So, I stood up in the middle of my life
gadé tout oliwon	Looked around me

gadé anho, gadé anba	Looked up, looked down
awa	Alas
yon sèl bagay mwen wè	The only thing I saw
sé ti poem-sala	Was this little poem
mwen di an tjè mwen:	I said in my heart
si sé sa sé sa	If it's thus, it's thus
mwen pwan kouway, mwen hélé	I took courage, I shouted
Kwik:	Crick:
poem-la wéponn	The poem replied
Kwak:	Crack:
èk mwen koumansé listwa	And I began the story.

Kendel Hippolyte

The responses of the students to this part of the questionnaire were analysed (below).

Analysis of the Written Work of the CCP Students

The following written work by the CCP students was available for analysis:

Speaker	For CCP	By Interview using the Literature Questionnaire
1	No	
2	Yes	
3	No	
4	Yes	Yes
5	Yes	Yes
6	No	
7	No	
8	No	
9	No	
10	No	
11	Yes	
12	No	
13	No	
14	No	
15	No	Yes

The total available written work done for CCP by the students, and the written work done as part of the literature interview with the writer were analysed for errors in English with allusions to French Creole features, which may have influenced the production of these errors.

Analysis of Creole Features in the Literature (Informal Speech) Responses of the Speakers

Speaker 4 — Informal Speech
Feature   Examples in French Creole
(Stabiliser)   *sé   kon   ha   yo   ka   palé*
                              "*Stab*like this they *Prog.* speak"
                              'That is how they speak'

(Catenation)   *bat*   *tanbou ai   alé   an...   laivyè*
                        "beat   drum   go   go   in...   river"
                               'beat drum and go to the river'

(Separable plural)   *sé   bagai   la*
                               "*pl.*   thing   the"
                               'the things'

(Suffixation of article and pronoun)
                               tanbou la — 'the drum'
                               "drum the"
                               lèspwi mwen — 'my brain/ideas/spirit'
                               "spirit me"

English insertions in the French Creole speech
                               because; sorry; about; I don't no ho, mean, you know; strict, ain't it, bed, yes, so.
                               Examples in English
                               it really nice
                               cf. French Creole
                               i   byen   bèl
                               "(s)he/it good   nice"
                               'it is really nice'
                               because me one living here
                               cf. French Creole
                               paski   mwen yon   ka   viv   isi
                               "because I   one   *Prog.* live   here"
                               when you see is you alone
                               cf. French Creole
                               lè   'w   wè   sé   ou   yon
                               "when   you   see   *Stab.* you(*sing.*) one"
                               'When you notice that you are alone'

French Creole Insertions in English Speech
Leonard Jones bat tanbou a mwen ja kwè   wi
"Leonard Jones beat drum the I (*Past*) think yes"
sa sé vyé nèg dansé tanbou
"that *Stab.* old negro dance drum"
'That is a worthless negro drum dance'

Items of Oral Literature Performed by Speaker 4
(a) Proverb in French Creole
(b) Prose narrative in French Creole
(c) Riddle in English

Items of Oral Literature not Performed by Speaker 4
(d) Songs
(e) Children's songs
(f) Songs for special occasions only.

Analysis of the Informal Speech of Speaker 4
The speaker made use of four Creole features and a number of individual English words in her French Creole informal speech.

In her English informal speech the speaker made use of a number of Creole features and a number of phrases in French Creole.

The speaker has a good command and repertoire of French Creole oral literature but, due to old age, her memory of some of this literature had begun to fade.

Speaker 5 — Informal Speech

Feature No.	Examples in French Creole
8 (Separate plural)	sé ban dòla la "*pl.* group dollar the" 'Those with a lot of money'
1 (Stabiliser)	nou sé maléwé "we *Stab.* unfortunates" 'We poor people'
8 (Suffixation of article)	dòla la "dollar the" 'the dollar'

Feature	Examples in English
Absence of the copula	"when you — at home" cf. Standard English 'when you are at home' Following French Creole structure, the copula is not used.

"they will — sorry for you" cf. Standard English 'they will be sorry for you'. The copula is not used again following Patwa structure.

"you concentrate upon the person — doing" cf. Standard English 'you concentrate upon what the person is doing' This, also reflects Patwa structure in the absence of the copula.

Omission/simplification   "even you is well educated" cf. Standard English 'even if you are well educated' in which 'if' is omitted by the student.

Items of Oral Literature Performed by Speaker 5
(d) Song
Items of Oral Literature not Performed by Speaker 5
(a) Proverb
(b) Prose narratives
(c) Riddle
(e) Children's songs
(f) Songs for special occasions.

Analysis of the Informal Speech of Speaker 5
The speaker used three of the Creole features previously mentioned as well as three other Creole features not, so far, mentioned in this study (see above).

Speaker 14 — Informal Speech

Feature No.   *Examples in French Creole*

11 (Suffixation of articles   *sik   li*
    and Pronouns)   "sugar (s)he"
                               — 'his/her sugar'

Items of Oral Literature Peformed by Speaker 14
None.
This older speaker may have been inhibited by the setting of the interview, i.e. a youth centre. It was inconvenient for her to allow me to interview her at her own home.

Analysis of the Informal Speech of Speaker 14
The speaker made use of one of the Creole features selected in her informal speech.

Her English informal speech had no Creole features at the structural level, although her intonation pattern was quite clearly that of a French Creole speaker.

Speaker 15 — Informal Speech

Feature Number and Examples in English Creole
None of the selected Creole features were used. However, other Creole features were evident:
a non-use of a plural marker, e.g. *fild* — 'fields';
faiv finge a planteen — 'five fingers of plantain';
and a non-use of past tense markers on the verb
e.g. *giv* — 'gave (*Past*)'.

Item of Oral Literature Performed by Speaker 15
The speaker only performed a prose narrative.

Analysis of the Informal Speech of Speaker 15
The speaker's informal speech reflects a more relaxed usage of Creole features than her formal speech which reflects the influences of Standard English.

Observations

Creole features reflecting Creole oral literature more closely were not used in Patwa formal speech i.e. catenation, emphatic repetition and the use of grammatical 'say'/'for'. These features were also not used because of Standard English influences on French Creole. In formal speech (both in French Creole and English), fewer Creole features were used by all speakers.

The older speakers used more French Creole oral literature than the younger speakers, and also felt more comfortable using it. Creole features evident in the French Creole oral performances of the students are also evident in the oral English of the same students.

When the French Creole speaker learns to read and write English (s)he carries on using the same Creole features in his/her use of spoken English. These Creole features are evident as 'errors' in the written Standard English which the French Creole students are trying to master:

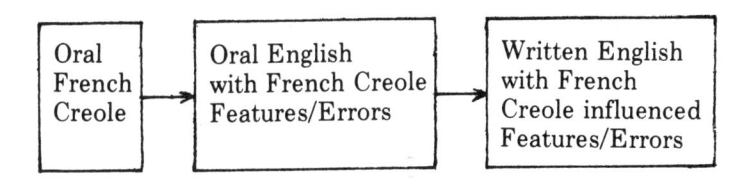

```
┌─────────┐    ┌──────────────┐    ┌─────────────────┐
│ Oral    │    │ Oral English │    │ Written English │
│ French  │ →  │ with French  │ →  │ with French     │
│ Creole  │    │ Creole       │    │ Creole influenced│
│         │    │ Features/Errors│  │ Features/Errors │
└─────────┘    └──────────────┘    └─────────────────┘
```

Creole Features in the Oral and Written Responses of Five CCP Students

Examples of Error in Spoken English   *Influencing Creole Feature*

Speaker 2

"I then asked if I *can* work in circulation"
Cf. Standard English
'I then asked if I *could* work in circulation'

Verbs are unmarked for tense. All tense(/aspect) is indicated by tense/aspect markers in French Creole e.g. *ka* — Prog.
   i   ka   vini
"(s)he *Prog.* come"
'(s)he is coming'
cf. i   kay   vini
     "(s)he *Fut.* come"
'(s)he will come'

"Yet again, still not sure of my future ..."
Cf. Standard English:
'Yet again, I was still not sure of my future'

Non-use of the copula (a form of the verb 'to be').
Cf. French Creole
mwen pa   té   sav
"I   Neg. Past. know"
'I was not sure'

... "so took a job"
Cf. Standard English
... 'so *I* took a job ...'

No apparent Creole influence but a non-use of 'I' as in the sentence above may imply a process of 'simplifying' Standard English in order to make it more Creole-like.

Speaker 4

"until you finish the washing"
Cf. Standard English
'until one finishes the washing'
or
'until the washing is finished'

Use of 'you(*Sing.*)' to mean 'one' e.g.:
lè   ou   wè   sa
"when you(*Sing.*) see that"

"... which I was put ..."
Cf. Standard English
'which I had put ... '

Cf. French Creole
ki   mwen   té   mété
"which I   Past   put"
'which I had put'

"It — no joke"

Non-use of the copula
Cf. French Creole
sé   pa   blag
"Stab. Neg. joke"
'It is not a joke'

"I — very glad"

Non-use of the copula. Cf. Patwa:
mwen   byen   kontan
"I   very   happy"
'I am very glad'

Speaker 5

"the music was hot very hot
Cf. Standard English
'the music was very
entertaining/enjoyable'

The concept of music as a sensory activity e.g. 'hot music' and 'hot girls' is typical of Creole language e.g.
i   sho
"(s)he/it drunk"
'(s)he/it is drunk'

"the Pope permission"

Cf. Patwa
pèmisyon   pop   la
"permission Pope the"
'The Pope's permission'
in which possession is implied by the juxtaposition of the items 'Pope' and 'permission'

"the members of the brotherhood *promise* to have no belongings"
Cf. Standard English
'the members of the brotherhood promised to have no belongings'

Cf. Patwa verbs which are uninflected for tense e.g.
yo   pwomèt   li
"they promised him"
'They promised him'

Speaker 11

"I am happy for go to school"

Cf. Patwa
mwen   kontan   pou   alé   lékòl
"I   happy for go school"
'I am happy to go to school'

"I shout for someone to come"
Cf. Standard English
'I shouted for someone to come'
"Chimney smoke come from the chimney"
Cf. Standard English
'Chimney smoke comes from the chimney'

"In August month is my birthday"
Cf. Standard English
'My birthday is in August'

The fact that the Creole verb is uninflected for tense influences French Creole speakers in their choice of the most uninflected forms of the English verb.

Cf. French Creole
mwa Sèptam
"month September"
'In the month of September'.
In French Creole the juxtaposition of two nouns, as above, implies possession. Note also the French Creole structure:
mwa   Awou sé
"month August *Stab.*"

birthday   mwen
"birthday   me"
'My birthday is in August'

The students' written work for CCP suggests that their French Creole mother tongue features are transferred in writing to their spoken English language output. The most frequent errors in spoken English were:
1. absence of past tense suffixes or past tense verb forms
2. absence of a copula
3. absence of 's possessive marker.

This gives support to the Resource Officer's categories of "tense" and "possessives" as a source of potential errors. Other sources of errors included simplication (deletions or omissions in Standard English) in order to make the English sentence shorter and more Creole-like; loan translations of Creole concepts into Standard English e.g. the idea of 'hot music' and the transformation of a Creole notion into Standard English e.g. "you" being used to mean Standard English 'one' is a transformation of French Creole *ou* — "you (*Sing.*)" which functions both as a subject pronoun as well as being used to convey the notion of 'one', 'generally people . . .'

Errors in Student Written Work in Response to the Literature Questionnaire (Part 3)

The following written work from interviews carried out between 14th and 21st January 1984 was available for analysis:

Example of Error in Written English	Influencing Creole Features
Student No. 5	
"It *make* me remember" Cf. Standard English 'It makes me remember' or 'It reminds me of';	Non-inflected French Creole verb e.g. *épi apwan mwen* "and learn me" 'and teaches me' The Creole verb has no suffixes.
and "*teach* me" Cf. Standard English 'and teaches me'; "he *wach* you do something" Cf. Standard English 'he watches you do something'; "and he *do* it" Cf. Standard English 'and he does it'	
Student No. 4	
'I never knew there is so much joy' Cf. Standard English 'I never knew there is so much joy'	No marker of past tense on the French Creole verb; Cf. French Creole *mwen pa té konnèt* "I Neg. Past know" 'I did not know'
Student No. 15	
"he would be *deid*" Cf. Standard English 'he would be dead'	No apparent influences.

As seen above, errors in student work can again be related to Creole features, especially the absence of past tense suffixes or other past tense markers on the verb.

Although a detailed analysis of spelling errors is not made in this study, one main factor is evident:
French Creole phonology affects the students in that they attempt to 'translate' French Creole sounds by the medium of English spelling, for example:
"notting" — Cf. Standard English "nothing" | nʌoiŋ |
and "forgetfool" — Cf. Standard English "forgetful" [fəgɛtfəl]
As neither [Θ] ("th") nor [ə] ("u") is an important sound (i.e. phonemic) in French Creole, the students have substituted them for French Creole sounds i.e. [tt] ("tt") for /Θ/ and [u:] ("o") for /ə/, in the spellings of "nothing" and "forgetful", respectively.

The 'translation' of these sounds through the English orthography is at least one source of mental confusion for the students, which leads to spelling errors.

Creole Features in the Oral and Written Work of Individual Students

Although most of the students' use of Creole features in their oral and written work can be summarised as 'errors' in Standard English, typical of the English of French Creole speakers, a number of Creole features were more typical of the language use of one student than that of another:
1. Speaker 4 was more sensitive to the non-difference in i — '(s)he/it' in French Creole in contrast to English.
2. Speaker 4 made a high use of English loans in her French Creole. This may well reflect the greater exposure to English loans that Speaker 4 may have had due to her former residence in the Castries urban area of St. Lucia, where English and English Creole are more frequently used than elsewhere in St. Lucia.
3. Speaker 5 often deleted the copula.
4. Speaker 2 often did not make use of the first person singular.
5. Speaker 5 often did not make use of the copula.
6. Speaker 11 did not make use of inflected verbs.

A Contrastive Analysis of Students' Work Before and After CCP

Of the 15 students under discussion, only the work of speakers 4 and 5 can be easily contrasted with respect to recent work and work previously done for CCP. The work of speaker 4 shows a difference between that done on first coming to CCP in 1981 and that done in 1984, after a period of non-attendance at CCP classes (below).

Work done for CCP by Speaker 4 during 1981

wash bay
I useb To live in The country.
People who are liveing There in country
washtheir cloThes in The River. I love
washing. I used to bo This This Be twice
a week monbay an SATARbay.
spersally on monbays when There is a Lot of white claThes. Because at The River I look a goob place near The Higbe edge of The waRTeR . . .

Using the first five lines of speaker 4's 1981 writing as a basis for comparison with her 1984 work (also the first five lines): there were five errors in five lines in her 1981 work in contrast to seven errors in five lines in her 1984 work.

A similar analysis of speaker 5's work while with CCP in 1984 indicates two errors in five lines, in contrast with four errors in five lines, after a period of non-attendance at CCP classes. (see below).

Work done for CCP by Speaker 5 during 1984

5. He went to Rome to ask the Pope
permission to start a
brotherhood.
6. The members of the brother
-hood promise to have no
belongings to tell people about Christ and to help those in need.
7. St. Francis visit North Africa, Spain, Egypt, Syria and Palestine.

Although this data is too limited to use as a firm basis for generalisation, it is evident that each student characterises an increase in the use of errors after they have ceased attending CCP on a regular basis, as have both speakers 4 and 5.

Other points at issue, however are:
1. the persistence in errors due to Creole structure in contrast to some improvement in spelling.

and,

2. the learning behaviour of the speakers in the formal CCP school setting is in contrast with student learning behaviour in the more informal setting of their own homes, where most of the interviews were carried out.

Written Response to the Literature Questionnaire (Part 3)

Speaker 4 (1984)

Passage A
Lennard is a praud man becaus he did nat want to beg so he has to larne any haw he can to keep his family.

Passage B
I like the poem I neve know here is so much much joy in side Patwa.

Speaker 5 (1984)

Passage A
The poem is a very good poem
It make me remember of home
And also teach me to no how to live on your own.

Passage B
Leonard did not go to school but he was very good. While I say that he wach you do something and he do it He must get.

Speaker 15 (1984)

Passage A
It was about survival in the world and struggle.

Passage B
He is saying if it wasn't th Pom in his haut he would be deid.

An Analysis of Students' Work while at CCP — Tutors' Perspectives

Using the tutors' comments on the CCP Student Registration Forms and CCP Student Assessment Forms as data, the following tutors' comments can be related to the following students, while they were attending CCP classes.

Student
No.   *Tutors' Comments on Student's Language and Education*
1. 8 'O' Levels and 1 CSE
2. Weak Caribbean Creole influence evident in pronunciation.
   Wants to learn to read and write English.
   Semi-literate, i.e. left school at 14.
3. Reading and spelling difficulties.
4. Left school when nine years old.
   Cannot spell.
   Cannot write very well.

5. Very little schooling.
   Left school at 14.
   Poor spelling.
   Poor reading.
6. Cannot read or write. Primary school only.
7. Can read. Difficulties with spelling.
   Fell behind in education.
8. No formal education. Cannot read or write.
9. Difficulties with spelling, writing and reading.
10. No comments available.
11. Below average reading.
    Spelling and writing needs improvement.
    Irregular school attendance. Left school before final year.
12. Cannot read.
13. Poor English.
14. No comment available.
15. Little to no formal education. Cannot read well.
    Difficulties with spelling and English grammatical structure.

The above comments of tutors suggest that the students who came to CCP were, in general, poorly educated and unable to read and write. The tutors' comments are, in fact, 'overfavourable' and perhaps euphemistic in the face of real inabilities in reading and writing on the part of their student clientele.

In the light of these severe student inabilities, CCP's achievements with at least three students interviewed (i.e. speakers 4, 5 and 15) who can now read and write, have been very good.

Recommendations on CCP's Language Policy
CCP should use the Creole features indicated as the basis for potential problems in the learning of Standard English by Creole speakers of both the English Creole and French Creole varieties.

The separate nature of Creole languages and English should be clarified in the minds of Creole speakers.

CCP should continue developing teaching materials that deal specifically with each Creole feature as part of a planned syllabus, e.g. ten lessons which heighten the need for some form of the verb 'to be' followed by six lessons giving practice in the use of English adjectives, preceded by a form of the verb 'to be' (see below for a brief analysis of CCP teaching materials which have Creole features in mind).

Practice should be given in oral English as well as written English.

A more intensive approach to the acquisition of Standard English, aimed at developing permanent attachments to the use of Standard English in the Creole speaker, is needed.

A Selection from CCP Teaching Materials which have Creole Features in Mind

In the student work files and exercise books, one 'filling in the blanks exercise' (cloze test), which related to students' lack of practice with English past tense verb forms, was frequently used.

Practice in the use of the copula (any form of the verb 'to be') is particularly relevant to Creole languages in which the use of the copula is largely absent. Such practice is provided in another part of the same 'filling in the blanks exercise'.

Theoretical Implications for the Education of Caribbean Adults

Caribbean adults represent a largely 'uneducated' group of migrant labourers who have settled in Britain. They are largely non-literate, due to the largely oral tradition of their Creole culture. Their mainly low status work has combined with their lack of education to make them unaware of facilities for continuing their education. The physically demanding nature of their work has also made them so exhausted after work that their 'higher' needs for education could not be easily satisfied.

The greatest drag upon their wish to further their education has been psychological. They have been usually viewed negatively by British society in their workplaces. To face the same society on an educational level in the evening may be to expose themselves to further negative perspectives. To confess to illiteracy in a largely literate society is to expose oneself as 'ignorant'. To expose oneself to potential ridicule is harder for an adult.

A bilingual approach should be adopted which validates and contributes to a positive approach to Creole culture, but sees it as clearly separated from English.

CCP's ability to offer help to these adults through Caribbean tutors goes some way to getting the students over these psychological hurdles.

French Creole speakers are a minority within an English Creole minority. Having a language substantially different from English gives them a perspective of their own separateness and marginality to all things English, both Standard English and English Creole. an overemphasis upon English Creole and the English Creole speaking islands, for example, Jamaica and Barbados, in CCP teaching material, serves only as reinforcement to this marginality and sense of difference. The 'official absences' of concentration and attention by the French Creole students is a mark of their decision to abandon the CCP course when they have found it too Jamaican or English Creole centred. Dual marginalisation both from English speakers and English Creole speakers leads to a duality of responses in the French Creole psychology.

Practical Implications for the Education of Caribbean Adults

CCP should expand its teaching materials with respect to French Creole features. CCP should carry out further research into the teaching materials, types of lesson plans and schemes of work which can be used for teaching literacy in English to Creole speakers. The materials and line of research with respect to Creole features, as used by the Resources Officer and expanded by the work of the writer and Mr Eglon Whittingham, should be used as the factual basis for the production of even more teaching materials for CCP's use.

Evaluation of CCP Practice

CCP's Caribbean centred approach to the students has been extremely helpful. Its recruitment of Afro-Caribbean tutors has been extremely useful in gaining the confidence of Caribbean adults who may otherwise never have confessed that they could not read or write.

CCP also provides a service to people whom British society and its educational systems usually hold in contempt, or at least marginalise. The attainment of educational development under such social conditions can only be to CCP's credit as an 'intermediary' organisation catering for 'Third World' adults in a 'First World' which, despite its rhetoric, does not cater for them as well as it could.

CCP's practice of, at times, placing tutors in the homes of the students is a useful one, especially where work, age and more often embarrassment at not being able to read and write, work against the student leaving his/her home. The confidence of being in their own home, in fact often provides a positive stimulus to students who are lacking in confidence.

CCP's wish to use skills already in the Afro-Caribbean community is also a good thing in that it helps extend the skills of that community and makes it less dependent upon the wider society.

CCP's engagement of the difficult questions of Creole language and culture is admirable in a world which, for at least 500 years, has been so externally hostile that even Creole speakers often deny their associations with Creole languages and culture. This denial has often been a source of negative learning, and CCP has had some measure of success in making both Creole speakers and outsiders view Creole culture as a positive resource in a multi-ethnic education, rather than a negative source for eternal despair.

On a more practical level CCP has trained many Creole individuals to read and write who had been illiterate.

CCP should, in order to streamline its objectives, write up its syllabus, its schemes of work and its experience in the use of textbooks i.e. whether they have proved useful or useless.

Conclusions, Including a Contrast with CCP's Stated Aims
Although CCP's constitution does state the Project's general aims as: "to promote literacy and other communication skills among adults of Caribbean origin and other people with similar needs", a more expanded account of CCP's aims can be inferred from its own documents which include a newsletter, its annual reports, its internal reports on its short-term aims and training programmes. From the latter the following implicit aims are evident:
1. CCP is not only Caribbean orientated but focussed upon the educational development of people of Caribbean origin.
2. CCP wishes a process to be initiated for a Caribbean orientated component in teacher-training in Britain.
3. CCP also wishes to include the participation of Caribbean tutors on a voluntary basis.
4. CCP wishes to have a competent staff on a permanent or semi-permanent basis.
5. CCP wishes to get permanent or semi-permanent funding.

The remarks that follow on aims, failures and successes are based on limited discussions with the four CCP students interviewed.

Failures in Achieving its Aims
i) In its larger general aim of providing literacy to Caribbean adults in general, CCP' success in qualitative terms, with respect to its French Creole students, has been low. The writing of the students analysed indicated that their learning from CCP has not been as permanent as desired. The Creole features in their use of English seem to have resurfaced more strongly after the students have terminated, or temporarily suspended, their contact with CCP.
ii) CCP has been unable to fund many paid posts for tutors.

Successes in Achieving its Aims
i) CCP has had great success, considering its size and financial constraints, in helping a large number of Caribbean adults begin to

address the problem of their illiteracy. It has had substantial success in providing some of them with a minimal level of literacy e.g. in the case of the student writing considered.
ii) CCP has been successful in its involvement of the Caribbean community in the problems of its education and especially its literacy or the lack of it.
iii) CCP has succeeded, to a limited extent, in making the wider community aware of Caribbean perspectives in teacher training.
iv) CCP has managed to achieve some semi-permanancy of funding through a series of impermanent grants.
v) CCP has managed to make other 'black' organisations aware of its existence and to publicise CCP initiative through their own media.

Recommendations

i) CCP should initially provide a scheme of work and syllabus for its students which clarify and give a practical dimension to its literacy aims.
 CCP should include with these aims a series of objectives which its students are to be expected to fulfill after certain points in their training.
ii) CCP should increase its efforts to get funding for its most valuable asset and productive force, i.e. its tutors.
iii) CCP should set up a teacher-training course related to the education of Afro-Caribbeans which it could advertise to interested teachers at a fee of say £3 per head every summer or Easter vacation.
iv) Funding also reflects the present circumstances of African peoples. CCP should, therefore, be selective about the few student places it can fund, and which it could expand as its circumstances improved.
v) CCP should fund its own pieces of research which it should sell. It should fund limited, short-term research projects of its own, which it could then sell as publications for a restricted market.

Appendix 1.

Speaker A.

CARIBBEAN COMMUNICATIONS PROJECT

NAME:........................ D.O.B.............
COUNTRY OF BIRTH:........................SEX:............
CREOLE SPOKEN (COUNTRY):........ B   M   A

	D	F	D	F	D	F	D	F	D	F	D	F	D	F
1. Unmarked plurals	12 81	1												
2. Tenses														
3. Subject/verb agreement														
4. Possessives														
5. Dropped words/ phrases	12 81	4												

KEY: D = Date   F = Frequency

Appendix 2.

Speaker B.

CARIBBEAN COMMUNICATIONS PROJECT

NAME:........................ D.O.B..............
COUNTRY OF BIRTH:........................SEX:............
CREOLE SPOKEN (COUNTRY):........ B   M   A

	D	F	D	F	D	F	D	F	D	F	D	F	D	F
1. Unmarked plurals	1 10 80	4	7 1 81	1	29 4 81	4	23 7 81	4	5 11 81					
2. Tenses	1 10 80	12	7 1 81	17	29 4 81	5	23 7 81	3	5 11 81	13				
3. Subject/verb agreement	1 10 80	3	7 1 81		29 4 81	3	23 7 81		5 11 81					
4. Possessives	1 10 80		7 1 81		29 4 81		23 7 81	1	5 11 81					
5 Aspivant H									5 11 81	1				

KEY: D = Date   F = Frequency

Appendix 3.

Speaker C

CARIBBEAN COMMUNICATIONS PROJECT

NAME:....................... D.O.B..............
COUNTRY OF BIRTH:.......................SEX:............
CREOLE SPOKEN (COUNTRY):........ B   M   A

	D	F	D	F	D	F	D	F	D	F	D	F	D	F
1. Unmarked plurals	16/9/81	1			11/81	1								
2. Tenses					11/31	4								
3. Subject/ verb agreement														
4. Possessives														
5. Spelling	16/9/81	4	10/81	5	11/81	5								

KEY: D = Date   F = Frequency

Notes

1. See Part IV, ch. 3 on the work of the CCP.
2. Labov, W., 1970, in Pride and Holmes, (eds.), 1972, p.200 and Dalphinis, M., 1981, p.274 and p.459.
3. Labov, W., 1966.
4. Trudgill, P., 1974.
5. Holm, A., 1976.
6. Trudgill, P., 1974, ch. 3.
7. Labov, W., 1976.
8. Dalphinis, M., 1981.
9. See p.12 of the General Introduction.

5. Recommendations for a Productive Use of Creoles in Teaching

For many years Africans transported to America, Britain and elsewhere, during the period of the Atlantic Slave Trade, have spoken various Creole languages. These languages and their speakers have been viewed negatively and oppressed within the systems they found themselves.

This background of negative attitudes and related oppression of their speakers is the context within which present debates on Creole languages by superliterates[1] and other manipulators of opinion are to be situated.

The Problem

The justification for this discussion would be some or more of the following 'problems' posed by Creole languages and their speakers within the British Educational system:
i) Creole speakers are inferior and their languages, consequently part of that inferiority;
ii) Creole languages interfere with the acquisition of Standard English by Creole speakers;
iii) Creole speakers have a poor understanding of their British and other 'host' cultures;
iv) Creole speakers have imbibed an inferior view of themselves and their languages through indoctrination by the societies in which they live;
v) Creole speakers do badly in the British Educational System.

The Solution

It seems to me that the above list, though touching on some key issues, represents only the tip of the historical iceberg within which our minds have been frozen.

The central problem remains that of oppression, as there are no linguistic or educational reasons why Creole languages and their speakers cannot be, at least partially, accommodated within their mainstream educational systems. The reasons why they are not remain in the present world power structure within which Africans and their descendants are exploited, both inside and outside Africa, and an international ideology of racism used as justification for this oppression, both by themselves and their oppressors.

The solutions I suggest firstly lie in a decision to include Creole languages within their respective mainstream educational systems. Brandt and others, I know, would argue against their inclusion, in the case of black youth in Britain.[2] However, I believe that the positive backing of Creoles through their inclusion in mainstream educational systems would have beneficial educational effects upon both the educators and the educated. I do not believe that the resistance of black youth, or indeed of blacks internationally, will end purely due to any inclusion of their languages in educational systems. The paramenters for conflict will merely change. If anything, the use of Standard English by groups other than the English, continues to be a use of English which is characterised by the cultural and socio-political resistance ot its speakers, e.g. the Black Americans and Black South Africans.

I have previously outlined methods to help correct some of the negative social attributes placed upon Creole languages and their speakers at various stages within their mainstream educational systems.[3]

Approaches towards a methodology

The following approaches have been successfully used by myself, at the various educational levels below, and are proposed here as a platform for discussion rather than as a prescriptive guide:
Primary: At the primary level oral work with Creole languages has been successful in the telling of a Creole story in Standard Enlgish, but with all the Creole/African intonations related to particular characters in the story. The following lesson is a typical example:
Aim: To improve oral and written communication. To provide an insight into the African and Creole culture.
Method:
Stage 1: The teacher tells the following story:
One day Mr Rabbit was fishing and had caught a big pile

of fish. Mr Lion came to Mr Rabbit and said: "I am the King of the Forest and I want your fish! I want your fish!" Mr Rabbit said: "Oh great one to hear you is to obey you! Take all my fish!" Mr Lion ate all the fish and went off. One day Mr Rabbit met Mr Lion and said "Oh great one, I know of some magic which will give you more fish". Mr Lion said: "Show me this magic!" Mr Rabbit said: "Let me tie you to a tree, and afterwards, the magic will bring the fish to you". Mr Lion said: "Oh yes! Oh yes!". So Mr Rabbit tied him tightly and then after warming a poker till it was red hot, Mr Rabbit stabbed Mr Lion with it and said: "That's for my small fish! That's for my big fish!"...
(The parts said by Mr Lion should be accompanied by the teacher's miming power, strength and speaking in a loud and regal voice. The parts said by Mr Rabbit should be accompanied by nasalised speech and, in most cases, a mime of feigned subservience.)

Stage 2: After telling the story the pupils are asked to write down whether they thought Mr Rabbit was a good or bad character, and the reasons why they thought either.

Stage 3: Pupils were each asked, in turn, whether Mr Rabbit was good or bad. If one pupil suggests that Mr Rabbit was bad, another pupil would be asked to argue against what was said or vice versa. Work at this stage could also involve drawings of Mr Rabbit and Mr Lion, or mime of the dialogue between Mr Rabbit and Mr Lion.

Secondary: At this level, an initial lesson or lessons aimed at indicating an awareness of different varieties of language is valuable, e.g. a list of the languages spoken by the pupils in the class; the varieties of language spoken in the school; or in a particular place in the world, in order to indicatethe varieties available in any one speech community.

These language awareness lessons can be followed by lessons of the following type:

Lesson A

Aim: To indicate some of the grammatical structure of Creole languages, its differences with Standard English and its own separate integrity within the context of a literary analysis of a text, within which some Creole, or a Creole use of English is used.
*Materials: Dubbing and Toasting (*in the appendix) and the poem *The Stone Sermon*[4]

Method:
Stage 1: The poem is read round the class by the pupils.
Stage 2: The poem is read by the teacher.
Stage 3: The words not understood by the pupils are explained e.g. "Halleluja" by discussion with the pupils.
Stage 4: The language elements in the poem indicating Creole and a Creole use of English are written up on the board and explained, e.g. *Walls-dem* = 'walls' (a Standard English plural noun) followed by the Creole plural *dem*. *Wuk-a-wukking* = 'walking a lot' (formed by the Creole structure of reduplicating words to show emphasis).
Stage 5: Other differences between Creole and English, as well as other Creole uses of English within the poem are discussed.
Stage 6: The meaning of the poem is discussed.
Stage 7: Written work on, e.g. whether the title of the poem is suitable, is set and done by the pupils.

Lesson B

Aim: Unlike Lesson A (above), this lesson explores some of the Caribbean Creole literary context, and attempts to relate it to some of the Caribbean musical heritage, with which many of the pupils are familiar.
Materials: *Dubbing and Toasting* and *The Stone Sermon*
Method:
Stage 1: Give out the handout 'Dubbing and Toasting' and discuss it with the pupils.
Stage 2: Discuss examples of what the pupils think of as 'dubbing' and 'toasting'.
Stage 3: Give out the poem *The Stone Sermon* and ask pupils to identify the chorus in this poem.
Stage 4: Discuss the uses of the chorus in other poems.

Tertiary: The following two course outlines would typify the kinds of Creole language and Sociolinguistic inputs within which an awareness of Creole languages in particular, and a use of language within the social context generally, could be developed.

Creole Course (A)

The course was given by the author at the Janako Art Centre in London, for the Hackney Adult Education Institute in June 1984. *Aims and Objectives*: To provide an introductory framework for the

study of Afro-Caribbean Languages, History and Literature.
Course Description: An analysis of the meaning of the term *Creole* was made. The course also analysed the historical and social background to the development of Creoles in the Caribbean, using the development of Patwa in Saint Lucia as a case study.

The grammatical structures of English-based and French-based Creoles were studied from the point of view of their common African language influences.

The influences of the Creole upon Caribbean literature (oral and written) were assessed.

The issues at stake for the British educational system were also discussed.

Course Outline
I   Definitions of *Creole*.
II   Historical background to the Development of Patwa in Saint Lucia.
III   Sociolinguistic Analysis of Patwa in Saint Lucia.
IV   African Grammatical Structures in Creoles.
V   English and French-based Creole Grammatical Systems.
VI   Portuguese-based Creole Grammatical Systems.
VII   Lexical Expansion in Portuguese, English and French-based Creoles.
VIII African influences in Creole Vocabulary.
IX   Creole and African Oral Literature.
X   The influences of Creole Oral Literature upon Caribbean Written Literature.
XI   Implications for the Education of Creole Speakers.

Creole Course (B)

This course was given by the author at the University of Maiduguri, Nigeria, 1982/1983 Session, and can be summarised as follows:
Aims and Objectives: The course aims to introduce university students to the basic concepts in Creole language studies, and highlighted the sociolinguistic and African language discussions of these Creoles.
Course Description: The course looked at pidgins and Creoles as a result for inter-ethnic contacts, African language influences, General Linguistic Theory with special emphasis on Sociolinguistics Historical Linguistics and theories of language variation.
Course Outline: The following topics will be covered in terms of *provisional* numbered sequence below:
1. A historical definition of pidgins and Creoles.
2. A general linguistic definition of pidgins and Creoles.

3. A Sociolinguistic definition of pidgins and Creoles.(diglossia and trigossia).
4. Relexification: i) African bias ii) European bias iii) As an independent process.
5. Relexification and Creole varieties: i) Portuguese ii) English iii) French iv) African languages.
6. Calques (analogy), convergence and loans (domain, prestige and Creole).
7. Lexical expansion.
8. African language structures and Creole sub-strata.
9. Creolization as a process i) African ii) Caribbean iii) Universal
10. Decreolisation.
11. Recreolisation.
12. Languages in contact (synchronic and diachronic).
13. Variation in Creoles.
14. Lects i) Acrolect ii) Mesolect iii) Basilect.
15. New Creole theories.
16. Revision of the course.

Further, Adult and Voluntary: As a former Acting Regional Coordinator, tutor and researcher in a Caribbean voluntary literacy organisation, the Caribbean Communications Project, the following approaches proved useful in tutoring pupils of Caribbean origin in whose written and oral use of English Creole features were evident.[5]

i) An introductory awareness of the differences between Creole language structure and English was encouraged by orally indicating the Creole structure equivalent to the Creole use of English made by the student. For example, the student may make a Creole use of English (a term coined by myself to mean all use of English in which Creole language features are evident). Pointing to the structural equivalences with Creole languages helps create the awareness of such differences:

Creole Use
of English :   It all happen when the Policeman name Eric ...
Patwa (French
Creole):   i tout fèt lè Polis-la nomen Érik . . .
English
Creole: i ol hapin wen di Polisman nem Erik .....

ii) These differences are then heightened by oral exercises in which the student practices the Standard English equivalent of his/her Creole use of English, in the above example 'It all happened when the Policeman named Eric . . .'

iii) Written work is given which consolidates the Standard English structure.

iv) Work is done with a text in which Creole or a Creole use of English is evident and to which the student responds to by written/oral work in Standard English.

Conclusions

The question of Creole languages in most societies is a political question related to the particular social system's view of the ultimate role of Creole language speakers in the society.

If the traditionally low status of Creole speakers and their languages in many societies is to be altered, then the above suggestions, based on my own teaching experience, may offer guidelines to the teacher.

They are, however, offered as working methods, for improvement and refinement rather than as directives.

As any teacher knows, actual practice of the most laudable aims has to be continually reshaped by any host of conditions 'at the chalk face'.

Appendix

Dubbing and Toasting

Dubbing and toasting are means by which a song or the music from a song is added to by a Disc Jockey who sings or chants his own words into a microphone while the original song or music is being played, for example, the Bob Marley song *Wake up and Live* can be 'dubbed' or 'toasted' by a Disc Jockey singing:

> An liv as a wud say
> As a wud say . . .

Record makers such as 'Island' saw this practice as a basis for making two versions of the same song: an 'A' side with the words and music of the song and a 'B' side with the music only for those who wanted to 'dubb' and 'toast'.

Singers also saw this as a reason for having a 'toasting' style of singing, for example, *U-Roy*.

The Caribbean Link

Such dubbing and toasting in Britain is, however, only a way of keeping some Caribbean literary (e.g. songs, poetry, stories) habits alive.

In the Caribbean, songs, stories and poetry are and were often sung and chanted with the idea that the people listening could join in also, for example, before beginning any story, the people listening have to give the storyteller a signal to show that they want to listen to him. In Jamaica, for example, the people listening signal that they want to listen by saying Krac!

The audience can also add to the story while it is being told, for example, the listeners may say:

> Jamaican: Well Ananci is like dat yu no!
> St Lucian: *ou* sav sé kon sa Ananci yé!
> (meaning: That's the way Ananci is!)

Stories and songs are also told by anyone who wants to do so. Because of this many people have many versions of songs and stories and can tell the same event either as a song or a story.

The African Link

In Africa the same uses were and are made of songs and stories, as in the Caribbean. For example, among the Hausa, singers may praise one of their heroes, Usman dan Fodio in songs such as:

> Babbar k'asa Shehu d'an Fodio
> 'Great country of the Leader d'an Fodio'

whereas most Hausa people can tell you a version of the song in story form.

In this way they are giving a story version of the song. They are 'dubbing' and 'toasting' the song in a story form.

Other Hausa singers sing about Usman d'an Fodio as a religious man rather than as a military leader. In this way they are often creating one or two dubbings/toastings or versions of the same song.

In Africa, as in the Caribbean, the singer often sang his song with some chorus singers who helped him. Bob Marley, for example, was assisted by the I-Three. The Hausa singer in Africa is assisted by a chorus (or 'Yan Amshi' meaning 'Sons of Answering'). In Britain, the 'toaster' or 'dubber' is taking the place of this kind of chorus.

Caribbean Written Literature

Because of these performer and chorus or performer and 'toaster'/'dubber' connections, Caribbean written poetry often leaves a 'space' for a chant or a 'toast', for example, in the poem *The Stone Sermon*, by E. Brathwaite, the 'toast' or 'dub' or chorus is:

> Stokey dead
> Stokey dead
> Stokey dead o

while the rest of the poem discusses the relationship between the death and Christianity.

Notes

1. Dalphinis, M.., 1984(c).
2. Brandt, G., 1984.
3. Dalphinis, M., 1984(c).
4. Brathwaite, E., 1969, pp.97-100.
5. Dalphinis, M., 1984(a) and 1984(c).

Bibliography

ABALOGU, U.N., ASHIWAJU, G., and AMADI-TSHIWALA, R. (eds) *Oral Poetry in Nigerian*, Nigeria Magazine, Lagos, 1981.
ACHEBE, C., *Things Fall Apart*, London, 1980 (reprint).
ALLADINA, S., 'Languages in Britain, Perceptions and Policies in Education'. Paper presented at the *National Convention of Black Teachers*, Institute of Education, Univ. of London, 1982.
ALLEYNE, M.C., 'Language and Society in St. Lucia', *Journal of Caribbean Studies*, 11, Univ. of Puerto Rico, 1961.
ANDERSEN, R.W., 'Creolization as the Acquisition of a Second Language as a First Language'. Paper presented at the *Conference on Theoretical Orientations in Creole Studies*, St. Thomas, Virgin Islands, 1978.
ANDRADE, E., *The Cape Verde Islands from Slavery to Modern Times*, United Nations, Dakar, Sénégal, 1973.
ARCHIVES NATIONAL, Dakar: Reference no. 2F4, *Relations du Gouvernement du Sénégal avec le Gouvernement de la Guinée Portugaise 1887-1891*.
BABALOLA, S.A., *The Content and Form of Yoruba, Ijala*, Oxford, 1976.
BAKER, P., *Towards a Social History of Mauritian Creole*, B.Phil. dissertation, Univ. of York, 1976.
BALEWA, A.T., *Shehu Umar*, Northern Nigerian Publishing Company, henceforth N.N.P.C., 1966.
BELLO, A., *Gand'oki*, N.N.P.C., 1972.
BEVER, T.G. and LANGENDOEN, D.T., 'The interaction of speech perception and grammatical structure in the evolution of a language', in R.P. Stockwell and R.K.S. Macaulay (eds.) *Linguistic Change and Generative Theory*, Bloomington, 1972.
BOLLÉ, A., *Le Créole Français des Seychelles*, Max Niemeyer Verlag, Tübingen, 1977.

BOULÈGUE, J., 'Aux Confins du Monde Malinké, le Royaume du Kasa (Casamanca)', *Manding Studies*, School of Oriental and African Studies, henceforth S.O.A.S., Univ. of London, 1972(b).

BRATHWAITE, E., *Masks*, Oxford, 1968.
Islands, Oxford, 1969.

BRANDT, G., 'British Youth Caribbean Creole — The Politics of Resistance', paper presented at the *Conference on Languages Without a Written Tradition*, Thames Polytechnic, 31 August-3 September, 1984.

BREEN, H.H., *History of Saint Lucia*, Longman, Brown, Green and Longmans, Longmans, London, 1844.

BRETON, R., *Dictionnaire Caraibe-François*, Auxerre, 1665.
Dictionnaire François-Caraibe, Auxerre, 1665.
Grammaire Caraibe, Auxerre, 1667.

BROUSSARD, J.F., *Louisiana Creole Dialect*, Kennikat Press, New York, 1972.

CALLENDER, T., *It So Happen*, Christian Journals Ltd., Belfast, 1975.

CARRINGTON, L.D., *St. Lucian Creole, a Descriptive Analysis of its Phonology and Morphosyntax*, Ph.D. thesis, 1976, Univ. of the West Indies.

CASSIDY, F.G. and LE PAGE, R.B. (eds.), *Dictionary of Jamaican English*, Cambridge, 1967.

CÉSAIRE, A., *Return to my Native Land*, translated by J. Berger and A. Bostock, London, 1969.

CHAUDRON, D.M.A., *Essai sur la Colonie de Sainte Lucie*, Neuchatel, 1779.

CHOMSKY, N., *Syntactic Structures*, Mouton & Co., The Hague, 1957.
Aspects of the Theory of Syntax, Cambridge, Mass., U.S.A., 1965.

COARD, B., *How the West Indian Child is Made Educationally Sub-Normal in the British School System*, London, 1971.

COHEN, A., *Two-Dimensional Man: An Essay on the Anthropology of Power and Symbolism in Complex Society*, London, 1974.

COMHAIRE-SYLVAIN, S., *Le Créole Haitien: Morphologie et Syntaxe*, Wettern, Port-au-Prince, Haiti, 1936.

CRAIG, D., 'Models for Educational Policy in Creole-Speaking Communities', paper presented at the *Conference on Theoretical Orientations in Creole Studies*, St. Thomas, Virgin Islands, 1978.

CURTIN, P.D., *The Atlantic Slave Trade: a Census*, Univ. of Wisconsin Press, 1969.

DALBY, D., 'The place of Africa and Afro-America in the history of the English language', *African Language Review*, vol. 9,

London, 1970/71.
'Ashanti survivals in the language and traditions of the Windward Maroons of Jamaica', *African Language Studies*, XII, London, 1971.
'The African element in Black English', in T. Kochman (*ed.*), *Rappin' and stylin' out: communication in urban Black America*, Univ. of Illinois, 1972.

DALPHINIS, L.B., *St. Lucian Education: Problems of Literacy and the Creole Question*, paper written as part of the Education in Developing Countries option of the P.G.C.E. course, Univ. of London Institute of Education, 1981.

DALPHINIS, M., *Gwendé Pou Peter Moses* (Dice for Peter Moses), French Creole poem read at the Black Arts Festival of West London, 1972, published in *Anthologie de la Nouvelle Poesie Créole*, Editions Caribéennes & Agence de la Cooperation Culturelle et Technique, Paris, 1984, pp.63-67.
'Various Approaches to the Study of Creole Languages with Particular Reference to the Influences of West African Languages upon those Creole Languages', paper presented to the *Africa Society*, King's College, Univ. of London, 1976. Published in the *Black Liberator*, London, 1978 & CCP Occasional Paper No. 2, London, 1982.
'A Synchronic Comparison of the Verbal Systems of St. Lucian Patwa and Guinean Crioulo', paper presented to the *Comparative Seminar on African and Creole Languages*, S.O.A.S., Univ. of London, 1977(a).

'A General Introduction to Creole Languages', paper presented to the teachers at *Holloway Comprehensive School, London*, 1978.
'Lexical Expansion in Casamance Kriul, Gambian Krio and St. Lucian Patwa', paper presented to the Conference on *Theoretical Orientations in Creole Studies, St. Thomas, U.S. Virgin Islands*, 1979(a).

'Historical Background to the Development of Patwa in St. Lucia', paper presented to the *Comparative Seminar on Creole and African Languages*, S.O.A.S., Univ. of London, 1977 (b), and the *Conference on Creole Studies and Development*, Mahé, Seychelles, 1979(b).
'The African Presence in West Indian Creole Literature', paper presented at the *Centre for Urban Educational Studies*, London, 1979(c).
African Language Influences in Creoles Lexically Based on Portuguese, English and French, with special reference to Casamance Kriul, Gambian Krio and St. Lucian Patwa, PhD Thesis, S.O.A.S., Univ. of London, 1981.

'The Social History of Caribbean Languages — The St. Lucian Case', paper presented at the *Third International Conference on Creole Studies*, Vieux-Fort, St. Lucia, 1981.

'The Writer and His Audience — Influences of the African Oral Tradition on Nigerian Literature (Oral and Written)', paper presented at the *Modern Languages Association of Nigeria, Annual Conference*, Univ. of Calabar, Nigeria, 1983(a).

'Portuguese Creole, French and African Languages: languages in competition in southern Senegal', paper presented in absentia at the *fourth International Conference on Creole Studies*, Louisiana, U.S.A., 1983(b).

'French Creoles' in *Language and the Black Experience in Britain*, (forthcoming) Blackwells, Oxford, 1985.

'French Creole' in the Caribbean Communications Project Report for the ILEA, Afro-Caribbean Language and Literacy Project, © ILEA, 1984 (a).

'Creoles and Ideologies of Return' paper presented to the *Conference of the Society for Caribbean Studies*, Heigh Leigh Conference Centre, Hertfordshire, May 1984 (b).

'Oral Languages, Power and Education: A Comparative Survey of Saint Lucian and English Practices', paper presented to the *Conference on Languages Without a Written Tradition*, Thames Polytechnic, August/September 1984(c).

'Island Carib Influences in Saint Lucian Patwa', paper presented (in absentia) to the *Conference of the Society for Caribbean Linguistics,* Univ. of the West Indies, Mona, Jamaica, September 1984 (d).

'Gwo Piton, Piti Piton', *Caribbean Quarterly,* Univ. of the West Indies, 1985.

D'COSTA, J., 'Language and Dialect in Jamaica', *Occasional Papers No. 1 of the Caribbean Communications Project*, London, 1980.

DELAFOSSE, M., and DEBIEN, G., 'Les origines des Esclaves aux Antilles', *Bulletin d'I.F.A.N.*, pp.319-405, Dakar, Senegal, 1965.

GASPAR, D.B., 'The Emancipation of the Free Coloureds in St. Lucia 1824-1831', paper presented to the *Eleventh Conference of Caribbean Historians*, Curaçao, 1979.

DELSOL, S., *The 'New' Black Teacher,* part 1, mimeographed booklet, London, 1984.

DE SAUSSURE, F., *Cours de Linguistique Generale*, Payot, Paris, 1969.

DU TETRE, *Histoire Generale des Isles de S. Christophe de la Guadeloupe, de la Martinique et Autres dans l'Amerique*, Paris, 1654.

EDWARDS, V., *The West Indian Language Issue in British Schools*, London, 1979.
EDWARDS, W., 'A Comparison of Selected Linguistic Features in Some Caribbean and Arawakan Languages in Guyana', paper presented at the *Society for Caribbean Linguistics Conference*, Barbados, 1978.
EYSENCK, H.J., *Race, Intelligence and Education*, London, 1971.
FANON, F., *Black Skin, White Masks*, Grove Press, New York, 1967, and Paladin, 1970.
FERGUSON, C.A., *Language and Social Context*, P. Giglioli *(ed.)*, London, 1975.
FIGUEROA, J.M., 'Notes on the Teaching of English in the West Indies in *Occasional Paper No. 1 of the Caribbean Communications Project*, London, 1980.
FINNEGAN, R., *Oral Literature in Africa*, Oxford, 1975.
FROSSARD, M., *La Cause des Esclaves Negres et des Habitans de la Guinée*, in two volumes, Lyon, 1789.
GIDLEY, C.G.B., 'Rok'o: A Hausa Praise Crier's Account of his Craft', in *African Language Studies, XVI*, S.O.A.S., Univ. of London, 1975, pp.93-115.
HAIR, P.E.H., 'Ethnolinguistic Continuity on the Guinea Coast', *Journal of African History*, viii, 2, pp.247-268, London, 1967.
HANCOCK, I.F., *A study of the Development of the Lexicon of Sierra Leone Krio*, PhD thesis, S.O.A.S., Univ of London, 1971.
HAYOT, E., *Les Gens de Couleur Libres de Fort-Royal*, 1679-1823 Société Française d'Outre-Mer, Paris, 1971.
HOCKETT, E., *A Course in Modern Linguistics*, Macmillan, New York, 1958.
HOFF, B.J., *The Carib Language*, Leiden, 1968.
HYMES, D., *(ed.)*, *Pidginization and Creolization of Language*, Cambridge, 1971.
IMAM, A., *Magana Jari Ce*, N.N.P.C., 1972 (reprint).
ISAYEV, M.I., *National Languages in the USSR: Problems & and Solutions*, Moscow, 1977.
JOHNSON, H.A.S., *Hausa Stories*, Oxford, 1966.
KIPARSKY, P., 'Linguistic universals and linguistic change', in E. Bach and R.T. Harms (eds.), *Universals in Linguistic Theory*, London, 1968.
KOELLE, S.W., *Polyglotta Africana*, London, 1854.
KOESTLER, A., *Act of Creation*, London, 1959.
KUCZYNSKI, R.R., *Demographic Survey of the British Colonial Empire*, Royal Institute of International Affairs, London, 1948.
LABAT, J.B., *Nouveau Voyage aux Isles de l'Amerique*, 6 vols., Paris, 1722.
LABOV, W., *The Social Stratification of English in New York City*,

Washington D.C., 1966.

'The Study of Language in its Social Context', 1970, in P. Giglioli, (ed.), *Language and Social Context*, London, 1972.

LAROUSSE, *Nouveau Petit Larousse Illustré*, Paris, 1927.

Dictionnaire d'Ancien Français, Paris, 1947.

Lexis Dictionnaire de la Langue Française, Paris, 1975.

LAURENT, J., and CÉSAIRE, I. *(eds.), Contes de Mort et de Vie aux Antilles,* Paris, 1976.

LAYE, C., *The Radiance of the King*, Collins (translation), London, 1956.

LEIBERMAN, D., *Bilingual Behaviour in a St. Lucian Society*, PhD thesis, Univ. of Wisconsin, 1974.

LE PAGE, R.B., 'De-creolization and Re-creolization: a Preliminary Report on the Sociolinguistic Survey of Multilingual Communities, Stage II, St. Lucia, *York Papers in Linguistics*, no. 7, 1977.

LITTLEWOOD, W., *Communicative Language Teaching*, Cambridge, 1981.

LITTRÉ, E., *Dictionnaire de la Langue Française*, Paris, 1873.

LORD, A., *The Singer of Tales,* Oxford, 1960, and Atheneum, New York, 1965.

LYONS, J., *Introduction to Theoretical Linguistics*, Cambridge, 1968.

MAHONEY, F., *Stories of the Gambia*, Government Printers, Banjul, The Gambia, 1975.

MARTIN, G., *Histoire de l'esclavage dans les Colonies Françaises*, Paris, 1948.

MAUNY, R., *Guide de Gorée*, I.F.A.N., Dakar, Senegal.

MIDGETT, D., 'Bilingualism and Linguistic Change in St. Lucia', *Anthropological Linguistics*, vol. VII, pp.158-170, Bloomington, Indiana, U.S.A., 1970.

MONTEJO, E., *Autobiography of a Runaway Slave*, London, 1970.

MUKHERJEE, T., 'E.S.L.: A Legacy of Failure' in *EFL Gazette*, London, October 1983.

MURRAY, J.A. *(ed.), A New English Dictionary on Historical Principles*, Oxford, 1888.

NGCOBO, A.B., 'Language Issues in our Multi-Cultural and Multi-Lingual Society', paper presented at the *Conference of the Campaign Against Racism in Education*, London, 1984.

NORRISH, J., *Language Learners and Their Errors*, London, 1983.

OGBALU, F.C. and EMENANJO (eds.), *Igbo Language and Culture*, (reprint) Oxford, 1975.

PALMER, F., *Grammar*, London, 1971.

PEI, M.A., *Glossary of Linguistic Terminology*, Colombia Univ. Press, New York, 1966.

PLANTERS and CITIZENS of ST. LUCIA, *Addresse des Planteurs et l'Isle St. Lucie à M. De Damas, Gouverneur et à l'Assemblée Coloniale de la Martinique 1791*, preceded by *Memoire de M. de Damas, Gouverneur de la Martinique sur les Troubles de Cette Colonie,* (copy available at the British Museum, London).
PUBLIC RECORDS OFFICE, London (P.R.O.), *Registry of Plantation Slaves*, St. Lucia, 1815.
Minutes of the Privy Council, 1826-1834.
Minutes of the Executive Council, from its formation in March 1832 to February 1834 (CO256, piece no. 2).
Minutes of the New Legislative Council, 1832-1833 (CO256, piece no. 3).
Reports of the Protectors of Slaves, July 1826 to December 1829 (CO258, piece nos. 5-15).
Journals of the Legislative Council, 1835-1839.
Administrative Reports, 1895-1904. A Report on the Primary Schools in Saint Lucia for the year 1895, Education Office, Castries, 1896, by V.S. Gouldsbury (CO256, piece no. 16).
Departmental Reports, St. Lucia 1932 (CO256, piece no. 36).
RICHARDS, J. (ed.), *Error Analysis*, London, 1974.
RICHMOND, J., *Dialect*, I.L.E.A., English Centre, London, 1966-1977.
RIDGEWAY, A., *Saint Lucia, Island of Conflict*, a broadcast talk, West Indies Pamphlet, folio number 804. Available at the Library of the British Colonial Office, London, date of publication: 1945.
Old West Indian Days, a broadcast talk on West Indian history, West Indies pamphlet, folio number 817, 1945, Colonial Office Library, London.
RINCHON, D., *Traite et l'esclavage des Congolais par les Européens*, Paris, 1929.
ROBERT, P., *Dictionnaire de la Langue Française*, Paris, 1967.
ROBINS, R.H., *General Linguistics: An Introductory Survey*, London, 1964.
ROCHE, C., 'Ziguinchor et son Passé (1645-1920)' in *Boletim Cultural da Guiné Portugesa*, vol. 28, no. 109, pp.35-59, Lisbon, 1973.
Conquête et Résistance des Peuples de Casamance 1856-1920, Univ. of Dakar, Sénégal, 1976.
RODNEY, W., *The Groundings With My Brothers*, London, 1969.
A History of the Upper Guinea Coast, 1545-1800, London, 1970.
ROMALIS, R., 'Economic Change and Peasant Political Consciousness in the Commonwealth Caribbean', *Journal of Commonwealth and Comparative Politics*, vol. XIII, no. 3, pp.225-241, London, 1975.

SANDSTROM, C.I., *The Psychology of Childhood and Adolescence*, London, 1961.
SELVON, S., *A Brighter Sun*, London, 1976.
SHAKESPEARE, W., *The Tempest*, in *The Complete Works of William Shakespeare*, London, 1958.
SKINNER, N., 'Lexical Evidence of Manding-Hausa Connections in *Manding Studies Conference Papers*, vol. 5, S.O.A.S. Library, London, 1972 (unpublished).
TAYLOR, D.M., *The Black Carib of Honduras*, New York, 1951. *Languages of The West Indies*, Baltimore, U.S.A. and London, 1977.
TEXEIRA da MOTA, A., MONOD, Th. and MAUNY, R., 'Description de la Côte Occidentale d'Afrique', *Centro de Estudos da Guiné Portugesa*, Bissau, Guinée-Bissau, 1951.
TOUZE, R.L., *Bignona en Casamance*, Editions SEPA, Dakar, Sénégal, 1963.
TOYNBEE, N.W., *A Visitor's Guide to Saint Lucian Patois*, 1969, Lithographic Press, St. Lucia, 1969.
TRUDGILL, P., *Sociolinguistics*, London, 1974.
VALKOFF, M.F., *Studies in Portuguese and Creole With Special Reference to South Africa*, Witwatersrand Univ. Press, Johannesburg, 1966.
VALLON, A., 'La Casamance, Dépendence du Sénégal', *Revue Maritime et Coloniale*, pp.456-474, Paris, 1862.
VERIN, P., 'Sainte Lucie et ses Derniers Caraibes', *Les Cahiers d'Outre-Mer*, no. 48, pp.349-361, Bordeaux, 1959.
WALCOTT, D., *In a Green Night*, London, 1962.
WALTER, J. (ed.), *Memória Sobre o Estado Actual da Senegambia Portugesa*, H.P. Barreto, Bissau, Guinée-Bissau, 1947.
WEINREICH, U., *Languages in Contact*, Mouton & Co., The Hague, 1968.
WHITTINGHAM, E., 'The Position of Black Teachers in Relation to the Place of West Indian Dialects in Language Teaching', paper presented at the *National Convention of Black Teachers*, Institute of Education, Univ. of London, 1982.
WHORF, B.L., *Language, Thought and Reality: Selected Writings of Benjamin Lee Whorf*, in Carroll, J.B. (ed.), MIT Press, Mass., 1956.
WILSON, W.A.A., *The Crioulo of Guinea*, Witwatersand Univ. Press, Johannesburg, 1962.